The Governance of S[...]

Recent reforms in the governance of schooling have affected roles, relationships and decision-making within schools and between schools and the wider community. Using empirical and theoretical approaches, this book describes, analyses and compares the effects of devolved management on secondary schools in a number of countries. It casts a critical light upon policy ideas and aims, challenging assumptions about the way policy works in practice.

Through a comparative international perspective, which looks at countries including the UK (Scotland and Northern Ireland as well as England) and the US, the conflicting options for school governance are addressed. These include:

- parental participation and school management policy
- professional, managerial and market principles in education
- school-based decision-making and the implementation of over-arching government policies
- devolution and centralisation

This is a timely study for practitioners in education, policy-makers in local and central government, academics and students of education policy and management.

Margaret A. Arnott is Lecturer in Political Science at Glasgow Caledonian University. **Charles D. Raab** is Professor of Government at the University of Edinburgh.

The Governance of Schooling

Comparative studies of devolved management

**Edited by Margaret A. Arnott
and Charles D. Raab**

London and New York

First published 2000
by Routledge
11 New Fetter Lane, London EC4P 4EE

Simultaneously published in the USA and Canada
by Routledge
29 West 35th Street, New York, NY 10001

Routledge is an imprint of the Taylor & Francis Group

Typeset in Goudy by Taylor & Francis Books Ltd
Printed and bound in Great Britain by MPG Books Ltd, Bodmin

British Library Cataloguing in Publication Data
A catalogue record for this book is available from the British Library

Library of Congress Cataloging in Publication Data
The governance of schooling: comparative studies of devolved
management/edited by Margaret A. Arnott and Charles D. Raab
Includes bibliographical references and index
1. School management and organization–Cross-cultural studies. 2.
School-based management–Cross-cultural studies. I. Arnott, Margaret A.
1967- II. Raab, Charles D.
LB2801.A1 G68 2000
371.2   99-057255

ISBN 0–415–19537–3 (hbk)
ISBN 0–415–19538–1 (pbk)

Contents

Tables

Contributors

Margaret A. Arnott is Lecturer in political science in the School of Social Sciences, Glasgow Caledonian University. She has been a member of several research teams studying devolved management of schools in England and Scotland, funded by the National Association of Head Teachers, the Economic and Social Research Council and the Scottish Office Education and Industry Department.

Lucy Bailey has taught Sociology at the University of New York in Prague since recently completing her PhD at the University of Bristol. Her research interests include educational sociology and the analysis of gender and identity.

Grainne Byrne is Lecturer in the School of Business, Retail and Financial Services, University of Ulster. Her main research interests are in educational management and education policy and she has been involved in a number of research projects which have assessed the impact of education reform and local management on schools in Northern Ireland.

Jørgen Grønnegaard Christensen is Professor of Public Administration at the Department of Political Science, University of Aarhus. His main research interests are public sector organisation and governance. His most recent publications include studies of Danish welfare institutions, Danish central government and privatisation. Currently he is researching managerial behaviour in public institutions.

Kerry Jacobs is Lecturer in Accounting in the Department of Accounting and Business Method at the University of Edinburgh and an associate research fellow in the Institute of Public Sector Accounting Research. Prior to 1996 he was a lecturer in accounting at the University of Canterbury, New Zealand. His recent publications have focused on accounting and accountability in the New Zealand public sector, particularly the reform of health and education and the changing role of public sector audit.

Penny McKeown is Senior Lecturer in the Graduate School of Education, Queen's University, Belfast. Her main research interests lie in the areas of education policy and management. She has researched school governance comparatively across the education systems of the United Kingdom and in Northern Ireland. She is currently working on the Selection Project, funded by the Department of Education for Northern Ireland, which is intended to provide an up-to-date information base for the forthcoming Assembly debate on academic selection at Eleven Plus.

Jane Martin is an education officer with responsibility for school governance at the Dudley LEA. Until September 1999 she was a research fellow at the University of Birmingham School of Education where she worked on a variety of projects in the field of education management and governance, including studies for ESRC, the DfEE and OECD.

Pamela Munn is Professor of Curriculum Research and Associate Dean in the Faculty of Education, University of Edinburgh. Her main research interests lie in school discipline, exclusion and truancy, the professional development of teachers and in school governance. She is currently visiting professor of education at the Graduate School of Education, University of Tokyo.

Jon Nixon is Professor of Education in the Institute of Education at the University of Stirling. His recent research and writing is elaborating the characteristics of a new teacher professionalism.

Charles D. Raab is Professor of Government in the Department of Politics, University of Edinburgh. His publications on education policy include (with A. McPherson) *Governing Education: A sociology of policy since 1945* (Edinburgh University Press, 1988), and many contributions to leading journals and collected works. He has held research grants from the Economic and Social Research Council and the Scottish Office Education and Industry Department, and is an editorial board member of the *Journal of Education Policy*.

Stewart Ranson is Professor of Education in the School of Education, University of Birmingham. His research has focused upon the changing governance of education and the emerging characteristics of a learning society.

Penny Bender Sebring is senior research associate at the University of Chicago and Co-Director of the Consortium on Chicago School Research. She is co-author of *Charting Chicago School Reform: Democratic Localism as a Lever for Change* (Westview Press, 1998), and lead author of two reports on education reform in Chicago. She has directed federally funded school students, and she was a high school teacher. She has published articles on a variety of topics, including students' course-taking patterns in high school, urban education, school leadership, and the utilisation of research and evaluation results. She graduated from Grinnell College, where she is a member of the Board of Trustees. She received a PhD in Education and Policy Studies from Northwestern University.

Priscilla Wohlstetter is Professor of Education and director of the Center on Educational Governance at the University of Southern California. She has a PhD from Northwestern University and an EdM from Harvard University. She is internationally recognised for her work on school-based management (SBM), particularly in the areas of politics, organisational policies and school-based budgeting, and was named a leading expert on SBM by the US Department of Education. Her publications include numerous articles on the politics, organisation and effects of SBM; links between policy and practice in charter schools; and the development of school networks to improve educational performance.

Acknowledgements

In editing this book and collaborating in the research upon which part of it is based, we have incurred debts to a number of organisations and colleagues whose assistance has been indispensable. The Economic and Social Research Council (ESRC) was generous in its financial support for the study of Devolved Management of Schools (grant no. R000233653) on which we, with others, worked between 1992 and 1996. No less helpful was the Scottish Office Education and Industry Department (SOEID), which funded the work of our research team between 1994 and 1996 on Devolved School Management in Secondary Schools in Scotland. The grant-holders for those projects, which were based at the University of Edinburgh, were Michael Adler, Pamela Munn and Charles Raab, and the research team included Margaret Arnott, Lucy Bailey, Lorraine McAvoy and Carole Moore.

Although Michael Adler has not authored a chapter, we acknowledge his sound advice concerning the compilation of the book His contribution to both research projects as well as to their final reports and to other co-authored publications based on them was invaluable and, we hope, is reflected in the contents of this volume. We are grateful to him and to Pamela Munn, as co-grant-holders with Charles Raab, for having entrusted us with the task of bringing our joint work to further fruition in this volume. We also wish to give our grateful recognition to the collaboration of all the research assistants, and to their contribution to the collegial spirit in which the research team worked.

The critical but helpful judgements of members of the Scottish Office research project advisory group should also be mentioned: in particular, Judith Duncan and Tom McDonald of the Scottish Office. A dissemination seminar held during the lifetime of the ESRC project brought to bear the observations of academics and practitioners, including Jørgen Grønnegaard Christensen, David Bell, John Fairley, Stewart Ranson, and Gwen Wallace. Although – in keeping with our undertakings on confidentiality – we cannot name them, we would also like, on behalf of the Edinburgh research team, to express our thanks to the teachers and head teachers, school staff, school boards and governing bodies, administrators in central and local government, and voluntary organisations, who allowed us access to their deliberations and gave generously of their time and resources during the lifetime of our projects.

We owe a particular debt to the other authors of chapters, whose willingness to contribute in a relevant and timely manner greatly eased the burdens of editorship, and with whom it has been a pleasure to work. We hope that they are pleased with the overall result of our collaborative efforts in putting together this comparative and international study of the devolved management of schooling. Thanks are also due to our editor at Routledge, Jude Bowen, for her guidance as well as for her patience and understanding when unforeseen circumstances delayed the delivery of our manuscript.

Finally, we would like, with much gratitude, to acknowledge the support of Helen and Ian Arnott and Gillian Raab during the preparation of this book.

Introduction

School governance in comparative perspective

Margaret A. Arnott and Charles D. Raab

Overview

The governance of school education in many Western countries under-
went important changes in policy and practice in the 1980s and 1990s
that portended profound consequences for roles and relationships in the
education system, and for educational outcomes. Controversy surrounded
governments' plans to redistribute power and influence in education
systems. They hoped to engineer this by moving responsibilities nearer
the school and the classroom, strengthening some decision-making arenas
and weakening others, empowering parents and community groups and
curbing the professionals' control, and inserting the style and substance of
modern business and financial management into the procedures of schools
and the work of their staff. With varying implications in different countries and localities, the cause of educational reform disturbed the settled
political and societal understandings in terms of the way in which education systems were to be governed, the nature of what was to be taught,
and the criteria and manner by which results would be assessed.

The effects of these changes – whether in management content and
style, in the ethos and 'success' of schools and pupils, or in the position of
schools in local communities and the society at large – are still unfolding,
taking sometimes unforeseen and unintended paths. Yet amidst the many
twists and turns of government policy and, perhaps particularly, its implementation in schools, patterns may be emerging with enough clarity to
indicate the implications of this shift towards new forms of educational
governance. In different countries, these forms go by various names:
devolved school management, site-based management, local management
of schools, school-based management, etc. In many, devolved management as such is part of a package of more comprehensive reforms of
schooling. Regardless of the label, the changes in governance signify, in
practical intention as well as normatively, the elevation in importance of

the school and its local-community environment in the governance of education, and an ostensible retreat from traditional, 'top-down' direction exercised through one or more hierarchical levels of officialdom. In some countries, the new forms feature a restructuring of relationships and power amongst levels of the policy-making system. New educational governance also has wide-ranging implications for what goes on within schools, among teachers, head teachers (or school Principals), administrative staff, parents, pupils and others.

This book aims to contribute to the understanding of these changes by describing, analysing and comparing the effects of devolved management, mainly on secondary schools. It is based upon empirical research and theoretical analysis in the education systems of the constituent education systems of the United Kingdom (UK) – England (and Wales), Scotland and Northern Ireland – and in other countries: the United States, New Zealand and Denmark. It deals, in particular, with changing approaches to school management, the effect of the market, public participation in school-based decision-making, the role of teachers as professionals, and the refashioning of systems of governance that include schools' internal management and their relation to other public authorities and loci of power.

The changes that are under investigation may share similar characteristics across countries and systems, yet they contrast in various ways. A number of broad, alternative theoretical explanations for their similarity may be imagined. These would include common responses to common problems, mutual influence across countries, and the dissemination of a prestigious model from a single source. Teasing out and refining such explanations are the province of studies of lesson-drawing and policy-transfer, and are an important part of policy studies to which the raw materials of these chapters may contribute, although their systematic exploration is beyond the scope of this book. The chapters dealing mainly with Scotland in Part I, along with those on England and Northern Ireland in Part II, for example, could point towards a systematic and detailed analysis of similarities and differences in policies and implementation amongst the several education systems within the UK. The second section of this Introduction, in fact, begins this kind of comparative study by describing variations, although it does not attempt to account for them.

Leaving the question of policy-transfer aside, comparisons (including, of course, contrasts) may be found in or across many of the present chapters, whether between national systems, localities, or schools of differing characteristics. Delving below the national level into comparisons across local education authorities and across particular schools, this book shows that there is room for further enquiry about policy lessons and variations in those arenas as well. Comparative analysis need not be always confined to whole systems; micro-level comparative studies may uncover explanatory factors that are overlooked at higher levels. We say this because much public policy research in the education field is likely to be conducted by school-based practitioners themselves. They may lack the resources of time and money that are required for undertaking national and international comparative research which investigates, in some depth, policy and implementation across many sites. Although this is often thought necessary for interesting and valid conclusions to be drawn, we believe that more modest comparative research is valuable as well, especially if framed within widely shared theoretical, conceptual and explanatory frameworks concerning educational governance, the nature of public policy, and the political or public issues that inhabit or influence policy-related action. We hope that this book will serve to stimulate such research.

The chapters in Part I all derive from two related research projects which the editors as well as the chapter authors conducted in Scotland and England[1] These chapters deploy some of the findings of the projects, which were conducted amongst a sample of schools in several education authorities in Scotland and one in England. The research facilitated comparisons between education systems at national levels, among education authorities at the local government level, and among roughly similar sets of schools that served contrasting catchment areas or communities. Further details of the research setting are given later on in this Introduction, and in the chapters of Part I. Taken together, the chapters deal with a number of overarching themes of educational governance. These include lay participation at the school level, 'managerialism', the effect of markets and parental choice of schools, teachers' professionalism, and relations between schools and other levels of governance. The macroscopic issues are also taken up, selectively, in Part II, where the chapter authors explore them in the context of devolved management and its equivalents in other education systems within the UK and abroad. In the UK context, both researchers and practitioners, perhaps especially teachers, have often found it difficult to separate devolved management from the package of education reforms which affect schools, relationships, roles and educational outcomes. This is because schools have been charged not only with increased administrative and financial responsibilities, but with, for example, the implementation of major, contentious and continuously modified reforms in curriculum and assessment, and in parental choice of schools. The combination of policies and programmes complicates the analysis of devolved management as a discrete factor in the perception of teachers and in the policy-related action within schools and between them and other levels. It has given rise to the education practitioners' complaint that schools have suffered an overload of innovation, and to contestation over the very meaning and reality of devolved management. These issues are reflected in some of the chapters presented here.

The next section of this Introduction gives a brief description of each chapter, highlighting the main themes and conclusions. The final section provides a background to the UK chapters of both parts of the book. It outlines and compares the main contextual and statutory factors that help to determine the implementation of devolved management in England and Wales, Scotland and Northern Ireland. It concludes by describing the methods used in the research projects on which the chapters of Part I are based.

Describing the chapters

Charles Raab places the study of the devolved management of schools in the context of broader theories, models and concepts in the field of public policy studies, especially with regard to the new emphasis placed on 'governance' as a term denoting new patterns of interaction between government and society. He explores meanings of governance with reference to the question of policy networks and steering, as well as to the respective roles of state and civil-society institutions, and the market. The position of the school is discussed, with reference to its head teacher, its internal hierarchy, and its governing body or school board under devolved management, and the changing nature of 'partnership' in the system under the new governance of education is considered. Raab draws upon research findings to illustrate and compare these changing relationships, roles and structures in Scotland and in England within the analytical categories developed earlier in the chapter, before concluding on a sceptical note concerning the effects of devolved management, and indeed how they can be evaluated.

Margaret Arnott's chapter is concerned with the effect of 'managerialism' on schools in these two countries, based again upon the findings of the research projects. She relates these effects to the market orientations of Conservative government reforms in the 1980s and 1990s, and to the shift in the pattern of accountability that these reforms represent. Viewing managerialism in a comparative perspective as between Scotland and England, Arnott focuses particularly upon the new position of teachers – the regulation of their work in schools, and external regulation of the profession – and the role of lay participation in school decision-making.

Looking at the impact of managerialism within schools, she highlights the changing nature of headship and the relationship between the head teacher and other teaching staff, and the workings of school boards and governing bodies, before drawing comparative conclusions about devolved management and the importance of the head teacher in the new managerial arrangements.

Further attention is given to the effects of devolved management and related changes on the school as a workplace (using a somewhat different conceptual framework), in Lucy Bailey's chapter, in which she focuses on teachers' changing position as employees in the education system. Based on the Scottish and English research evidence in the light of sociological theories of teachers' work, she examines critically changes in the labour process, in management, and in employment conditions. Three key areas of analysis are highlighted in this chapter: conceptions of professionalism, changing hierarchies and working conditions, and effects on teachers' day-to-day experiences of work. Looking in detail at teachers' relationships in schools and at their discourse about work, Bailey contrasts the argument that teachers are being deskilled and their work intensified, with a more complex understanding of how teachers' professional values mediate but are also changed by the pressures of devolved management. She emphasises the importance of seeing how teachers conceive their role in order to assess the effect of particular policies, arguing that devolved management itself is part of a wider reform and cultural change in schooling.

Part I concludes with Pamela Munn's discussion of parental participation in the Scottish and English schools that were the subject of the research on which this part draws. The government's policy intentions were to subordinate the influence of professionals and local-authority administrators and to elevate that of parental and other lay participants in decision-making. Placing this aspect of devolved management in a context of other reforms in educational governance, Munn considers whether Scottish school boards and English school governing bodies have fulfilled policy expectations as vehicles for greater responsiveness and accountability of schools to the community outside, and for a shift in the balance of power, as integral parts of devolved management. Looking at what actually happens at meetings of these boards and bodies, she explains why the outcomes have fallen short of these expectations, illustrating, for example, the staying-power of traditional patterns of power and deference in relationships between the school and the parent that contrive to blunt the effect of deliberate change. This account provides an object-lesson and explanations of the gap between policy-making and implementation. Munn speculates on the implications that another form of devolution – the creation of a Scottish Parliament in 1999 – might have for the part played by civil-society institutions in the workings of centralised, state-provided systems and services, such as education.

Part II opens with an analysis of devolved management in a number of disadvantaged schools in England and Wales, by Jane Martin, Penny McKeown, Jon Nixon and Stewart Ranson, based on research that covered all parts of the UK. Like Munn's, their chapter concerns civil society, considered here at the local level, where they see community-based restructuring as an essential component of learning and professional authority as well as of governance. Divergence between schools' responses and the values and aims of the legislated, 'managerial' and market-driven education reforms is one of the themes of this chapter, resonating with similar findings in others. This testifies to the ability of schools and their communities to shape opportunities within the framework of reforms that often appear determinative, although there were important variations in the 'regimes' that schools adopted for this. Three school case-studies are used to illustrate further variations within the most progressive pattern of this restructuring, in which new relationships between schools and parents are forged.

Turning next to Northern Ireland, Penny McKeown and Grainne Byrne discuss the way in which policies common across the UK in the 1980s and 1990s operate in the education system of that country. In the context of Northern Ireland education's distinctive structural and administrative arrangements, including academic selection at 'eleven-plus', different emphases and, in some cases, different policies have led to some variations in the impact and outcomes of the reforms, compared with those elsewhere. The authors focus on parental choice (open enrolment) – a 'market'-related reform – and on the relationship of schools to their communities of parents. As in other chapters, this shows the extent to which central policy initiatives are susceptible to mediation at the regional, local and school level. They discuss variations among types of secondary schools in terms of the effect of devolved management, specifically concerning the ways in which selective and non-selective secondary schools have responded to the challenge of competition in safeguarding or extending their enrolment. Some strategies involved cultivating new forms of relationship with parents and with the world beyond the school. McKeown and Byrne conclude that the (selective) grammar schools have benefited from parental choice at the expense of the rest, exacerbating inequalities.

In another sense, contrasts between improving and struggling schools also feature in the chapter on school-based management (SBM) in the United States. Priscilla Wohlstetter and Penny Bender Sebring discuss the

SBM experiments that are prevalent in nine school districts. These innovations have been introduced as a way of raising educational performance by situating decisions about finance, staffing and pedagogy at the level of the schools, whilst leaving the framework of standards and goals to be set at higher levels of governance. In the light of this rationale, and based on large-scale research conducted in Chicago and in other school districts, the authors highlight the variety of approaches that have been taken in implementing SBM. Focusing on identifying the conditions that are characteristic of 'successful' SBM schools, including the distribution of power between schools and district offices concerning budgets, personnel, curriculum and instruction, they assess the difference that it makes to the roles and relationships of education professionals and parents, and explain the factors that produce differences amongst schools. Noting that under SBM, variations in performance across schools can become more marked, they contrast the contributions of school Principals, teachers, parents and district offices between the struggling and the improving schools, and discuss the relationship between autonomy and accountability. This research points up the complexity and variability of interdependent factors and players at different levels of governance that may explain why devolved management 'works', or fails to, in different settings.

With some comparative reference to the UK, Kerry Jacobs' chapter looks at the sweeping education reforms that have taken place in New Zealand. He focuses on their effect on four Christchurch schools of differing characteristics, after describing the political and policy background that generated legislation embodying the reforms at the end of the 1980s and its implementation in the 1990s. Financial and administrative responsibilities were devolved to schools, but they became subject to intensive external indirect control from the centre in terms of auditing and accountability, including performance measurement and standards-setting. Interview material gathered from teachers, school Principals and administrators is used to describe the experiences of the schools under devolved management, to illustrate the effects on different roles in the school, and to portray the tension between autonomy and control. Jacobs' study raises questions about the meaning of devolution and about the nature of the teaching profession, casting light on important themes in the general governance mode of analysis as well as in the more specific understanding of education.

Finally, Jørgen Grønnegaard Christensen analyses the Danish school system with regard to devolved management and new forms of governance. In the 1990s, Danish head teachers' authority was strengthened, parental choice of school extended, and schools given directly elected school boards. After describing the system's history, complexity and distinctive characteristics, including the presence of a significant private sector, Christensen explains the variations in devolved management, which result from: the different legal status of types of schools that affect the degree to which they are subject to national regulation; the historical legacies of the different types that powerfully shape the implementation of devolution; and important political factors. Whilst the existence of parental choice of schools in Denmark, as elsewhere, places public schools on their mettle, the Danish reforms illustrate once again the difficulty faced by national policy-makers in achieving the goals of new governance uniformly across an education system. An important observation is that – as in Scotland, perhaps – the channel of user-democracy afforded by school-level boards has neither excited very much interest nor altered substantially the responsiveness of schools to parents.

Devolved management of schools in the United Kingdom

The existence of distinctive education systems within the UK offers researchers the opportunity to study the impact of legislative developments on a comparative basis, yet relatively few researchers have taken this opportunity. Until July 1999, policy generation was undertaken within a unitary *political* framework but there were, in fact, three clearly distinct school systems in the UK, those of England and Wales, Northern Ireland, and Scotland. In Scotland, for instance, the schooling system and its governance had a distinct institutional arrangement within the UK framework. Separate educational legislation for Scotland was passed in the UK Parliament in Westminster, and it was the Scottish Office, not the Department for Education and Employment, which had responsibility for Scottish education. Traditionally, there have been a number of administrative institutions which are unique to Scotland, for example the Scottish Office Education and Industry Department, the Scottish Qualifications Authority, the Scottish Consultative Council on the Curriculum and the General Teaching Council. At various times, new bodies were created, others have passed out of existence, and names have changed. Thus, even within a unitary political framework, the administration of education policy was conducted in a distinctly Scottish network of institutions.

Recent developments in education policy, especially policies on devolved management of schools, reveal that contextual differences between the UK education systems affect the formation of policies. Those differences which had the most direct bearing on the way devolved management has been implemented in each system include the diversity of school types; the structure of local government; the extent of religious segregation and church involvement; and traditions of parental involvement in schools. Table 0.1 summarises those contextual differences at the local and school levels which affected the way in which devolved management was introduced across the UK schooling systems.

It is clear that concessions have been made by central government to territorial diversity; the most obvious being the establishment of territorially based central-government departments such as the Scottish Office and the Northern Ireland Office. These departments were not, however, intended to have a policy-making function in the political sense. The convention of administrative devolution implied that central government would pursue common policy objectives across the UK but would tailor policies to accommodate the distinctiveness of the different education systems. In practice, however, the theoretical line between 'policy' and 'administration' is blurred. Thus, Scotland and Northern Ireland were largely able to make or adapt education policy through their distinct administrative institutions, under the aegis of the central-government departments in each of their countries. As we shall see in Part I and in McKeown and Byrne's chapter in Part II, this has been the case with devolved management of schools. McKeown and Byrne emphasise, for instance, that the academically and socially divided nature of Northern Ireland's schooling system has affected the way in which the policy of open enrolment has combined with formula funding, introduced under LMS, to exacerbate inequalities which existed before the implementation of these policies. In particular, they argue that the hierarchical structure of the schooling system has not only been reinforced but extended.

Conservative governments wanted to restructure the education systems of all the UK countries to enhance consumerist and managerial modes of accountability, but had to start from a different basis in each of these systems. Also, if central government wanted to ease the path of implementation, policies had to be drafted to accommodate the distinctiveness of each of the education systems. Current constitutional reforms offer the possibility of greater policy diversity in the UK in the future. This is especially the case in Scotland where the new Parliament has a much stronger overt policy-making role than its Welsh counterpart.

Turning now specifically to the implementation of devolved management of schools, elsewhere we have argued that there are four main policy themes evident in this policy initiative (Raab *et al.*, 1997):

• increasing competition among schools in attracting pupils, with school budgets largely determined by the number of pupils at the school;

Table 0.1   School governance: key contextual differences

Type of provision	England and Wales	Northern Ireland	Scotland
Compulsory provision	Ages 5–16	Ages 4–16	Ages 5–16
Local government	Recent reorganisation in England created a hybrid system of unitary authorities, two-tier authorities and metropolitan authority areas. In Wales twenty-two new unitary authorities were created in April 1996. Responsibility for maintained schools remains with local education authorities.*	No local government reorganisation. In 1973, education was removed from local government's remit, and responsibility for schools now lies with five Education and Library Boards (ELB), which are appointed by the Secretary of State for Northern Ireland.	In April 1996, the two-tier system of Regional and District authorities was replaced with thirty-two unitary authorities. Local government's relationship to the Scottish Parliament is under review in 1999.
School types	Mostly co-educational comprehensives: county, voluntary, grant-maintained (GM)	Religious segregation, selective. Compared with the rest of the UK, there is a higher proportion of single-sex schools and smaller Controlled (Protestant), voluntary grammar, grant maintained integrated (rather than GM), and maintained fully funded schools.	Co-educational comprehensives: state-funded Catholic schools and non-denominational schools. The vast majority are state 12–18 comprehensives. Secondary system is structurally homogeneous.
Lay participation	Governing body comprising parents, teachers, LEA nominees and co-opted governors.	Governing body comprising parents, teachers, ELB representatives, church representatives and non-voting head. ELB nominees are not party political appointments.	School boards only created in 1989 comprising parents (in the majority), teachers and co-opted members. The head has advisory status.
Responsibilities	Management, curricular and financial responsibilities, including the appointment and dismissal of staff.	Management, curricular and financial responsibilities, including the appointment and dismissal of staff.	School board has only a consultative role in DSM. Responsibilities are delegated to the head, not to the school board.

Source: Adapted from McKeown, P. et al. (1996) 'Issues in Comparative Education Policy Research: School Governance in the UK Education Systems', Paper presented at the Annual Conference of European Educational Research Association, University of Seville.

Note:
*The 1993 Education Act established a new appointed body – the Funding Agency for Schools (FAS) – to administer GM schools. It would also share responsibility with an LEA for planning provision where 10% of schools had acquired GM status and FAS would assume complete control once 75% adopted GM status.

- promoting lay, especially parental, participation in school decision-making;
- enhancing teachers' and other educational professionals' accountability to parents;
- greater delegation of decisions to school level, with (local) education authorities adopting a strategic and enabling role and providing only a small number of services to schools.

These themes were applied throughout the UK, but have been implemented differently in each of the UK education systems. The various policies associated with devolved management of schools, such as Local Management of Schools (LMS) in Northern Ireland, England and Wales: Devolved School Management (DSM) in Scotland; and open enrolment, evince a number of differences (see Table 0.2 for fuller discussion).

For instance, if we compare the responsibilities of governing bodies and school boards, important variations become apparent. The responsibilities of governing bodies have been greatly expanded: as pointed out by Levacic (1995), the official model of local management in schools in England and Wales portrays the governing body as a board of directors with the head teacher as the chief executive. In this model, the governing body sets the goals and objectives of the school, determines policy, allocates resources, monitors school performance and holds the professional managers to account, while head teachers are responsible for the day-to-day running of the school. In contrast, DSM delegates responsibilities to the head teacher rather than to the school board. School boards were introduced in Scotland rather later than in England; thus it was not until the School Board Act 1988 that there was a Scottish form to governing bodies. Under the terms of the 1988 legislation, boards have very limited powers and responsibilities; their main power being the ability to request information on a range of matters, including assessment and discipline (Munn 1993). As stated in the last education White Paper issued by the former Conservative government, *Raising the Standard*, 'school boards are a channel for the flow of information between parents, schools and education authorities and are in practice involved in all aspects of school life' (Scottish Office 1997).

In Northern Ireland the implementation of LMS has varied in some important respects from that in the rest of the UK. Two elements of the schooling system are worth considering briefly. In contrast to the rest of the UK, responsibility for the schooling system lies outside the remit of local government. This has been the situation since 1973 when the Westminster Parliament assumed responsibility for matters, including education, devolved to the assembly in Stormont. Responsibility for the

Table 0.2 Comparison between LMS and DSM

- LMS was introduced in England and Wales by legislation in 1988, which was reinforced by prescriptive administrative guidelines, whereas DSM was introduced in Scotland by more flexible guidelines, without prior legislation, in 1993. In Northern Ireland, equivalent reforms were introduced in the Education Reform (Northern Ireland) Order 1989.
- In Northern Ireland, England and Wales, governing bodies have been given statutory powers on a range of matters, including staffing, curriculum, and discipline. In Scotland, school boards have a largely consultative role, and powers have been delegated to the head teacher.
- School boards and governing bodies differ in their composition. Scottish boards have an in-built parental majority, but they do not have an equivalent to governors nominated by the LEA. Head teachers are the powerful professional advisers to school boards, but, in governing bodies in England, Wales and Northern Ireland, they cannot be full members. In Northern Ireland, the churches are represented on governing bodies of maintained and controlled schools.
- Scottish education authorities have more flexibility than their English or Welsh counterparts in applying their own funding formulae and devising schemes of delegation to schools. For instance, the formula could give schools actual salary costs, rather than average salary costs calculated across the authority as a whole. In Northern Ireland, Education and Library Boards, which are appointed by the Secretary of State for Northern Ireland, are responsible for the schooling system.

Source: Adapted from Raab, C. *et al.* (1997) 'Devolving the Management of Schools in Britain', *Educational Administration Quarterly*, 33(2): 143–44.

schooling system was passed to five area boards – Education and Library Boards (ELBs) – whose members, including representatives from local government, are appointed by the Secretary of State for Northern Ireland. Therefore LMS has not reduced or redefined the role of local government but rather affected the position of the ELBs within the schooling system. Responsibilities have been shifted from these appointed bodies to governing bodies.

Another dimension of the schooling system in Northern Ireland which has affected the implementation of LMS is the traditional division between the Catholic and Protestant religious communities. Religious segregation within the schooling system has affected the composition of governing bodies, with a much greater involvement for the churches in controlled and maintained schools. Steps have been taken by central government to try to develop an integrated schooling system where the churches have much less input. However, this sector accounts for only a small proportion of schools.

Description of projects in Part I

As mentioned earlier, the chapters in Part I are based upon two research projects in which the authors and their colleagues were involved. The first was an illustrative comparative study of devolved management of schools in Scotland and England; the second was a qualitative case study of the implementation of DSM in Scotland. The latter study built upon the Scottish element of the first project and offered a rare opportunity to collect longitudinal data for six of the case-study schools. For the first study, three (local) education authorities were selected: Lothian and Strathclyde in Scotland, and Newcastle-upon-Tyne in England. These authorities were selected to provide contrasts along two dimensions: centralised/decentralised decision-making and strong/weak parental influence. Lothian represented a traditional, centralised management style with very limited experience of devolved management and relatively weak parental influence. Strathclyde Region had played a leading role in developing devolved management with its scheme of Devolved Management of Resources.

In each authority four case-study schools were selected. The sample within each authority was intended to illustrate the effects of devolved management upon schools in a range of circumstances. These were an affluent area with mainly owner-occupied housing, an area of high socio-economic deprivation, and two intermediate areas: a 'mixed' area and a 'traditional' working-class area. The schools' relative market position was also noted; that is, whether they had gained or lost pupils as a result of parental choice legislation. A number of variables were, however, held constant. For instance, all the chosen schools were non-denominational secondary schools.

This research design facilitated comparisons at a number of levels. First, comparisons could be drawn at national level between the experiences of different forms of devolved management. Second, comparisons could be drawn between (local) education authorities in their approaches to devolved management. Finally, looking across the twelve schools allowed comparisons to be drawn at institutional level. The chapters in Part I deal primarily with comparisons at national and school levels.

Four methods of investigation were used. The range of methods was chosen to provide different kinds of evidence on the effects and perceptions of devolved management and thus provide a fuller understanding of them. The methods used were: observations of school board and governing body meetings in each school; semi-structured interviews with selected members of boards and governing bodies, the head teacher, selected members of staff, key politicians and officials at local and national levels, and pressure group leaders; a telephone survey of a sample of parents at each school; and analyses of official documents and various types of school documentation such as minutes, school-development plans and handbooks.

A similar methodology was adopted in the second funded project. In addition, the two Scottish authorities from the first project – Lothian and Strathclyde – were retained and a third was selected to extend the study into schools with less predominantly urban catchment areas. Three schools were selected in each authority. The Lothian and Strathclyde schools had been included in the previous study. Criteria employed in the first study were also used to select the schools in the third Scottish authority.

Notes

1   These were: *Devolved Management of Schools*, conducted in 1992–96 under Economic and Social Research Council (ESRC) grant no. R000233653; the research team consisted of Michael Adler, Margaret Arnott, Lucy Bailey, Carole Moore, Pamela Munn and Charles Raab; and *Devolved School Management in Secondary Schools in Scotland*, conducted in 1994–96 under a contract from the Scottish Office Education and Industry Department (SOEID); the research team consisted of Michael Adler, Margaret Arnott, Lorraine McAvoy, Pamela Munn and Charles Raab. Details of these projects and their methodology are available in final reports to sponsors.

References

Levacic, R. (1995) *Local Management of Schools: Analysis and Practice*, Buckingham: Open University Press.

McKeown, P., Arnott, M. A. and Bullock, A. D. (1996) 'Issues in Comparative Education Policy Research: School Governance in the UK Education Systems', Paper presented at the Annual Conference of the European Educational Research Association, September 1996, Seville, Spain.

Munn, P. (1993) *Parents and Schools: Customers, Managers or Partners?*, London: Routledge.

Raab, C. *et al.* (1997) 'Devolving the Management of Schools in Britain', in *Educational Administration Quarterly*, **33(2)**: 143–44.

Scottish Office (1997) *Raising the Standard: a White Paper on Education and Skills Development in Scotland*, Edinburgh: HMSO

Part I

The governance of schooling

Themes in Scottish-based research

1 The devolved management of schools and its implications for governance

Charles D. Raab

Introduction: Theoretical perspectives on the new governance of education

Devolved School Management (DSM) in Scotland, and Local Management of Schools (LMS) in England and Wales are related manifestations of the changing governance of education. They involve changes in the exercise of power and leadership within schools and in the relationship of schools to the wider system of management and control. They resemble trends in other countries, holding out the promise of useful comparisons beyond the English/Scottish ones. As mentioned in the Introduction, there are several variations in labels across and within countries; these often reflect differences of emphasis amongst various elements in devolved or decentralised management. Levačić (1998: 331) concisely defines the generic 'school-based management' in terms of two elements:

1. decentralization to school level of responsibility for decision making ...
2. the sharing of decision-making power amongst the key stakeholders at school level – head teacher, teachers, parents, students, other community members.

She argues that, in LMS, it is predominantly the first element that is emphasised, although there are also greater powers for school governors and parents. She also notes that there is a milder form of school-based management in Scotland as compared with that in England (Levačić 1995: 15).

The research reported in this chapter, and in the rest of Part I of this book, deals with both aspects. It does not relegate the second element because the widening of participation beyond the traditional confines of the 'vertical' axis of central government, local government and teachers in schools is seen as an important potential development that casts considerable light on the full meaning of the new governance of education.[1] The research is based on the view that the new governance of education in Scotland and England, as exemplified by devolved management, represents a restructuring of:

- *roles and relationships* within schools, and between schools and a range of external environments that include levels of government as well as other actors or stakeholders; in particular, lay, and especially parental, participation in school decision-making is promoted;
- *the pattern of accountability* of teachers and other education professionals to each other; accountability to parent and other community 'stakeholders' is emphasised;
- *the pattern of governance* between or among levels of the decision-making system, including strategies and mechanisms of control; there is greater delegation of decisions to schools, and education authorities, whilst losing many traditional powers, adopt a strategic and enabling role whilst providing fewer services to schools;
- *the flow of resources*, principally money, and the mechanisms that arbitrate its flow (e.g. quasi-markets); schools compete with each other to attract pupils, as school budgets directly reflect the number of pupils;
- *the educational and other values* that underpin schooling; there is a heightened emphasis on measured performance, on targets for learning, and on the management of resources, and less emphasis on teachers' traditional collegial values.

This research enables the devolved management of schools and associated education policies, such as parental choice of school, to be considered as major components of the new governance. Educational governance can be seen in the context of the general analytical framework of 'governance' in policy and governmental studies, where there is now an array of theoretical and conceptual constructs (e.g. steering, dependence, networks) that point up the significance of crucial aspects of change, but do not necessarily explain them. While these terms help to reclassify data about roles, patterns and actions in policy systems, the explanation of change lies elsewhere, in the macro, meso, or micro processes of the society, economy and polity. Moreover, similarities as well as differences of new forms of governance across countries or sites may invite explanations based upon alternative theories. These include political and institutional causation, economic influences, international and cross-sectoral borrowing or 'lesson-drawing', ideological fashion or cultural change. Although the research discussed here does not go that far, it casts light on the implementation of education policies that exemplify the new governance in different national, local and school settings; only further comparative research could help to address larger issues of policy explanation.

The policy studies literature contains a number of varying and imprecise 'governance' definitions of broad applicability. Without getting drawn too far into semantics, it is worthwhile looking at some that bear upon the way in which educational governance can be understood. For Rhodes (1997: 53), governance in Britain 'refers to self-organizing, interorganizational networks', signifying that government centralisation now coexists with fragmentation and interdependence. In this differentiated polity, policy networks characterise the policy process; a segmented executive features bargaining games between and within networks. Government interventions and direct management create unintended consequences and implementation gaps. 'There is a persistent tension between the wish for authoritative action and dependence on the compliance and actions of others' (Rhodes 1997: 15).

Rhodes' stipulative definition thus equates 'governance' to these network phenomena and structures whilst acknowledging other meanings of that term. At the heart of the new public management, for instance, is the idea of 'steering', which Rhodes sees as synonymous with governance (Rhodes 1997: 49). Unfortunately, he introduces needless confusion in the applicability of 'governance' by defining it in terms of network *structures* whilst also equating it with governance as a norm-setting *process* or activity. Compounding this incoherence is an apparent endorsement of the view that governance is also 'the *result* of interactive social–political forms of governing' (Rhodes 1997: 51; emphasis added). Matters are not helped by the variety of perspectives on the concept of 'networks' itself (e.g. Marsh and Rhodes 1992; Jordan and Schubert 1992; Raab 1992). Nevertheless, if 'governance' is a more radical development of the policy-network approach purporting to denote a new way of governing that is now characteristic of Britain, it refocuses attention upon interdependent relationships among an array of structures at various levels. Although definitional issues are unresolved, 'governance' usefully signifies a departure from the presumption that a hierarchical, formally authoritative 'government' must always be the most important actor. An empirical issue for comparative analysis would concern the relative (un)importance of governmental institutions in different fields of policy. This would require analysts to demonstrate, rather than assume, *a priori*, the superior or inferior potency of government within the networks.

Yet an important question is whether 'governance' denotes a real and recent change in policy-making and government, or whether previous policy histories – including, for example, what occurred at different stages, especially perhaps implementation – could indeed be credibly rewritten in terms of the new concept. The idea that governance through networks is a new phenomenon in Britain, and that governments are no longer so capable of exercising authority, should be viewed sceptically (Peters 1997). There are two issues here: one concerns the concentration or dispersion of decision-making; the other concerns the part played by government in these processes. For Smith (1999: 15; emphasis in original), the contemporary 'shift from a directive state to a more fragmented one' has influenced 'notions of *governance* as a flexible form of control rather than *government* as direct control'. This conflation of structural properties with modes of action is awkward, especially in that the identifiable differentiation and network activities are said to occur not only between Whitehall and outside groups, but within the 'core executive' itself – the co-ordinative heart of the government machine. This is an important observation. However, the core executive has arguably for a long time been composed of multiple, interdependent institutions, whose work is done through complex network relationships; and, indeed – considering the Treasury as one of the core's mainstays – whose ability to exert direct control has never gone unchallenged. Recent reforms in British government may have exposed the fragmentation of policy processes and posed severe challenges to co-ordination (Rhodes 1995) but they are more likely to have exacerbated these tendencies than to have created them anew.

Although relationships have varied in their degree of tightness and in other dimensions of structure and action, interdependence amongst public and private groups, decision centres, governmental levels and appointed bodies has for long been recognised as a common feature of governance – not least in the nineteenth century – in what is formally a 'centralised' state. Scottish education, for example, has for generations been characterised by policy-making and administrative interactions within clusters of institutions that included levels of government (and various institutions at each level), appointed bodies ('quangos'), and representative associations (Raab 1980). At least from the 1940s to the 1980s, these were laced together by networks of connections amongst participants in a policy community in which the dynamics of trust and distrust were played out in terms of recruitment to the network and its policy activities (McPherson and Raab 1988). It is not a contradiction to say, also, that central authorities tried to use their powers and legitimate authority, albeit with varying degrees of success. There is ample evidence of how interdependence and the distribution of exchangeable resources throughout the network prevented government from always getting what it wanted, and of how the government's attempts to steer the policy action and to shape the networks in which it participated were by no means certain to prevail. The authority and will of government were, and are, indispensable, although insufficient.

Rhodes certainly recognises that government may still exert some control (Rhodes and Marsh 1992: 202–3), but the main message of the new approach is that the networks of governance, of which government is part, now prevail. Perhaps 'steering' is the key concept, denoting new and subtle ways in which governments remain potent actors. This is also a central theme in Kooiman's (1993) perspective on governance, in which social complexity, dynamics and diversity are handled by new government–society interactions. 'Interactive social–political governance', for Kooiman (1993: 3), 'means setting the tone; creating the social–political conditions for the development of new models of interactive governing in terms of co-management, co-steering and co-guidance'. Interaction, rather than government action, sums up this approach to governance. 'Steering at a distance' is the way that Kickert (1995) describes the situation of new governance in Dutch higher education, but he emphasises that this 'is not a form of government withdrawal, a partial abolition of government steering capacity' (Kickert 1995: 153) either in intention or effect. Government in the Netherlands gave greater autonomy to the higher education sector in order to increase the effectiveness of steering towards the goals of better quality, more efficiency and achieving innovations by concentrating on steering the outputs more than the inputs.

Thus, for any policy field, a governance perspective based on an analysis of networks runs the risk of neglecting the important directive and leadership roles that governments and the machinery of the state may, and often do, still perform. The extent and manner of this is obviously an empirical question, field by field, and should not be defined out of existence. Smith (1999), who adopts the 'governing without government' definition of governance, nevertheless acknowledges that governments may still seek to exercise authoritative control, as in education under the Conservatives: '[i]f the notion of governance is to be used at the domestic level in Britain then it cannot be governing without government' (Smith 1999: 28). However, control is not assured because departments compete for authority and must form alliances, exchange resources and engage in games through a range of networks that are horizontal as well as vertical in extent.

This perspective comes nearer the mark, but it is not new. It has generally been overlooked that, long before the recent conceptualisations of governance, Kogan and his colleagues (1984) criticised and supplanted the traditional description of educational government in Britain along some of the same lines. That received description was of a liberal, top-down model, based on legislation, in which local education authorities provided education and made key decisions circumscribing the work of the schools. Note that, especially in the English education context, it was not inappropriate to focus upon a rather shortened hierarchy that left the central government departments to some extent in the background in the day-to-day running of the system. In any case, traditionally and paradoxically, head teachers had great discretion over the curriculum, resource allocations, and external relations with the community and other organisations. Considering the role of local government, Kogan's team looked sceptically at the hierarchical assumptions of the model on the basis of administrative theory, sociology and political science:

> Theory challenges traditional managerial models by asking ... whether policy-making originates solely from within the local authority's authorised channels, or whether values are generated more diffusely. It asks whether the processes of arriving at policies take place more widely within the policy-making system and also among those groups who press upon that system ... The structure is in fact diffuse and complex ... Policy is made or modified by the interaction within a *network* of organisations and groups which each fulfil functions in local education governance. Conflict is possible and negotiation becomes necessary.
>
> (Kogan *et al.* 1984: 12–13; emphasis added)

This reformulation has a further contemporary ring in its identification of exchange and dependency theory, as well as of resources and intergovernmental relations, at the heart of the education policy system in which school governing bodies are situated:

> Essentially, it views social and political actions as a process of exchange within a political model in which relationships between levels of government form a complex network of institutions, interest groups, and the like. The groups live in an environment of uncertainty produced by the scarcity of resources. They pursue interests and acquire strategic resources by creating dependencies among other actors. Authority and power provide critical bargaining levers to manipulate exchange relationships in the network ... Working through a system of exchange, the operation of the intergovernmental network is shaped by the pattern of resource ownership and the structure of dependencies. This model of exchange and power is known as resource dependency theory.
>
> (Kogan *et al.* 1984: 16–17)

The attention devoted to policy networks thus engages debates about the role of the state, or at least of formal governmental institutions, in the policy process (Raab 1994). Atkinson and Coleman (1992: 168) are emphatic that 'proceeding to analyze the policy process as if broad state institutions are irrelevant is a misuse of the concepts of network and community'. If networks by themselves do not sum up 'governance', let us detour briefly to acknowledge the market as another principle and a co-ordinating mechanism of governance; the question of the market in education is treated at greater length in Arnott's chapter of this volume (Chapter 2). Some writers use the term '*quasi*-market' partly because price and other market mechanisms do not operate as such in schooling. Quasi-markets combine market and hierarchical principles (Frances *et al.* 1991: 8). Indeed, as Levačić (1991: 23) observes, 'market coordination could not function in the absence of the other modes of coordination'. Government is necessary to provide a legal framework of rights, and civil society is necessary to establish conditions of trust and social expectations that underpin the market and individual choice. The interdependence of market choice with these other principles and institutions suggests that markets may be deliberately structured by the state, that individual 'rational' choices are also institutionally constrained, and that sellers' marketing strategies are also calculated as well as conditioned by the state and civil society.

'New Right' governments, but not only they, have brought markets into play as partial alternatives to governments and networks as allocators of values and resources in public policy. This is emphatically so in educa-tion. The effect of markets has run deep, manifested in such devices as parental choice of school (open enrolment), voucher schemes, and the strengthening of the private sector, as several chapters of this book show. Of course, the market in education exists in some tension with, and perhaps contradicts, the 'strong state' dimension of New Right philosophy and policy, exemplified by central control of the curriculum and of the major levers of statutory requirements, sanctions, and finance. Its tendency to individuation in terms of parental choice – one meaning of 'participation' – may cut across the solidaristic norms of civil society and its structures of collective participation.

Although these issues of ideological and policy coherence between markets and other principles and practices are important (Gamble 1988; Raab 1993a), they can be set on one side here. But they further point up the necessity of seeing governance as a pattern of policy and control that may combine elements of several principles, often in novel and change-able permutations. Various ways of understanding these combinations are available to be applied to understanding changes in the governance of policy fields. For Pestoff (1993), there is now a 'new welfare mix' among modes of service provision and production that includes the state, civil society and the market. This approach maps on to another, which high-lights hierarchies, networks and market choices as three principles and instruments of control and co-ordination (Thompson *et al.* 1991; Maidment and Thompson 1993). This trio is closely related to, if not isomorphic with, the dimensions of 'governance' seen above. To the extent that the relationship (or 'mix') of modes is changing, we may talk about new patterns of interdependence amongst the organisations through which governance takes place, new co-operative (but also conflictual) relationships amongst organisations and actors at different levels, and new implications for the role and authority of governmental institutions. The research findings in this book illustrate these for educa-tion systems.

In this sense, to ask, 'what is the governance of education?' is not necessarily to invite an answer solely in terms of policy networks, but in terms of possible mixtures of machinery or processes. Government steering, therefore, is not just a matter of steering networks, but of steering markets and hierarchies as well, albeit not necessarily with success. Moreover, the organisational and decision-making processes of the state and civil society, or of hierarchies and networks, are related to the market principle and individual choice in so far as the latter provide some of the subject-matter of public policy agendas and some of the rationale for insti-tutional and network change. This relationship is very important, because devolved management and the new governance involve, in theory, not only a juxtaposition of several control or decision-making mechanisms or strategies, as with a checklist, but their interweaving in various patterns of harmony or tension as befits the idea of a new *system* of governance (Kooiman 1993) which has ostensibly been created in the recent past.

A closer look at the state and civil society in education

Leaving the market aside for the purposes of this chapter, it is worthwhile approaching concepts of the state and civil society, and the related ones of hierarchy and network once again in the context of education and the devolved management of schools. *The state* is a much-debated concept both generally (Dunleavy and O'Leary 1987) and with regard to educa-tion (Dale 1983, 1989, 1992; Ozga 1990; Raab 1994). It refers here to the formal political, administrative and legal arrangements for schooling. In the United Kingdom's education systems, central government, local authorities and schools are involved in hierarchical patterns of authority and accountability. Hierarchical principles also underlie the school's internal authority structure which ranges typically from the head teacher and senior management to the classroom teacher. Hierarchical relationships have changed under devolved management: although management is theoretically devolved to the school, it is in many respects accompanied by an increase in formal central powers and by the erosion of local government control – the middle level. An interesting new pattern suggested by the data is that the hierarchical relationship of these other levels of the education system to the school is in some ways loosened – as government policy has professedly desired – in favour of steering by means of new patterns of incentives and controls. Meanwhile, one result of many of the new responsibilities placed upon schools is that hierarchy has tended to become more formalised within the school as between the head teacher (or management team) and the rest of the staff, although this is not universally so and may be mitigated by more collegial styles of operation.

The new governance of education therefore involves, in part, changes in the patterns of authority under new 'managerial' pressures, and therefore changes in the part that hierarchy plays within educational institutions in which norms of professional collegiality are challenged. These changes in hierarchical relationships, from state to school, relate to what has been described as the demise of an older professional/bureaucratic 'partnership' in education (Raab 1992), and in central–local relations generally, in favour of a newer one which enfranchises parents and the laity, and which incorporates civil society ideals and practices, as described further on.

The extent to which there has been a transition from some degree of top-down regulation to the self-regulating (or self-managing, or self-governing) school, varies across locations, but cannot be said to be large in any of the research settings discussed in Part I of this book. Theoretically and generally, the state may be becoming more 'responsive': Sørensen (1995: 67) says that 'the market and civil society intervene more and more in what were formerly defined as areas suited for state-organized governance'. If so, then we should be able to note the consequences, for state-provided institutions like schools, of 'user'-dominated mechanisms of what Hirschman (1970) calls 'exit' (e.g. individual parental choice, or the school as a whole 'opting-out') and 'voice' (e.g. participatory structures like school boards and governing bodies). We should also be able to assess the bearing that the market and self-governance have upon schools' decision agendas and decision-making patterns, and upon participants' perceptions of the effects of new sources of influence upon the school.

Civil society, and its relation to the state, is also a subject of debate.

Recent academic interest in the concept has not settled on an unambiguous meaning or on the concrete institutions to which it refers. For some, 'civil society' refers primarily to societal institutions outside the state: families, households, neighbourhoods. For others, it is (also) the world of interest groups, self-help associations and voluntary organisations. Martin *et al.* (1995: 3) use the concept to describe 'a network of non-governmental intermediary institutions between the family and the state', although they do not define 'state'. Nevertheless, in discussing the governance of education, they see civil society exerting a necessary braking effect on the market in a complex arrangement in which the (limited) state protects and guarantees educational institutions, whilst civil society provides democratic accountability to the citizenry. Concerning contemporary reforms, they write:

> The state provides a framework of schools and their curriculum with more open funding arrangements and equality of access albeit regulated through the market. The state provides ... , guarantees ... , and undertakes to protect the service. Society, through its citizens, has an interest in ensuring the availability and quality of that service for all. Educational institutions are at the same time separate from the state and yet bounded by the state.
>
> (Martin *et al.* 1995: 7)

Classifying the institutional status of schools is slightly problematic. Private (independent) schools can be regarded as mainly civil-society institutions. Although state-maintained (public) schools are state institutions in the formal sense, as described above, they may exhibit many features that distance them from direct state control, and they may come to regard themselves, or be culturally regarded, as outwith the state, operating on collegial, non-bureaucratic lines, and to some extent as autonomous. This depends to a considerable extent on the potency of professional values and control, and upon the scope of decision-making at school level. Neither of these two factors may be wholly determined by the school itself: it may only be as autonomous and collegiate as it is allowed to be by the organs of the state that establish, finance or regulate it. There may be an unresolvable structural tension between state and civil-society modes of schooling, perhaps manifested particularly in terms of the control of the curriculum.

In a legal sense, in the United Kingdom, devolved management does not change schools' 'state' character and neither does the opting-out of schools from local-authority control. Yet both these aspects of governance have consequences for schools, in so far as, in principle, the locus of major decision-making, the functions of co-ordination and control move away from the formal levels of the state hierarchy and towards the school itself, characterised as a 'self-governing' school. Although Scottish legislation (and a growing English usage) pre-empts the meaning of that term by associating it with 'opted-out' schools, the broader usage adopted here refers not to its formal status but describes a school that has a substantial degree of budgetary control and decision-making autonomy, along with a network of connections outward to the local community and the representation of the interests of lay, civil society on its governing body or school board.

From this perspective, we might be seeing the transition of schools from being state institutions to becoming civil-society institutions. At least, schools may be acting more in the manner of the latter. Thus they are supposed to respond to and be accountable to social groups, negotiate relationships with parents and others, and forge networks that partially replace – or coexist uneasily with – hierarchical dependencies and accountability relationships (see Martin *et al.* 1995: 7). This, at least, may be the vision, although the current and prospective reality may fall short (see Munn's chapter in this volume (Chapter 4)). Change is not wholesale or without apparent paradoxes – for example, 'self-governing' schools implementing a formal, state-devised curriculum and being monitored by outside inspectors – and there are important research questions concerning the effects and extent of this shift. Schools may be in flux between state and civil-society roles and expectations, between orientations 'upwards' in the hierarchy of control and 'outwards' to the local communities that they serve. On the other hand, we are likely to be witnessing a hybrid form that incorporates different and maybe contradictory elements that require to be managed; or, if they are not managed, that may generate acute problems.

In any case, research findings indicate that the head teacher, and perhaps senior management staff, are the pivotal roles. Changes in the role of the head teacher (or school Principals in other systems), and the importance of head teachers in contemporary managerial reform, are also emphasised in the studies by Wohlstetter and Sebring (Chapter 7), Jacobs (Chapter 8) and Christensen (Chapter 9) in this volume. Heads stand between, and may also mediate, conflicting (or transitional) elements such as professional and managerial styles and philosophies of leadership, and the requirements of hierarchical and lateral accountability. The governing body or school board is, in principle, another pivotal institution as the main formal arena for such reconciliation or, conversely, as the locus of tensions between conflicting tendencies and obligations. If schools are becoming an intermediate form, they can be said to be 'quasi-civil-society' bodies, but we might expect that schools vary in how they perform this role. Some will develop more pronounced internal hierarchies than others; or will be more permeated by influences from the local institutions and elements of civil society than others, whether through reaching out to them or through unavoidable influences from them. Some will accommodate pressures from the local education authority and central government, whilst others may resist them.

This hybrid nature of schools means that the state still plays a powerful part in terms of finance, law, and policy influence. Many would argue that the extent of devolved management is minimal, and that central governments in the United Kingdom have tightened their grip despite political claims to the contrary. Central (and local) structures still govern or 'steer' them, but some of the instruments differ from those used before, as a result of devolved budgeting and devolved management. In particular, the controlling role of local education authorities has been diminished within the new governance. An intensive use of devices such as performance indicators, targets for literacy or numeracy, and inspection reports, enhances this steering capacity, but these also contribute to the perception that the reins have tightened; such perceptions are important, becoming themselves part of the action.

It is important, however, to separate rhetoric from reality. The formal state hierarchy in education has not necessarily dictated the realities of decision-making and initiative-taking. Central government, although armed with legislative powers, did not traditionally preside over a *dirigiste* education system. Nevertheless, hierarchical relations counted for much. In Scotland in particular, a deferential education culture sustained and legitimised these. Educationists typically looked to central government for a lead (McPherson and Raab 1988); that was much less so in England, where considerable power and influence resided in local education authorities. Therefore, the extent to which schools could act as (quasi-) autonomous, professionally led institutions was always questionable; neither, for that matter, could teachers act fully as a self-governing profession. Moreover, the scope that schools had, and indeed the latitude that was possible at the level of the education authority, were circumscribed as much by politics and bargaining as by statutory imperatives.

There has always been some degree of arm's-length relationship between schools and government. This was demonstrated in the long experience of professional control of education, in the state's traditional non-interference with the day-to-day running of schools, and in the teachers' determination of curriculum and pedagogy. This was precisely the government's complaint about 'falling standards' in English and Welsh schooling, which were attributed to a professional/(local) bureaucratic monopoly that excluded parents and resisted the assertion of central government's political leadership. Malaise about 'standards' was absent or muted in Scotland, reflecting perhaps a certain complacency. However, central government's intention on both sides of the border, under recent Conservative governments at least, was that schools must be freed from 'pernicious' local-authority direction. This was not so that they could become unreformed bastions of professional domination, but so that there could be incorporated, in 'self-governing' (opted-out) institutions, a significant societal element in decision-making which, when coupled with the logic of the market operating through parental choice, could make an arm's-length relationship safe for pupils.

This resonates with the two-level model described for Denmark: a combination of a parliamentary chain of governance plus self-governing public institutions that 'rests upon the junction of organisational features belonging to state, market and civil society' (Sørensen 1995: 82). But such a model risks disintegration unless co-operation between the two levels is institutionalised. Observational research at the level of the school shows that this requires considerable political work to be done there – in its board or governing body, and between the head teacher and the staff – as well as between the school and both the civil-society interests in the local community and the state interests in local and central government.

Political rhetoric has often depicted the changes of the 1980s and 1990s as a structural decentralisation to schools and their governing bodies or school boards, and to the exercise of 'exit' powers by newly enfranchised or empowered 'consumers'. Using financial and legislative levers, significant structural changes have been made within the governance of education, to which the erosion of local authority powers is ample testimony. There are also important new, and potentially transformative, involvements of the wider society in the life of the school, which may yet develop into a strengthened civil society; Munn's chapter in this book (Chapter 4) weighs the likelihood of this in Scotland. Moreover, the 'consumerist' ethos, reinforced by resource allocations consequent upon individual choice, has exerted a powerful, albeit not an all-powerful, influence.

On the other hand, the effectiveness of any devolution to the world of education outside government and its agencies has been very variable. Change has been neither revolutionary nor wholesale: we have not witnessed the abdication of government, the birth of participatory democracy and of an educational civil society, or the full fledging of informed consumer choice, whether in intention or in outcome (see Pierson 1998). The extent of central control in Britain, under Conservative governments as well as their Labour successor, has remained considerable; debates about the extent of its tightness have themselves become part of the politics of education. However, there are at least some elements of a newer pattern in which the state steers at a distance rather than governs in traditional ways, and in which societal initiative has been enhanced and legitimated. Government institutions at different levels – central and local – remain part of the policy network, although their relative influence has shifted dramatically. Moreover, the network itself has incorporated changes in organisations and roles; for example – and most notably – the greater prominence of OFSTED (the Office of Standards in Education) in England and Wales.

An important related change in the governance of education has been in the conceptualisation and implementation of 'partnership'. This concept and its exemplification in recent education policies have been extensively discussed elsewhere, against a backcloth of previous understandings and settlements amongst the players (Raab 1993b). The old 'partnership' of central government, local government and teachers has been supplanted (under the Conservatives) or at least augmented (under Labour), in normative value and in many practical instances, by a newer, civil-society one of schools, parents, and local networks or institutions.[2] It is sometimes not clear who, if anyone, is excluded, and what the roles and contributions of the respective 'partners' should be. The traditional bureaucratic–professional partnership was a fragile one: trust was often at a premium and consensus was perhaps more fictitious than real, as Kogan et al. (1984) claim. It excluded lay participants, but also shunned party politicians; the new partnership envisaged in Conservative policy turned instead to parents, industry and elements of local communities, but also, with less fanfare, gave national political actors – education Ministers and the Prime Minister – a leading role. In the new partnership, however, relations between parents and schools remain strongly affected by what happens in the vertical dimension, for parents' roles in schooling are shaped by legislation and by local-authority implementation as well as by the local policy climate. All of these form not only the statutory and financial framework within which parent–school partnerships may occur, but also many of the outside expectations about the scope and content of these interactions. If, in addition, one considers 'partnership' as a feature of inclusive, national consultation in the shaping of legislation and policy, it is difficult to distinguish this clearly from pluralist pressure-group politics. It may betoken a loosening of the texture of the networks of policy-making, such that new players may participate, although it may not be so certain whether the influence of longer-standing members is challenged effectively.

The position of the local education authority within any new partnership has been under attack, with occasional political proposals for its abolition. Although the extent of its control over schools has been reduced under devolved management, the local level remains crucial to the implementation of education policy. This may be seen, for example, in recent proposals for performance targeting in Scotland, where SOEID, the central government education department, envisaged roles for the traditional partners:

> targets should be set, evaluated and reported upon by schools, educa-tion authorities and SOEID, working in partnership ... The nature of the partnership is crucial, balancing the requirement for consistency and rigour across Scotland with the need for local ownership and flexibility. Schools, education authorities and The Scottish Office each have a role to play.
>
> (Scottish Office 1998, paras 4, 6)

Schools were given what was described as the key role, in terms of ownership and commitment; the education authority would be consulted by schools and would support them. The education authorities' quality-assurance role and responsibility for strategic management were seen as critical to better school performance. SOIED would ensure national consistency. Of course, the central inspectorate (HMI) had earlier paved the way through its Audit Unit's work and advice on a range of perfor-mance indicators, which underpins the new initiative for targets, and HMI will retain an important role in benchmarking, national target-setting, and support and advice to schools and local authorities. In addition, this initiative was developed with the help of a Ministerially appointed Action Group on Standards in Scottish Schools, which will have a continuing role in monitoring and reviewing progress towards the national targets. All this is based on another 'partnership' mechanism, the Quality Initiative in Scottish Schools, which promotes school self-evaluation and involves all education authorities in working with the HMI Audit Unit.

This illustration shows some of the complexity of relationships that are still characterised as the work of a partnership, but one in which there is ostensibly an important role for the middle and lower levels under the steering influence (at least) of the top. How far this is 'distance' steering in the mould of new governance, given the political importance of a national drive to improve standards and performance by engineering the technical and organisational means for things to happen, cannot be gath-ered from documents and plans alone. However, it points up the close interdependence of actors, or partners, in relationships that constitute a policy-implementation network. Moreover, as far as education authorities are concerned, it indicates a facet of their continuing relevance.

Empirical illustrations

With these conceptual and theoretical perspectives in mind, let us turn selectively to the data to consider the way in which Scottish school boards or English governing bodies, head teachers and other relevant participants perceive the changes that are in train with the new governance, and interpret the modified roles and relationships that are brought about through devolved management and related policies. Of particular interest in any assessment of the extent to which theory translates into practice are the tensions or conflicts that are manifest in the transitional bedding-down of new practices, values, roles and relationships within schooling. Interview and observational data on school boards and governing bodies permit an exploration of these areas of harmony and tension amongst elements of devolved management. They also enable an assessment of the extent to which policy-makers' and legislators' expectations have been fulfilled. In particular, focusing upon roles and relationships within the school, and between the school and the education authority, as well as the school's position within civil society as represented mainly by the governing body or school board, casts light on the changing nature of power relations and interactions that are bound up with hierarchies and networks, as well as with markets as discussed in Arnott's chapter in this volume (Chapter 2).

There are important differences between England and Scotland with regard to the law, practice and timing of devolved management. The 1988 Education Reform Act established the main lines in England and Wales. Whereas Scotland's school boards derive from Scottish legislation of 1988, DSM did not take effect until 1994. However, Strathclyde Region's devolved management of resources (DMR) preceded this by some three years, giving the Strathclyde schools more experience upon which their head teachers, staff and board members based their comments. In the Lothian Region research, by contrast, remarks about DSM were more speculative, concerning what was about to happen, although Lothian school boards had operated for several years under market-oriented policies embracing 'exit' and 'voice'.

A Department for Education (DfE) Circular for England and Wales captures two of the main dimensions that are illustrated here, corresponding to the relationship between the school and the state, and between the school and the local society:

The underlying purpose of schemes of local management should be to ensure the maximum delegation of responsibility to governing bodies that is consistent with the discharge by the Secretary of State and by the LEA [local education authority] of their own continuing statutory responsibilities ... [T]his devolution of responsibility has already had a clearly perceptible effect in terms of the responsiveness of schools to their clients: pupils, parents, employers and the local community.

(Department for Education 1994: para. 10)

Schools and hierarchies

Under devolved management, relations between the school and the state cannot be seen purely in functional and formal terms. They are also the subject of negotiations and discussions in which the governing body/school board and the head teacher play an important part. The governing body of a Newcastle school spent almost one hour with an officer from the LEA, considering responsibilities for school meals. The complex position had to do with contractual arrangements between schools and the LEA, schools' decisions whether to remain within LEA meals provision, including free school meals for eligible pupils, the DfE's role in specifying the financial framework for these possibilities, and even the requirements of European Community employment directives and domestic social-security legislation. The officer reported that the LEA wanted to devolve as much as possible to the schools, and that surveys of heads, parents and pupils were being conducted in order to inform the Education Committee's specifications document. But central-government policies remained to be clarified, and the officer said that 'the LEA can only move at the pace of the DfE and they have been quite slow to pick up the issue'. In addition, this officer reported that the LEA had 'fought and won a lot of other battles'; the officer's job 'is to fight the battles of schools' within the local authority and beyond.

On the other hand, the Chair of the board of governors thought that teachers had little confidence in local education officers, and little faith in politicians' will to solve problems; these feelings were apparently shared across the LEA's head teachers and Chairs. Relations between this school and the LEA were very strained over other financial issues, including renovations and ways to manage budget deficits, in which this school felt disadvantaged by the effect of government cuts and the funding formula. Whilst the 'opting-out' of schools from local-authority control is a possibility on both sides of the border, it had not become a reality in Lothian and Strathclyde Regions in Scotland, or in Newcastle. Nevertheless, the potentiality of 'losing' a school threatened the education authority and thus played a part in the political game played between schools and education authorities, sometimes giving the school a plausible bargaining counter. There is a hint of this with respect to the Newcastle school just mentioned, and in another one over the question of the permitted intake number of pupils. In some schools, the head teacher could enlist the school board as a pressure group in relations with the education authority; this has been discussed elsewhere (Arnott *et al.* 1996).

Looking within the school itself, in many of the research settings described in Part I it was not unusual for teachers to remark that devolved management redefined the role of head teacher in terms of financial and managerial responsibilities. This is consistent with earlier English research (Bowe, Ball with Gold 1992) in demonstrating teachers' belief that devolved management alters, or may alter, relationships between senior staff and classroom teachers. The routines of management and bureaucratic authority within the school cut across a valued professional and collegial ethos. Thus, whilst devolved management may partially uncouple schools from a traditional hierarchical relationship to the education authorities which control them, many teachers feared that it might impose it more tightly between heads and other teachers. However, there was limited evidence of real conflict with older educational values and priorities. Easing such tensions may depend more on the choices, strategies and styles of heads and teachers as they develop their schools' approach to devolved management, albeit within externally determined parameters, and less on the institutional imperatives of new governance.

The delegation of responsibilities from the education authority, especially in Scotland but in England as well, poses questions about the heads' ability to reconcile new managerial requirements and role-definitions with older ones that concern professionalism and educational values. The handling of managerial and professional facets affects the internal workings of the school, and thus the relationships between heads and other teaching staff. It is not easy to identify the extent to which a head handles this as a result of his or her choice as a professional with a deliberate strategy or a personal style, on the one hand, or as a result of the situational constraints that provide the range of possibilities within which any head operates. Nevertheless, it is evident that the style of headship is central to the managerial and decision-making machinery and processes that develop. The perception that DSM and LMS redefine the role of the head in terms of financial and managerial tasks was shared by many staff in all three areas.

Whereas in England it is the governing body to which powers are devolved, Strathclyde's own relatively modest scheme of DMR, as well as the later DSM, delegated functions to the head teacher. These formal distinctions, however, appear to have made little difference to the head's role in practice across these sites. In the Newcastle schools, especially, teachers and heads referred to the financial and managerial roles of the head rather than to her/his role as educational leader. One head had seized the possibilities with alacrity: a Newcastle teacher said that the head 'couldn't wait to get his hands on the money, in that he had plans for this for a long time … He had spent the money before it arrived.' At another school in Newcastle, a Head of Department replied, when asked about the role of the head:

> you have got to be so much more financially aware of things, you have got to go out there and promote the school; you are no longer a head teacher, you are a manager or a managing director. And that has got to be difficult, because basically what the head is, is a teacher who has gone up through the ranks … Our head has made quite a positive step to make sure to do some teaching – which our previous head didn't do. But I do think that he is going to find that he is going to have to move further and away from that.

A teacher at a third school in that city had a similar view of LMS:

> I think it is a bit of a nightmare, to be honest, for someone who has trained as a teacher to come in and have to be a sort of an accountant at the same time … [I]t just seems wrong to me that a head should have to deal with all the financial side. I mean a head teacher who had to oversee redundancies was put in an awful position.

In Lothian, where DSM was only beginning, one teacher put the same point even more dramatically, in speculating on what might happen: a situation in which the head, although not fitted for the role, effectively becomes an accountant, because 'money becomes everything and educational values tend to be sidelined'. An Assistant Head at the same school anticipated that, when DSM was in full operation, the head teacher would have to spend a great deal of time on financial decisions and setting priorities and would have to delegate more tasks, so that 'the management team will have to shoulder a bit more and we will have to delegate our responsibilities down'. Another Lothian head teacher made the point about his new DSM role with especial poignancy:

> I see my job essentially as a manager of resources, but mainly as a head teacher … whose responsibility is to ensure that the quality of education that the kids are getting is the best that we can achieve.

And that in itself is a huge complex task … And anything that takes my time away from that process, I would find undesirable. So if … I am going to have to spend more time looking at budgets and nego-tiating contracts … then I would be unhappy … Philosophically I opposed it because it seemed to me to be the first [step] in dismant-ling the concept of a centralised education service which … tried to deliver quality education for everybody … The other reason I opposed it was … to do with where I want to focus my job which is about impacting on the … quality of teaching and learning … It has a positive spin-off, of course, apart from our ability to vire money [transfer across expenditure categories] which allows us to be a bit more innovative … The other spin-off … is in terms of the quality of service that the Region provides centrally, because a number of parts of the organisation are realising that if they don't get their act together the schools are not going to use them.

In Strathclyde Region, a Principal Teacher with DMR experience observed with some misgivings the 'trend towards an increasing manage-rial element in schools', complete with the ethos and terminology of business management and training as well as 'a trend to increase the powers of the head teacher', which this teacher thought was more true in England than in Scotland.

The obverse side of this coin is the way in which teachers perceived their own participation in decision-making, and their new place in the school hierarchy. A key theme that emerges is that of consultation. Broadly speaking, teachers see their main involvement as consultative rather than as direct participation; one Head of Department in Newcastle succinctly and sceptically characterised the change:

We discuss it, and we decide what has already been decided … A long time ago I think we did discuss and collectively we came to decisions. Then we went through a period when we were informed. And now we are in a period when we are encouraged to think we are discussing, but I don't think we are … It is quite carefully managed.

A teacher described what happened in another Newcastle school, alluding to the way in which there was now an increasing sense of hier-archical relationships within the school, such that the locus of decision-making has shifted upward to an inner group consisting of the Head, the Deputy and three Assistant Heads, with some decisions made in discus-sion with the school Bursar, 'and some of those decisions you find certainly have been made before you get a chance to discuss them; consultations are very brief'.

These Newcastle findings seem generally to confirm others (Bowe, Ball with Gold 1992) in showing that teachers perceive that devolved management actually or potentially opens a divide between managerial staff and classroom teachers in which bureaucratic authority threatens to overtake the collegiality of professional relations and decision-making. Although the Lothian schools had less experience of devolved management, teaching staff speculated about the likely consequences of DSM for the relationship of the head to other teachers. A Lothian Deputy Head argued that there was a danger that the head and the board of studies would become more remote from the rest of the staff because of the weight of other activities. A teacher at one of the other Lothian schools shared this view:

> He says his priority is the financial well being of the school and I know I'm being very old-fashioned here, but to my mind a head teacher's priority is the education of his pupils, or seeing to the effectiveness of that. It also leaves the staff without a head as well, if you know what I mean; it is not just the pupils who require a figurehead.

A second Lothian teacher also saw that DSM activities might lead to a growing separation between head teachers and other teachers, including the senior management team. On the other hand, in a Strathclyde school there was a feeling that devolved management was to be welcomed because it could make the head more accountable to staff. The head could be trusted to protect the school and the teachers' best interests. Teachers at a different school in that Region expressed a similar sentiment. In these two schools, the personality or inclination of the head teacher may explain these views, for the heads' style emphasised collegiality and thus encouraged trust in themselves as educational leaders.

To summarise themes that emerge from this evidence: tensions between professional and managerial conceptions of the role of head teacher appear to be more keenly felt by teachers and heads as a result of the particular characteristics of devolved management. This is not an exceptional finding.[3] Although devolved management in principle loosens the hierarchical relationship between schools and higher levels of the state, in the minds of many it tightens it between heads and other teachers as managerial and financial routines are brought inside the school itself, to sit very uneasily alongside the professional culture and values of education. Bailey's chapter in this volume (Chapter 3) explores these and related issues of professionalism. However, tighter hierarchies and top-down control need not be inevitable results of such institutional change if, as proponents of 'loose–tight' management practices argue (Peters and Waterman 1982), centralised control can be combined with the decentralised, flexible, quasi-autonomous work patterns of teachers, seemingly in accord with norms of teachers' professionalism. Head teachers themselves can 'steer at a distance', using new tools of governance within the school, and there is some evidence of this style of leadership. Whether this fortuitous marriage can be made to work in schools under devolved management may therefore depend less on the institutional logic of the new arrangements, and more on the choices, strategies and styles adopted by heads and teachers as they evolve their school's approach to DSM or LMS, within a range of variation that is determined externally.

Schools and civil society

Turning now to the second issue: the extent to which school boards and governing bodies represent an increased incorporation of local community interests and civil-society values into the decision-making of the school, such that the school is re-invented as a civil-society institution, albeit with a legal position inside the state. Although, as noted earlier, this element of devolved management has been rather less emphasised in the United Kingdom. But this question is not wholly separate from the first one, because one consequence of the altered relationship between the school and the local education authority is that there may be more opportunities for negotiation, for pressure to be exerted upon education officers on behalf of the school, and indeed for conflict between newly enfranchised participants and bureaucrats as the school takes on greater responsibilities within the overall framework of the law and of local authority policy. This is not a clear-cut, before-and-after situation: local councillors and others have always interceded with local education departments to promote the interests of 'their' schools, and governing bodies in England and Wales were not a new invention of the late 1980s or early 1990s. But in arguing for a 'new partnership' for schools, the Taylor Report (Department of Education and Science/Welsh Office 1977) emphasised that parents, in particular, should play an important part.

Scottish policy and legislation is of a piece with this 'partnership' philosophy in principle, although quite different in practical arrangements.[4] The illustrative evidence presented here only gives glimpses of the way in which boards and governing bodies are involved in the decision-making processes of the school; a fuller analysis of findings concerning Scottish school boards may be found in Arnott et al. (1996).

School boards have far fewer decision-making powers than do governing bodies, and therefore less scope to become involved. Unlike their English counterparts, boards have very limited financial powers and no direct involvement in the curriculum. Flying in the face of government policies that seek to reduce the power of 'producers' in favour of 'consumers', there is considerable reluctance amongst Scottish parents to dabble in what they regard as 'professional matters' that are best left to teachers. Indeed, in some schools, boards have been very difficult to constitute and some have ceased to exist.

Scottish boards, therefore, appear to be peripheral to the decision-making procedures of their schools, although not without roles to play that are felt to be important to schools. Arnott *et al.* (1996) show that the boards under investigation deferred to the head's judgement, regardless of school size, the nature of the catchment area, or the length of time of the head's incumbency. Some boards discussed and debated issues more than others, but in only one instance were they observed to have overruled the head, and that only on a matter of detail. The remarks by the Chair of one school board in Lothian Region illustrate perceptions of the board's role as a

> 'talking shop, talking through the variety of ... policy proposals that come through the Scottish Office ... It's discussing those things, not necessarily taking any direct action ... The decision has always tended to be passed ... to the teaching body and to have as little as possible to do with the day-to-day running of the school, and not to interfere ... The function of the school board at the moment is basically ... just to support the head teacher, to a large extent. Maybe actually to protect the head teacher from excessive parent involvement.

In another Lothian school, even where the board had a formal part to play in the choice of a new head teacher, it could find itself marginalised. A parent member said that the board had discovered that the short list had been drawn up and 'that all we were being asked to do was to rubber-stamp something that clearly had already been decided'; general policy was still driven from the centre and there was not much scope for an change of emphasis at school level: decisions were 'delegated, not devolved'.

Nevertheless, board members as well as teachers in a number of schools saw the boards as playing important supportive roles. A Lothian head teacher described his board's support, saying that 'they have never expressed any desire either collectively or individually to become deeply

involved in what's happening in the school'. He thought that it was difficult for them to make clear judgements about curriculum policy or
financial matters; he gave the board the background but they merely rati-
fied the per capita allocations. Nonetheless, he felt that 'the concept of a
clear formal involvement of parents in the school is very important', but it
was hard for schools to get members who were prepared to make the
necessary commitment. In terms of the board's role in relation to parents
as a whole,

> it has to be a bit more pro-active in terms of making its contacts with
> the parents. If it's going to be representative in any sense of the
> parents, which I think it ought to be, it needs to have some means of
> contacting them, gathering information on how people feel about
> things and feeding that back into the meetings.

An Assistant Head Teacher at one of the Strathclyde schools, who was
once a teacher-representative on the school board, also took the view that
boards could be supportive, for example with regard to issues like school-
uniform policy and repairs to the building. But she thought that the board

> should be a force of its own. I don't think it should be doing just what
> the staff want it to do or the head teacher wants it to do. I think they
> should be deciding on their agenda. I think two very important roles
> – one is a kind of liaison between us and the rest of the parents; and
> the other one is really to do what they can to improve everything
> about the school.

She believed that it depended a great deal on the personalities of board
members: they tended to be supportive but were reactive, and did not take
the lead; in addition, other parents were not really interested in what the
board was doing, and did not want to get involved.

Teachers in several of the Scottish schools saw boards as playing an
insignificant role, and did not wish to see it expanded. One thought that
the board was a useful sounding-board with whom the head and the staff
were not in conflict, and that it could play a useful role in staffing decisions (although a teacher at another school saw this prospect as
'horrifying'), but that this would require a considerable sacrifice of time.
However, he pointed out that parental apathy meant that the board was
not a very effective communication link. Another teacher welcomed the
moderate stance of the board in guarding against the dangers of 'extreme'
proposals that might damage the school, and praised its supportive attitude which was respectful of the professional judgement of teachers. One

teacher in a Community School thought that the board's role was 'to represent the wider views of the user community ... and to do the same thing in reverse – to try and interpret and relay ... what the school's trying to do for the wider community'.

Board members' own outlooks also provide insights into the role of the board within the school and in relation to the outside world. The co-opted Chair of one school board saw an increased role for it in the future under DSM, but was concerned about the difficulty of recruiting members. He himself spent time at parents' evenings to publicise the board and to bridge the 'big gap' between the board and the parental community. On the other hand, as with other schools in both Scotland and England, parents are involved in campaigns to rescue the school from the threat of closure, or in other crises. This Chair claimed to have good links with the Region's education department and with elected members of the local authority, so that his contacts with them could be productive.

The former Chair of a Community School in a relatively socially advantaged part of Lothian came from the business world and saw the main areas of the board's involvement in terms of issues of money and the strengthening of the school's management staff as the number of pupils expanded. But the board also looked outward to the local area: it was involved in local enterprise initiatives and in decisions concerning the development of recreational parkland. Lobbying the Region for resources involved the board in inviting leading local politicians and officials, as well as government Ministers, to visit the school and to discuss issues with the board and others. He described this as a positive role in which the board was trying to explain or convince, 'rather than one of bitching or demonstrating', although they clashed with the Region over the size of the school roll and the calculation of non-pupil user-hours for the school's facilities. However, despite the board's apparent sophistication in mobilising its influence externally, links with parents were not strong. A parent member of the same board remarked upon its reluctance to increase its involvement in time-consuming staffing appointments, and also on the board's satisfaction with the way the school was run.

Variations amongst school boards in regard to their discussions and decision-making concerning the school's local market position and its image, the way in which information was handled, and its relations with the world outside the school have been discussed in Arnott *et al.* (1996). These differences owed much to the school's socio-economic position, which was largely reflected in the board's self-confidence and in its 'cultural capital' in being able to take on decision roles and external activity. If civil society is to make an impact on the life of state institutions such as schools, skills and political sophistication are required as well as goodwill and legislative provision for formal participation. Boards which were well connected to the outside world tended to adopt a more active role and to be less deferential to the head. The 'outside world' consists of significant influential groups, organisations or persons in the educational, business or political worlds beyond the school. Networks of these connections are useful to a school when they can be mobilised in the pressure politics of relations between the school and the education authority or the local community. The research suggests that, where a school board, through its lay members, was well connected outside the school, the head was able to use it as a supportive mechanism in dealing with local and central government officials further up the hierarchy.

Governing bodies in England and Wales have stronger powers and can, in principle, play a larger part in schools' decision-making and in wider activities. In Newcastle, a teacher at a school that had been faced with closure described how the governing body and especially the parents had saved the day. The aim now was to prevent a future threat by becoming 'that much part of the community that they'll not even try and shut us'. A department head at this school, however, saw such community concern as evanescent, although the school had developed an education/business partnership and there were other links to local educational institutions and to industry. This teacher was sceptical about the ability of governors to run the school because, despite the training they receive, they were unable to get an overall view of what it meant to run an educational establishment.

The head of another Newcastle school was unimpressed by the role of governing bodies in LMS in terms of community relationships. Instead of parents and business people being involved on a democratic basis, 'the reality is that there are tiny cliques generally at the top of the pyramid of the governors, the Chair or Deputy Chair' who tended to be academics with time to spare. They were needed, he thought, but the rest of the governing body do not have any sense of what LMS is about: 'it is the head and a couple of others who are in a sense managing it ... I don't believe that the community has been one jot enfranchised by that.' The same head teacher thought that LMS had increased the tension between himself and the governing body:

> governors who were once useful to call upon for friendship and advice have become our masters/mistresses and again can be used sometimes to hide behind ... there are some smashing people but there is also ... huge ignorance of schools, education, how they work, particular problems here.

He pointed to factors that inhibited the school from cementing itself into the local area. Although regarded as a 'good' school, its extreme diversity meant that there was 'no overall community or parental body', no geographical indicators of place, no sporting clubs named after the area: 'It's almost as if the place is refusing to admit to an identity.'

These glimpses are only illustrative, but they suggest that it is difficult to see a clear pattern in which schools under devolved management are redefined as 'owned' collectively by their local communities rather than by the professional 'producers' of education or, indeed, by the state. One of the Scottish schools, in fact, witnessed the demise of its board during the course of the research project. 'Civil society', in its socially impacted area, was more concerned with housing issues than with education, and local parents had little participative energy to spare for the school. With variations, teachers, heads and board members or governors in all schools interpreted their role in the normative terms of 'support' for the school and its professionals. In addition, whilst some saw the board or governing body as playing a very small role in practice, there was little desire to see participation extended. Indeed, there was some indication that, in the Newcastle schools, governors were thought to be wading into issues beyond their knowledge and understanding. Moreover, although boards and governing bodies existed alongside other means of involving parents in the school, such as PTAs, there was little indication of a more general and vigorous 'partnership' between schools, parents and the local community that could be interpreted in terms of a sea-change.

Conclusions

The limited evidence adduced in this chapter does not enable a firm conclusion to be drawn about the success or failure of devolved management in improving school management, teaching and learning, or democratic participation. Neither does it allow precise statements about the factors that explain variations across schools or education authorities in the changing patterns of relationship that have been brought about by DSM or LMS. On the other hand, the research findings do not appear to bear out many of the optimistic assumptions underlying the legislation and policy initiatives that brought about devolved management, and they lend weight to sceptical views. The critical argument of Deem *et al.* (1995: chapter 2), that English school governors' accountability to, and representation of, the local community must be doubted, can be adduced; so too, can Munn's chapter in this book (Chapter 4), based on Scottish evidence, which offers little comfort to the view that devolved management has transformed relations between schools and parents.

Some literature on LMS (Levačić 1998) has gone further into the question of the effect of this aspect of the new governance upon school performance, and has not found it easy to show a causal relationship. Moreover, Levačić (1998) points out that the very rationale for LMS is itself poorly developed in terms of explaining why better teaching and learning should result from either better resource management or more democratic decision-making; the same could be said for DSM. As argued elsewhere (Adler *et al.* 1996: chapter 5), the policy goals of DSM were ambitious, although they were laid down in broad, often non-specific and unquantified terms. Whilst it does not clearly indicate 'success' or failure', the Scottish research has shown the following:

- It is difficult for both participants and outside observers to disentangle the effects of DSM from those of other education policy developments and from other changes in governance. Yet DSM has altered the head teacher's role and brought about new procedures, new structures and new responsibilities for teachers, although awareness of DSM often failed to penetrate to the level of the classroom teacher.
- Heads and other teachers have broadly welcomed DSM, with reservations, and have tended not to want further delegation of education authority functions. DSM's benefits are broadly appreciated in terms of flexibility, control, and greater speed in effecting repairs and ordering supplies. While these are important, teachers do not seem to perceive that DSM has had a direct bearing on teaching and assessing pupils, or on learning. They have welcomed the freedom to arrange the school's in-service training, but have worried about the lesser role played by the education authority's advisory services, and about their additional workload, although the latter is not attributed specifically to DSM.
- School boards play a limited role in DSM, and seem to be of greater importance as pressure groups on behalf of the school, rather than as deliberative or decision-making bodies. This is not inconsistent with the formal place allotted to them, but board members as well as teachers appear content with this supportive role, in which boards defer to the professional and managerial skills and leadership of the professionals.

These findings provide some indications of partial achievement, or perceptions of achievement, whilst leaving the question of progress towards other goals in the realm of the unknown, and indeed of the unknowable. Short of transforming the culture and working patterns of schools, DSM has borne in on the consciousness of some school staff the importance of new financial arrangements and has altered the decision-making infrastructure at school level, and between it and the education authority. These seem to be modest gains, but they may not be negligible in terms of the environment for teaching and learning in the school. On the other hand, their effect on the morale of heads and teachers as they see the results of increased school-level control may be a more telling benefit than any hoped-for increase in the efficient use of educational resources and better value for money, the determination of which depends upon the application of techniques that are open to dispute. Moreover, whether DSM can improve the quality of education is, as mentioned, very difficult to answer unless the criteria for judging 'quality' can be made explicit and their connection with the elements of DSM can be clarified.

DSM has had other effects that were perhaps unintended or unforeseen, but which bear upon governance. First, it has added to the burdens placed upon schools, not least upon administrative and clerical staff. Second, DSM has also raised the possibility of a divergence between managerial requirements and traditional educational values, although whether a satisfactory consonance between these can be brought about may depend upon a mixture of skills, 'styles' and circumstances – financial, demographic and educational – that are only partially within the power of the school to effect. A third effect, which does not so much belie the aims of policy as cut across it, has been to elevate training for management, decision-making, or participation to prominence as an issue in itself. These roles and tasks are part of the essential wherewithal for governance. Fourth, whilst policy-makers in Scotland cannot have realistically supposed that an important element of DSM was to satisfy any appetite for parental power, neither has it served to whet it.

Comparing DSM with LMS, the absorption of the former into Scottish schools with relatively little acrimony or sense of disruption may have been due to its relative flexibility and to a rather more favourable financial formula regarding teachers' salary costs than in England and Wales. The implementation of LMS, by contrast, was marked in many places by conflict and apprehension in a context of political arguments over the continued role of local education authorities. LMS was a policy departure of considerably higher political salience, both in political party terms and in terms of a climate of significant political and popular distrust of education professionals. It was farther-reaching than DSM in that it devolved power to school governing bodies rather than to head teachers, rested upon a more prescriptive governmental approach with less local financial flexibility, and gave schools only average rather than actual salary costs. These features, along with the atmosphere into which they were introduced and the simultaneity of so many other innovations under the 1988 Education Reform Act, contributed to the difficulty of implementing devolved management as a discrete element of the transformation in educational governance; but in this respect, although for rather different reasons, implementing devolved management in Scotland has not been that much easier.

A final conclusion returns us very briefly to some of the ramifications of 'governance' discussed earlier. The means chosen for achieving the ends of devolved management was a chain of interdependent implementation agents, with scope for choice at each step, and much scope for steering in networks as well as hierarchies, with markets playing an important role as well. Thus, in accordance with Scottish central policy guidelines, education authorities prepared their own DSM schemes and restructured their relationships with schools and with central government. Schools, and especially head teachers, devised their methods of dealing with budgets, decisions, and processes within the framework of the authorities' schemes, and many formed linkages with each other. Teachers took on new roles and relationships within the assumptions and routines required by DSM. School boards learned to play a limited, but potentially important part, in the bedding-down of school-centred management within a context of parental participation and choice; they too created networks across the system, as did many parents' groups.

The 'success' of devolved management depends in considerable part on the coherence and consistency of action along and across this complex constellation, with observable results, if any, to be found within the school, the education authority, the board or governing body as it represents the local community, and within central government as well. Devolved management makes a difference to them all. But the quality of 'results' that can be taken as the criteria of 'success' is debatable, and evidence is not easy to gather or evaluate. 'Governance' may provide fresh concepts to describe what happens, and it may even be amenable to design in order to achieve certain ends (Hanf and O'Toole 1992); but the controversial politics of education may follow a different and unsteerable logic.

Notes

1   This chapter draws upon findings from, and papers written within, the ESRC-supported project on Devolved Management of Schools (grant no. R000233653) and the Scottish Office Education and Industry Department-supported project on Devolved School Management, including Raab *et al.* (1995), Adler *et al.* (1996), Arnott *et al.* (1996) and Raab *et al.* (1997).

2   That this remains a potent vision in Scottish policy terms is signalled by a ministerial statement on a forthcoming education bill by Sam Galbraith in

the new Scottish Parliament, in which he included parents, pupils and schools in the 'partnership' alongside the two levels of government and the teachers, and implicitly accepted a suggestion that employers and the police were included as well (Scottish Parliament 1999).
3 See, for example, Levačić(1998: 337–8), Levačić (1995: chapter 6), and the references cited in these works.
4 The rhetoric and reality of 'partnership' and parental participation in British devolved management of schools generally has been discussed in Sallis 1988; Macbeth 1990; Baginsky *et al.* 1991; Munn 1993, and Raab 1993b.

References

Adler, M., Arnott, M., Bailey, L., McAvoy, L., Munn, P. and Raab, C. (1996) *Devolved School Management in Secondary Schools in Scotland, a Report to the Scottish Office Education and Industry Department*, University of Edinburgh, Department of Politics: SOEID.

Arnott, M., Raab, C. and Munn, P. (1996) 'Devolved Management: Variations of Response in Scottish School Boards', in Pole, C. and Chawla-Duggan, R. (eds) *Reshaping Education in the 1990s: Perspectives on Secondary Schooling*, London: Falmer.

Atkinson, M. and Coleman, W. (1992) 'Policy Networks, Policy Communities and the Problems of Governance', *Governance*, **5(2)**: 154–80.

Baginsky, M., Baker, W. and Cleave, S. (1991) *Towards Effective Partnerships in School Governance*, Slough: NFER.

Bowe, R. and Ball, S. with Gold, A. (1992) *Reforming Education and Changing Schools*, London and New York: Routledge.

Dale, R. (1983) 'Review Essay: the Political Sociology of Education', *British Journal of Sociology of Education*, **4(2)**: 185–202.

Dale, R. (1989) *The State and Education Policy*, Milton Keynes and Philadelphia: Open University Press.

Dale, R. (1992) 'Review Essay: Whither the State and Education Policy? Recent Work in Australia and New Zealand', *British Journal of Sociology of Education*, **13(3)**: 387–95.

Deem, R., Brehony, K. and Heath, S. (1995) *Active Citizenship and the Governing of Schools*, Buckingham: Open University Press.

Department for Education (1994) *Local Management of Schools*, Circular **2/94**, London: Department for Education.

Department of Education and Science/Welsh Office (1977) *A New Partnership for our Schools* (The Taylor Report), London: HMSO.

Dunleavy, P. and O'Leary, B. (1987) *Theories of the State*, London: Macmillan.

Frances, J., Levačić, R., Mitchell, J. and Thompson, G. (1991) 'Introduction', in Thompson, G., Frances, J., Levačić, R. and Mitchell, J. (eds) *Markets, Hierarchies and Networks*, London, Newbury Park and New Delhi: Sage.

Gamble, A. (1988) *The Free Economy and the Strong State: the Politics of Thatcherism*, London: Macmillan.

Hanf, K. and O'Toole, L. (1992) 'Revisiting Old Friends: Networks, Implementation Structures and the Management of Inter-organizational Relations', *European Journal of Political Research*, 21(1–2): 163–80.

Hirschman, A. (1970) *Exit, Voice and Loyalty*, Cambridge, MA: Harvard University Press.

Jordan, G. and Schubert, K. (eds) (1992) *European Journal of Political Research*, 21(1–2): Special Issue: Policy Networks.

Kickert, W. (1995) 'Steering at a Distance: a New Paradigm of Public Governance in Dutch Higher Education', *Governance*, 8(1): 135–57.

Kogan, M., Johnson, D., Packwood, T. and Whitaker, T. (1984) *School Governing Bodies*, London: Heinemann.

Kooiman, J. (ed.) (1993) *Modern Governance*, London, Newbury Park and New Delhi: Sage.

Levačić, R. (1991) 'Markets: Introduction', in Thompson, G., Frances, J., Levačić, R. and Mitchell, J. (eds) *Markets, Hierarchies and Networks*, London, Newbury Park and New Delhi: Sage.

Levačić, R. (1995) *Local Management of Schools: Analysis and Practice*, Buckingham: Open University Press.

Levačić, R. (1998) 'Local Management of Schools in England: Results After Six Years', *Journal of Education Policy*, 13(3): 331–50.

Macbeth, A. (1990) *School Boards*, Edinburgh: Scottish Academic Press.

McPherson, A. and Raab, C. (1988) *Governing Education*, Edinburgh: Edinburgh University Press.

Maidment, R. and Thompson, G. (eds) (1993) *Managing the United Kingdom*, London: Sage.

Marsh, D. and Rhodes, R. (eds) (1992) *Policy Networks in British Government*, Oxford: Clarendon Press.

Martin, J., Ranson, S., McKeown, P. and Nixon, J. (1995) 'School Governance for the Civil Society: Redefining the Boundary Between Schools and Parents', Paper presented at the Symposium on the Local Governance of Education, British Educational Research Association Annual Conference, Bath, September.

Munn, P. (ed.) (1993) *Parents and Schools: Customers, Managers, or Partners?*, London and New York: Routledge.

Ozga, J. (1990) 'Policy Research and Policy Theory: a Comment on Fitz and Halpin', *Journal of Education Policy*, 5(4): 359–62.

Pestoff, V. (1993) 'Exit and Voice – Complementary Consumer Responses in Restructuring the Relationship Between the State and the Third Sector', Paper presented at the Workshop on Rebuilding Civil Society: the Politics of the New Welfare Mix, European Consortium for Political Research Joint Sessions of Workshops, Leiden, 2–8 April.

Peters, G. (1997) 'Shouldn't Row, Can't Steer: What's a Government to Do?', *Public Policy and Administration*, 12(2): 51–61.

Peters, T. and Waterman, R. (1982) *In Search of Excellence*, New York: Harper-Collins.

Pierson, C. (1998) 'The New Governance of Education: the Conservatives and Education 1988–1997', *Oxford Review of Education*, **24(1)**: 131–42.

Raab, C. (1980) 'The Changing Machinery of Scottish Educational Policy-Making', *Scottish Educational Review*, **12(2)**: 88–98.

Raab, C. (1992) 'Taking Networks Seriously: Education Policy in Britain', *European Journal of Political Research*, **21(1–2)**: 69–90.

Raab, C. (1993a) 'Education and the Impact of the New Right', in Jordan, G. and Ashford, N. (eds) *Public Policy and the Impact of the New Right*, London: Pinter.

Raab, C. (1993b) 'Parents and Schools: What Role for Education Authorities?', in Munn, P. (ed.), *Parents and Schools: Customers, Managers or Partners?*, London and New York: Routledge.

Raab, C. (1994) 'Theorising the Governance of Education', *British Journal of Educational Studies*, **42(1)**: 6–22.

Raab, C., Arnott, M., Adler, M., Bailey, L. and Munn, P. (1995) 'Devolved School Management and the New Governance of Education: Preliminary Findings', Working Paper prepared for the ESRC Invitational Seminar, Edinburgh, 6 October.

Raab, C., Munn, P., McAvoy, L., Bailey, L., Arnott, M. and Adler, M. (1997) 'Devolving the Management of Schools in Britain', *Educational Administration Quarterly*, **33(2)**: 140–57.

Rhodes, R. (1995) 'From Prime Ministerial Power to Core Executive', in Rhodes, R. and Dunleavy, P. (eds) *Prime Minister, Cabinet and Core Executive*, Basingstoke: Macmillan.

Rhodes, R. (1997) *Understanding Governance: Policy Networks, Governance, Reflexivity and Accountability*, Buckingham: Open University Press.

Rhodes, R. and Marsh, D. (1992) 'New Directions in the Study of Policy Networks', *European Journal of Political Science*, **21(1–2)**: 181–205.

Sallis, J. (1988) *Schools, Parents and Governors: a New Approach to Accountability*, London: Routledge.

Scottish Office (1998) *Setting Targets: Raising Standards in Schools*, Edinburgh: Scottish Office.

Scottish Parliament (1999) *Official Report*, **1: 11**, 23 June, cols 665–74.

Smith, M. (1999) *The Core Executive in Britain*, Basingstoke: Macmillan.

Sørensen, E. (1995) *Democracy and Regulation in Institutions of Public Governance*, Unpublished Ph.D. thesis, Institute of Political Science, University of Copenhagen.

Thompson, G., Frances, J., Levačić, R. and Mitchell, J. (eds) (1991) *Markets, Hierarchies and Networks*, London, Newbury Park and New Delhi: Sage.

2 Restructuring the governance of schools

The impact of 'managerialism' on schools in Scotland and England[1]

Margaret A. Arnott

Introduction

During the 1980s and 1990s, managing the system of state schooling became an increasingly politicised issue in the United Kingdom (UK). The government was, at least in terms of its rhetoric, attempting to shatter what it regarded as the cosy relationships which had developed within the education community since 1945. As the public sector had expanded, so had the role and influence of professionals within the welfare bureaucracies. Prevailing assumptions about the organisation and the management of the schooling system were to be challenged. The Conservative governments promised that local government and educational professionals would no longer be left to determine the management of the schooling system. Central government would take a more direct role in shaping the management of schools at local level than had been the case in the forty years or so following the Education Acts of 1944 (England) and 1945 (Scotland).

In both Scotland and England, these Acts had established a 'national system, locally administered'. Responsibility for the administration of the system was devolved to the educational professionals. Rarely – as Hoyle and John (1998) have noted – was the term 'management' used in relation to education. Within the public sector, the term 'administration' was used, whereas the term 'management' was judged to be more applicable to the private sector (Ranson and Stewart 1994). That central government from the late 1970s increasingly referred to the 'management' of the education system rather than to its 'administration' was not just a symbolic change. It signalled a shift in attitude by central government towards the post-war 'partnership' which had existed between central government, local government and the teaching profession. Broadly speaking, the roles adopted by these three partners had been as follows: that central government in consultation with the educational professionals would enact legislation and provide resourcing; local authorities would be responsible for implementing legislation whilst ensuring local needs were met; and the teaching profession would be responsible for the curriculum and assessment.

Strain was evident among the partners in England from the mid-1970s onwards. In response to concerns about the poor performance of the system of comprehensive schools, central government had begun to question the post-war tripartite partnership (Chitty 1989; Riley 1998). Debates about educational reform in England took place against a background of concern about the perceived failure of comprehensive schools. There was no equivalent to the 'Great Debate' in Scotland. However, by the late 1980s, relations between the post-war partners in the governance of the education systems in both countries were becoming uneasy. These relations became increasingly tense through the 1990s as successive Conservative governments attempted to redefine the role of the educational professionals in the governance of education. In Scotland especially, teachers were central to the opposition of Thatcherite education reforms (Arnott 1993). The government's intention was that educational professionals would be permitted less influence over how the education system would be administered, while central government, parents and business would all gain influence and power.

For Conservative governments, public-sector bureaucracies had been 'captured' by the professionals, and this capture had been a contributory factor to the post-war industrial decline of Britain. Such thinking was consistent with public choice critiques of the welfare-state bureaucracies, as the views of Niskanen and Buchanan, among others, were becoming increasingly influential in government thinking (Boyne 1998). Weberian bureaucratic structures within the welfare state were targeted for particular criticism. These structures had given prominence to models of bureaucratic and professional accountability which, according to the public-choice theorists, had created an environment in which professional self-interest had flourished at the expense of society's best interests. By introducing competition into the public sector, government could alter the behaviour of the professionals. Think tanks were an important bridge between government and the ideas of public-choice theorists. Groups such as the Hillgate Group, the Centre for Policy Studies and the Adam Smith Institute were arguing for radical changes in the way secondary schools were run (Denham 1996). It was to these groups that government turned for ideas about how the schooling system might be reformed.

Through the promotion of market-based reforms, the government hoped to replace bureaucratic and professional models of accountability with managerial and consumerist models. To achieve this end, government engaged in a wide-ranging programme of reform which encompassed both structural and organisational changes to the welfare state. To advance these new models of accountability successfully, the government would need to challenge the assumptions and values which permeated the Keynesian welfare state. The roles as well as relationships both between and within the different levels of the schooling system were to change significantly. The freedom which educational professionals had under the post-war tripartite partnership to shape the administration of schools was to be challenged. Local government's role in shaping school management would be reduced and its role redefined to that of the 'enabling' authority (Stoker 1999). Parents, through school boards and governing bodies, were to be given a direct role in school decision-making.

This, then, was the backdrop to moves in the 1980s and the 1990s towards a more consumerist and managerial system of schooling in both Scotland and England. There are important similarities in the changes to the environment in which schools in both countries found themselves operating. The emphasis on competition, the promotion of lay, especially parental, participation in school decision-making, and the delegation of decisions to school level from (local) education authorities, were shared themes of educational reform. The most significant difference between the two countries arguably lay with reforms to curriculum and assessment policy. In England, the National Curriculum gave teachers a limited control over curricular issues (Hoyle and John 1998). In Scotland, in contrast, curricular reforms such as the development of the National Certificate and the 5–14 Programme were more consensual and a greater level of professional autonomy was retained (Fairley and Paterson 1991).

However, the distinct political and cultural environment of the Scottish education system meant that differences were not confined to curricular issues. The absence of any equivalent to the 'Great Debate' has already been mentioned, but questions about the legitimacy of the Conservative government to introduce policies perceived to be Thatcherite were raised by both educational professionals and the wider public (Brown *et al.* 1998; Holliday 1992). This is not to argue that in certain parts of England, especially in the North, there was not wide-ranging opposition to the Conservative governments' plans to reform education and other areas of the welfare state, but in Scotland, where the Conservatives had only a small minority of seats in the UK Parliament and controlled few, if any, local authorities, the opposition had a 'nation-alist' dimension. The education system was and remains an important component of Scottish national identity (McCrone 1992). Policy-makers and educational professionals have long believed that there are certain distinctive features to the education system (Arnott 1993; McPherson and Raab 1988; Paterson 1994; Raffe 1998). Policies which impact on these distinctive features therefore run the risk of facing opposition which strikes 'nationalist' chords. In Scotland in the 1980s and 1990s, this was the situation in which Conservative governments found themselves concerning reforms to school governance.

While arguing that the content of policy at national level is an important consideration, it is worth raising a cautionary point. There is a risk that discussing the nature of school governance policies at national level underplays the impact that (local) education authorities and schools can have in shaping policy outcomes. We shall see below, for instance, that the style of headship had a direct impact on managerial and organisational cultures within schools. It is important to consider the extent to which policies meet their stated objectives. What were the similarities and differences on the ground between the governance of secondary schools in England and Scotland? Differences which existed on paper between the countries may have been less apparent when viewed from the 'bottom up'. In other words to what extent was there territorial diversity in policy outcomes? Until May 1999, the convention of 'administrative devolution' implied that central government would follow common objectives in education policy in the UK, but would adapt these policies to the differing national contexts. But to what extent did these differences in the technicalities of policies result in divergent systems of management developing in the Scottish and English schooling systems? Was it the case, for instance, that the organisational culture of English schools was more 'managerialist' than was the case for Scotland?

This chapter is in three parts. The first sets out to review the ideas and principles which underpinned the Conservative governments' attempts to reform the 'management' of schools. It is necessary here to place our consideration of education in the wider context of evolving forms of governance. The second section looks back on policy developments in the last ten years or so; comparisons are drawn at national level, in terms of how policies were framed and whether there was a distinctive Scottish dimension to the 'managerial' reforms introduced by central government. Here it is necessary to look at both the rationale and the technicalities of the policies which were introduced. The third section examines how these policies were implemented or translated into action at school level. In particular, it considers the extent to which bureaucratic and professional modes of accountability within the governance of schools were replaced by managerial and market-based models. The chapter concludes by reviewing the impact of recent 'managerialist' reforms.

'Managerialism': Shifting forms of accountability

Before addressing managerialism in education it is necessary to say a few words about how managerialism fits into the broader picture of public-sector reforms. As Eliassen and Kooiman (1993: 11) remind us, we should consider wider developments in the management of the public sector when analysing the internal management of public organisations:

> Managing public organisations concerns both the management of the public sector as a whole and the internal management of public institutions. These two levels of management are closely linked.

Over the past twenty years or so, central government has attempted to change or adapt the means by which it manages the public sector. In broad terms, attempts have been made to restructure the welfare state. The result, as discussed by Raab in Chapter 1, has been that government has emphasised new modes of governance. As Pyper and Stoker (1997: 1) argue:

> New, or at least refashioned, policy delivery mechanisms have emerged, and public–private 'partnerships' become common currency, as governments have attempted to come to terms with the 'hollowing out' of the state while adopting new modes of governance as enabler, contractor and regulator.

A shift away from traditional public administration models was an essential element of Conservative governments' attempts to promote new modes of governance. 'New public management' would replace models which had stressed hierarchical line management but allowed room for professional discretion (Hood 1998; Rhodes 1997). Here the influence of New Right and public-choice thinking on government policy is clear. The public sector, so the government argued, had become stifled by the interests of the bureaucrats and the professionals. Reforming the management of the public sector was the key to reversing its perceived problems. Clarke and Newman (1997: 45) point to the negative connotations which bureaucracy had for Conservative governments:

> bureaucracy embodied and exemplified the worst features of corporate ossification: an approach to corporate organisation that systematically privileged stability over adaptation, repetition over innovation, rules over responsiveness, hierarchy over performance, and roles over people.

From the late 1980s onwards, attempts to reform the management of the public sector were a prominent part of the Conservative governments' political agenda. The post-war assumption that bureaucrats and professionals could be trusted to ensure that the welfare state served the public interest was viewed with scepticism, to say the least. What followed was a series of reforms which were designed to change the organisational culture of the welfare state.

It is in this context that 'managerialism' has become something of a contentious term in recent years. 'Managerialism' is, as Pollitt (1993) has argued, an ideology, and, as such, has been politically motivated in its attempts to reform the welfare state. For Pollitt (1993: 1), the term has both positive and negative connotations. It can be viewed positively on the grounds that 'better management will prove an efficient solvent for a range of economic and social ills'. For instance, in education, positive interpretations of managerialism have welcomed attempts to adapt theories and techniques used in the private sector into the education service. After all, as Bottery (1992: 21) has argued, 'education had very little management theory of its own'. However, Pollitt also highlights that for those who view managerialism negatively it has become a 'term of abuse'.

From the late 1980s onwards, reforms to 'privatise' the schooling system were heavily informed by the New Right, and, in particular, neo-liberal thinking was a clear influence on some of the more managerialist reforms such as local management of schools in England (Raab 1993). For Chitty (1997: 45; emphasis in original), attempts to 'privatise' were not confined to promoting the techniques of the private sector, but extended 'to embrace some of the privatisation processes *within* the maintained sector which had the effect of blurring the boundaries between the private and the state sectors'. 'Managerialism' should be viewed within the context of these processes. Bureaucratic management of the welfare state has been replaced by decentralised management, in which accountability is viewed in terms of the market (Fairley and Paterson 1995).

A diverse range of educational reforms attempted to promote 'managerialism'. Local management of schools (LMS) in England, Devolved School Management (DSM) in Scotland, performance indicators, the move to fixed-term contracts for teachers, and school development planning were all part of the managerialist drive. The government did not necessarily follow a consistent and coherent programme of reforms to advance managerialist ideology, but there were common threads running through reforms from the late 1980s onwards. The desire to make schools responsive to new forms of accountability was central to the school governance reforms north and south of the border. Both externally and internally, schools would have to be responsive to a new set of actors, although to varying degrees.

That parents were to adopt the role of 'consumers' and the educational professionals that of 'producers' is a well-rehearsed argument. Since 1979, several important policies have promoted the rights of parents *vis-à-vis* the educational professionals. For example, the introduction of parental choice and nursery vouchers gave parents individual rights over the selection of their child's school or nursery education. The publication of information on school performance was intended to give parents information which could inform their choice. Although the new rights given to parents were premised on an individualistic philosophy, further policies were introduced which were intended to enhance the collective rights of parents in the day-to-day running of schools. The introduction of school boards in Scotland and the expansion of the remit of governing bodies in England were the principal steps here. These new parental rights were a prerequisite to the creation of a 'market' and attempts to restructure the education system.

Looking comparatively at recent developments in school governance in Scotland and England, it is helpful to draw a distinction between those steps which were taken by government to promote market-based accountability and control and those designed to develop managerial controls. Attempts to promote market-based accountability and managerialism were closely related. Both, for instance, attempted to challenge the position of the professional in the education system. The use of performance indicators, a central feature of management theories, would serve the dual purpose of providing another means of monitoring the performance of professionals, while also providing the information which parents could use to inform their choices in the educational market. However, while the links between managerialism and market-based reforms were close, they were not synonymous. It was managerialism rather than the 'quasi-market' which arguably had a more direct bearing on professionals in schools, from classroom teachers through to head teachers.

This chapter deals primarily with the effects of managerialism on school governance, and in particular its impact on roles and relationships within schools. However, the influence of the market context cannot be ignored in any account of devolved management. This is emphasised particularly in Adler's (1997) extensive discussion, and in the chapter on Northern Ireland by McKeown and Byrne in this volume (Chapter 6).

'Managerialism' attempted to replace bureaucratic and professional regulation within the teaching profession with externally set criteria and standards. As Ball (1994: 54) has argued, management and the market 'are "no hands" forms of control as far as the relationship between education and the state is concerned'. They are examples of 'steering at a distance' (Raab, in Chapter 1 of this volume). There was a switch in emphasis, from the bureaucratic concerns of monitoring of processes and procedures within the profession, to a concern with outcomes (Laffin 1998). Consumerism and the promotion of 'market forces' did impact on the external context of schools, and had a significant effect on the role of the head, but in terms of what is perceived by teachers as having a direct impact on their role, it is managerialism that is more usually identified. This is not to deny that, in those schools in the research studies which were 'losing' pupils as a consequence of parental choice legislation, market forces directly impinged on teachers. But even in these situations, there is some evidence to suggest that heads would attempt to shield their staff from the full impact of market reforms in order to maintain staff morale (Busher and Saran 1995).

'Managerialism': A comparative perspective

It has been argued above that the managerialist drive in Scotland and in England shared common themes. Forms of devolved management were introduced in both countries, and sought to alter power relations among parents, teachers, head teachers, (local) education authorities and central government. Responsibilities were devolved from local authorities to schools, and governing bodies and school boards were central to attempts to promote lay participation in school decision-making. However, whilst important thematic similarities were evident, there are significant differences in the way in which managerialist policies were framed. As a consequence, it is possible to draw some important distinctions between managerialism in the Scottish system as opposed to its English variant.

Three strands have been evident since the late 1980s: the first strove to place teachers within a regulatory environment shaped by performance management; the second attempted to restructure the external regulation of the teaching profession; and the third encouraged lay participation in school decision-making. Each of these strands is now considered in turn.

Ball (1994: 62) has argued that, rather than being seen as 'partners' in the government of education, teachers are now 'to be managed'. Teachers are to be held accountable according to a range of performance indicators identified by central government. Outputs or outcome measures have gained prominence. Schools now must publish information on a range of indicators, such as examination results, school costs, truancy rates and school-leaver destinations. In addition, financial delegation, a central component of both DSM and LMS, means that the three Es – economy, efficiency and effectiveness – are also monitored.

This strand of managerialism has affected the regulation of teachers within the school. The culture of performance management, however, appears to have gone further in England than in Scotland. For instance, the Scottish Office, unlike the Department for Education and Employment (DfEE), does not publish data about examination results in the format of 'league tables', although the Scottish press, especially the popular press, publishes them in league-table format. But it is when the impact of curriculum and assessment reform and its relationship to performance management are considered that the experiences of Scotland and England begin to diverge more sharply.

The National Curriculum was imposed by the politicians upon the teaching profession (Chitty 1992). As Hughes (1997: 193) has argued, 'the development of the 1988 National Curriculum was an essentially political process in which the views of teachers and other educational professionals were effectively marginalised and ignored'. From the mid-1970s onwards, central government had expressed concern about the failure of the comprehensive system in England. Prompted by the argument of the neo-conservative wing of the New Right, that a national curriculum would help to raise standards, the Conservative government was also attracted to such a reform because it would reduce the influence of the teaching profession over an area where they had traditionally exerted a considerable degree of autonomy. The publication of Standard Assessment Tests (SATs) in England gave an added dimension to the culture of performance management.

Experience of curriculum and assessment reform in Scotland has been somewhat different. With the possible exceptions of the initial stages of the introduction of Technical and Vocational Educational Initiative (TVEI) and the introduction of national testing in 1992, the process of reform has been more consensual, with educational professionals retaining a role at each stage of the process of reform. When the Scottish Office initially sounded out the idea of testing in its 1987 consultation paper, it faced concerted opposition from teachers, parents and local authorities (Hartley and Rodger 1990). However, there was a consensus that reform was necessary. The 5–14 Programme emerged from concerns about the poor performance of pupils in the early years of secondary schooling. As Brown (1994: 76) notes, 'the 5–14 Programme has always been "marketed" by the government as being based upon existing practice and not as a radical innovation'. From 1992, a modified form of testing was a feature of assessment policy in Scottish schools, but it was quite different in nature from that imposed on their English counterparts. For instance, the testing was more limited. More important, though, for a consideration of the effect of performance management, was the discretion for teachers to decide when a child was ready to be tested at a new level of attainment. There was also to be no central collection of results. What this suggests is that the regulatory framework teachers found themselves in may have been less politicised than in England. To explore this argument further, let us turn now to the second strand of the new managerialist regulatory framework, namely external regulation.

Following the 1988 Education Reform Act there has been a number of developments which have had implications for the external regulation of the teaching profession. The cumulative effect of these developments was the erosion of self-regulation which had been central to notions of professionalism in the post-war welfare state. In the wake of the 1988 legislation, a new appointed body, the Schools Examination and Assessment Council, was created by Ministers to review all aspects of curriculum and assessment policy. Reflecting government's wish to extend the use of such agencies in the policy process, several new bodies were established in the education field, such as the Funding Agency and the Teacher Training Agency. These 'quangos' and agencies, as Johnston and Riley (1995: 287) note, have 'created the scope for indirect government intervention and influence', although they were not a novel device in educational governance (Raab 1982). Government's increasing reliance on these arms-length bodies was a consequence of its attempt to shift power and control from professionals at local level to central government (Johnston and Riley 1995; Stewart 1995).

The most significant challenge to post-war notions of professionalism in England came with the privatisation of the schools inspectorate in the 1992 Education (Schools) Act. Taken alongside legislation passed in the following year to deal with 'failing schools', this initiative had profound implications for the teaching profession. Hoyle and John (1998) concur with such an assessment, arguing that for central government, '[i]nspection … was seen then as a central plank in the recasting of teacher professionalism'. Her Majesty's Inspectorate of Schools (HMI) was replaced by a new system of privatised inspectors. The Office for Standards in Education (OFSTED), which the 1992 Act established, was another new appointed body that now has responsibility for school inspection. Hargreaves and Evans (1997: 8) argue that inspections are now conducted within the discourse of school failure, 'a discourse in which teachers' positive qualities and the need to engage them could find little space'. Developments concerning school inspection indicated that the Conservative government was eager to continue the process of reforming the management of schools (Pierson, 1998).

In contrast, teachers in Scotland have been able to retain a greater degree of professional self-regulation. The absence of any equivalent legislation to the 1992 and 1993 Education Acts in England meant that there was a greater professional input into the external regulation of the teaching profession. The General Teaching Council (GTC) maintained standards of entry to the profession, and the HMI was not abolished. Indeed, the HMI retains considerable influence in the Scottish education system. Inspections while still conducted by the HMI did, however, begin to encompass some of the aspects of performance management discussed above. Nisbet Gallagher (1999: 140), former Senior Chief Inspector of the HMI, has alluded to the changing environment the Inspectorate faces: 'the encouragement and support of wider quality assurance arrangement has been a feature of Inspectorate activity in the 1990s'.

Why the difference in approach between Scotland and England? The lack of any equivalent to the 'Great Debate' arguably meant that the traditional professional standing of teachers remained high. The Inspectorate was also seen as a guardian of the Scottish education system (McPherson and Raab 1988). This, added to the electoral unpopularity of the Conservative government in Scotland, created a different policy-making environment. Brown *et al.* (1998) argue that the Scottish Office may have retained a strong corporatist approach for much of the period of Conservative government. The reform process had to be more gradual if government wanted to maximise its chances of successfully implementing its 'managerialist' policies; there could be no 'big bang' approach to educational reform in Scotland.

In an attempt to break down professional and bureaucratic accountability, the government also sought to give parents a direct involvement in school-level decision-making. This was the third strand to the new managerial framework. The government's expectation was that educational professionals would become more accountable when they had to respond to the wishes of the 'consumers'. School boards and governing bodies were the main mechanisms that government used to achieve this end. There are a number of differences between school boards and governing bodies in composition and in their statutory responsibilities. Scottish school boards, for instance, have a largely consultative role under DSM, while their English counterparts have executive powers on a range of matters, including staffing, curriculum and discipline. Given the relevance of these bodies to attempts to restructure accountability within the education system, a brief consideration of their impact on the role of professionals within schools is offered in the next section, but the position of parents in governing bodies and school boards is considered at length in Munn's chapter in this volume (Chapter 4).

To sum up: managerialist reforms which were introduced in England and Scotland shared the same ideological intention, that bureaucratic and professional control of the teaching profession should be replaced with managerial forms of control. All three strands of managerialism discussed above have been evident in Scotland and in England, but to varying degrees. Arguably, the greatest differences between the two countries lie with the second strand, that is, the external control and regulation of the teaching profession. Granted that it is possible to argue that educational professionals in Scotland have less influence in the government of education today than they did, say, twenty years ago, they have not experienced the same loss of autonomy as their counterparts south of the border. Let us now turn to the impact which these strands of managerialism have had upon roles and relationships within the case-study schools.

'Managerialism': Impact on roles and relationships within schools

This section examines the impact of education reforms upon the internal management of schools. It focuses primarily on teachers' perceptions of reforms to school governance and in particular to the management of schools. Broader issues of changing notions of professionalism and teachers' changing work conditions are explored in Bailey's chapter in this volume (Chapter 3). Extracts from interviews illustrate the impact which managerialism has had upon roles and relationships within schools, and are representative examples of teachers' perceptions. Three areas are considered: the changing position of the head, relations between head teachers and the school's teaching staff, and between the staff and the school board or governing body. Each provides an insight into recent changes to the governance of schools and has particular relevance to government's attempts to change the forms of accountability in the direction of managerial and market-based control. By assessing the nature of roles and relationships within schools, we can begin to understand the impact of 'managerialist' policies at school level.

Changing headship

The importance attached to the role of the head within managerialism has been noted by a number of writers (Angus 1989; Gewirtz *et al.* 1995; Grace 1995; Whitty *et al.* 1998). Writing within a managerialist paradigm, Caldwell and Spinks (1992: 202) have argued in somewhat evangelical terms of leaders having

> a commitment to and a capacity to articulate a vision of self manage-
> ment where schools are, quite literally, at the centre of the system,

with a culture of service pervading every aspect of arrangements for direction and support. They have the strength of will to see the complex and demanding processes of change to realisation.

One question posed at the start of the chapter was the extent to which the differences in the implementation of devolved management in Scotland and England had implications for the ways in which relationships and roles developed within schools in each country. For instance, in Scotland under DSM, responsibility for delegated functions lies formally with the head, whereas in England it lies with the governing body. Has this had any bearing on the way styles of headships have developed in the two countries? In order to answer this question, the impact of both managerialism and the market are considered. Arguably, at school level it was the head more than any other professional who was affected by the increasing emphasis in government policies on the market.

LMS and DSM have been central to the restructuring of the management of schools. The delegation of financial and staffing responsibilities to head teachers raises questions about the ability of the head to reconcile new managerial requirements and roles with older ones which emphasise professional and educational values. The ways in which managerial and professional roles are handled have implications for the internal workings of the school, and thus relations between heads and staff. The style of headship, as mentioned in Chapter 1, is pivotal to the organisational structures and the decision-making processes that develop in schools.

An awareness of the head's changing role came from both heads themselves and teaching staff. There was the perception that the delegation of functions from (local) education authorities to schools had led to tensions between financial management functions of the head and the role of the head as an educational professional, concerned with the curriculum, teaching and learning. Tension was evident between these competing roles as patterns of accountability were restructured along managerial and market-based lines. Across all of the case-study authorities, many staff-teaching and non-teaching – thought that the role of the head had been re-defined in terms of financial and managerial tasks. In Tayside, for instance, one Principal Teacher (PT) alluded to the changing role in these terms:

> He sees himself and his time as an accountant. He naturally has less time for the children and for the staff. He never says, 'no'. He doesn't close the door and say, 'I have got my DSM hat on, I wouldn't speak to you.' But he is not a full time head teacher because of DSM.

The tensions were more noticeable in Newcastle, where there was greater experience of delegated budgets. Findings confirm other research evidence that devolved management tends to drive a wedge between 'managerial' staff and teaching staff (Bowe *et al.* 1992; Deem *et al.* 1995; Gewirtz *et al.* 1995). At one Newcastle school, a head of department reflecting upon the role of the head teacher stated:

> you have got to be so much more financially aware of things, you have to go out there and promote the school; you are no longer a head teacher, you are a manager or a managing director. And that has got to be difficult, because basically what the head is, is a teacher who has gone up through the ranks. The head is not someone who was brought in from outside who has been a manager of General Motors or something like that.

The Scottish evidence was not so clear-cut. Some teachers speculated about possible conflict in future, but had not yet perceived radical changes in the head's role. The style of headship appears to be as important a factor as institutional structures in any tensions between contrasting responsibilities. Current concerns with educational issues in Scotland, particularly the *Higher Still* reform of curriculum and assessment, have emphasised the educational role of heads, who have been widely consulted about the nature, purpose and implementation of curriculum reform. This may have served to highlight the head's leading role in implementing the curriculum.

As the introduction of DSM progressed, financial management and managerial issues generally were thought by heads and also by many teachers across the Scottish schools to have become an increasingly important aspect of headship. This changing role was well expressed by one head teacher who had considerable experience of headship:

> [DSM is] just another change that has to be taken on board. It's what I call the ethos of management which has been the biggest single development in my time as head teacher.

Similar sentiments were expressed by other heads. For instance, a Lothian head pointed to the increasing emphasis on their managerial skills, saying that, 'there is certainly a far bigger focus on management effectiveness of the head teacher in the school'.

For some heads, their increasing involvement in managerial issues, particularly financial matters, was a welcome development. This was primarily because they thought they had the opportunity to distribute resources according to the school's priorities. But for others, there was concern about this aspect of headship becoming more prominent. One explained:

> I am not a great believer that the head teacher should be spending time on things economical and financial. But I am prepared to go along with it as far as I can. I am glad that there are people who can give me advice that I can trust, and let them get on with it.

It is important to emphasise that the changing role of the head was not solely due to DSM or LMS. Other, and sometimes not unrelated, changes were also affecting the head's position. The head who was just quoted, for instance, went on to say that 'the big issue was not DSM', but rather the 'monitoring of teaching and learning'.

Another relevant change to the role of the head identified by both heads themselves and staff was that they now spent more time away from school. Without exception, the heads of the case-study schools were finding it necessary to spend more time out of school. In the words of a head of one of the Scottish schools, 'I think taking head teachers, particularly perhaps the senior ones, out of school is a trend that's developed over the past couple of years, more than they did in the past.'

One reason for this trend in the Scottish schools was the increasing number of meetings that heads had to attend in preparation for the introduction of the new unitary local authorities, which succeeded the previous pattern of local government, in which Lothian, Strathclyde and Tayside were Regions. A closer relationship between heads and the authority had been anticipated by head teachers and teaching staff before this reorganisation. In the words of one head, '[heads] are now more involved in policy making at authority level' than they have been before. This was not felt to be the result of changing personalities, as this head was largely dealing with the same people, albeit in different roles. Rather, the authority had been actively consulting head teachers on a range of issues and involving them in working groups and policy forums, because it was setting out 'in a very enthusiastic way to look for the advice of people in the authority, especially senior people'. Examples of issues on which head teachers' advice was now being sought included staff training, quality development, the replacement of the education development service, and other personnel issues.

Though all of the heads in the school under study were spending more time out of school, their grounds for doing so were not necessarily the same. It is here that the differential impact of policies designed to promote market forces in Scotland and England begin to manifest themselves. Interestingly, in contrast to the research on Newcastle schools and other research on market reforms in English schools, it was not found that heads of the Scottish schools were spending more time away in order to 'market' their school. While they were keen to ensure that their schools had 'good' images in the local community, with the possible exception of two heads, they did not set out to compete directly with neighbouring schools for pupils. In several schools, rather than identifying the financial benefits of having more pupils, heads worried that an increased number would lead to overcrowding. Another possible explanation was a general reluctance, shown by both heads and staff in several schools, to compete with one another for pupils. The emphasis was on maintaining pupil numbers, rather than seeking to increase the school roll. One head drew a distinction between competing for pupils and communicating with parents:

> [Our school] could market [school B] into oblivion if it wanted to, which is completely wrong, because [school B] is just as good a school and has great leadership. The head and I get on really well. But because people think this school is better, we could really go for it if we wanted. We've not got the room, but we could do that. But I think that this all wrong; it is counter-productive. What we have tried to do is to improve what we do put out … We try to communicate effectively with parents – I think that is quite important … This is an important issue with parents – communication between the school and home. But we don't spend a huge lot of money, it is all home-made stuff.

Another illustration of the reluctance to compete actively with neighbouring schools was in Tayside. One PT was aware of the importance of pupil numbers to the school's budget, but when asked if the school had made active attempts to increase pupil numbers, replied:

> The honest answer to that is 'no'. I don't think that as a school we set out to, in effect, poach from other schools.

Similar sentiments were expressed, first by a PT and then by an Assistant Head Teacher in another school:

> I wouldn't have thought that the school is making specific efforts to increase our roll, other than doing the sort of liaison with primaries that would now be expected of any school … It was more tied with 5–14 [Programme] than attracting the pupils.

The heads [in the Authority] work very very closely together. I think that they always have, long before unitary authorities were introduced. We generally have an agreement that aggressive marketing is not the kind of thing that we want ... We do not poach each other's pupils – we try not to take each others' problem kids either.

In the Newcastle schools, the market had an important, though varying, impact on the way in which the role of the head had developed. Here the findings echo those of Gewirtz *et al.* (1995), who argue that the market conditions in which schools find themselves have an important bearing on the style of headships. At one school, which recently had to make some staff redundant, a head of department alluded to the pressure which the market had placed upon the head, arguing that as a consequence the head was now more accountable:

Certainly more accountable although I'm sure the [previous] head teacher would have said he was accountable, but I don't think that they were as accountable as the head teacher is accountable now. It's this marketing promotion. Schools were schools. People went to the school that was nearest to them. Things were stable. Now it's every which way, market forces are governing everything. And that obviously has a bearing on how head teachers spend their time.

Arriving at an explanation of why there should be this difference in the role of the head between the Scottish and English schools is not straightforward. After the 1988 Education Reform Act, both Scotland and England had similar parental choice legislation, but other market-based reforms had not gone as far in Scotland as England. Specifically, whilst both DSM and LMS advanced formula funding, the former allowed for actual salary costs to be included in the formula devised by education authorities. As a result, schools in Scotland did not experience the same pressures as English schools if their numbers fluctuated between school years. One could also point by way of explanation to the argument that in Scotland there remains a greater commitment to the principles of comprehensive education than in England (Adler 1997).

In sum, changes to the way schools are managed, in particular the development of financial and staffing delegation, have impacted on the role of heads across the UK. When we come to consider the impact which the market has had on heads, some interesting variations begin to emerge. Whilst, as Gewirtz *et al.* (1995) argue, heads respond to the localised markets in which their schools are located, there appeared to be less evidence in the Scottish case-study schools of heads adopting an active marketing role.

Head/staff relations

Whether or not Conservative governments were able to reform the management of schools, hinged upon the attitudes adopted by teachers (Hatcher 1994). According to Hatcher (1994: 41), 'the management of the service is inseparable from the management of the workforce'. In this section, the perception of teachers with regard to wider changes in the governance of schools is considered. That the role of the head was developing along more managerialist lines has been demonstrated above. What implications did this development have for relations within the school? One strand of managerialism which had particular relevance to evolving relations within schools was the culture of performance management. But to what extent did this aspect of managerialism impact upon notions of professional authority and control?

Echoing the findings of other researchers (Gewirtz *et al.* 1995; Levacic 1995), the perception of many teachers was that staff relations were now based much more upon managerial authority than professional authority. As a consequence, relations within the school were often seen as more hierarchical and managerial. Schools, especially secondary schools, have always been hierarchically organised, but was there less room for professional discretion from the late 1980s onwards? Advocates of DSM and LMS argue that, by delegating functions from local authorities to schools, teachers would have greater autonomy and a greater say in the management of their school. However, in reality these arguments were more pertinent to the position of the head than to teachers. In Scotland, for instance, the government envisaged that teachers would have a consultative role in DSM and that decision-making should be done on a consensual basis (SOED 1993). However, by delegating functions to head teachers, the pattern of staff involvement in the self-managing schools became even more dependent on the style of headship. For instance, in one Lothian school a PT alluded to the staff's lack of knowledge about decision-making processes in the school:

> We have bulletins three times a week, and there was a small insertion in one of the bulletins saying that if anyone wants to join a committee or come off it please see to it by such and such a date. It was something that a lot of people have felt we were kept in the dark about. We hear that something was decided by such and such a committee – 'What committee?' So at least we know the names of these committees.

Heads, however, did not necessarily enjoy increased professional autonomy. As Ball (1994) – among others – argues, after a long period in power the Conservative government had significantly enhanced its control over the management of schools. By advancing the culture of performance management, central government had been able to 'steer at a distance'. Hoyle and John (1998) labelled such developments as examples of 'neo-bureaucracy'. These developments, they argue, have been legit-imised by a discourse of empowerment. Mission statements, working parties, sub-committees and appraisals, whilst being presented as means to enhance participation, have not promoted collegiality but reduced profes-sional freedom at school level.

The research findings are that devolved management of schools had led to a renewed emphasis on sub-committees and working parties. Their number, remit and composition varied across the case-study schools, but heads tended to use them as consultative rather than as decision-making bodies. In the Scottish schools where staff committees had a decision-making function, it was of limited nature. For instance, in one school the DSM committee had an opportunity to make expenditure-related deci-sions only if there was an unspent balance at the end of the financial year. Experiences in the Newcastle schools were not dissimilar, despite the greater statutory responsibilities of governing bodies. Interviews with staff who were not members of the 'senior management team' revealed that staff involvement in school decision-making was largely consultative, with the head exercising ultimate authority. What was new about this situation was that the head was exercising his or her authority in areas in which teachers traditionally had professional autonomy. In sum, new managerial forms of control, especially performance management, allow heads to regulate the work of teachers in ways that impinge upon post-war notions of professionalism. Ozga (1995: 34) succinctly refers to this devel-opment as:

> the head-as-manager, working within a framework of regulations, and using management of the culture to internalise controls and ensure compliance.

Lay participation in school decision-making

The final aspect of managerialism to be considered is the attempt to use lay participation in the running of schools as a further mechanism to regu-late and control professional influence in school management. In Chapter 4 Munn considers the extent to which school boards and governing bodies fulfilled policy expectations, but of particular relevance for the present chapter are the ways in which the development of school boards and governing bodies dovetailed with managerialism. We have seen above that the use of internal managerial controls by heads impacted upon staff–head relations and that, as a consequence, hierarchical relations within schools were increasingly influenced by managerial responsibilities rather than professional authority. Boards and governing bodies can be viewed as part of this process of restructuring hierarchies within schools. The involvement of governing bodies in this process has gone further, at least in terms of the way the policies were drafted, than that of Scottish school boards. However, despite the differences in their statutory roles, governing bodies and school boards in the schools were supportive of the head. In other words, neither governing bodies nor school boards appeared to be using their enhanced role in the running of schools as a way to challenge the head. The following comment by the chair of a Lothian school board is illustrative of the attitudes of many parent board members and parent governors:

> In the case of our school board the decision has always tended to be to pass on all decision-making things to the teaching body and have little as possible to do with the day-to-day running of the school and not to interfere.

The significance of boards and governing bodies was not that they had assumed responsibilities for the running of schools but rather that, arguably contrary to the government's expectation, they had enhanced the position of the head. To give one illustration from a parent governor in one of the Newcastle schools:

> I think that this governing body would rubber stamp almost anything that the head puts in front of them, because they have confidence and trust in the man ... If it's the head's recommendation then the answer is yes, 100 per cent.

There was perhaps a greater tendency for heads in the Scottish schools to inform their boards rather than actively to consult with them or indeed to seek their direct involvement. This could be explained by the limited executive functions of boards compared to governing bodies. However, the trend across the (local) education authorities appeared to be that heads were mobilising the support of their governing body or school board to enhance their authority. As demonstrated in Munn's chapter, this manifested itself most obviously in relations with the (local) education authority, but the involvement of boards and governing bodies gave an added dimension to staff–head relations. In some of the Scottish schools, head teachers had brought parent board-members on to sub-committees and working parties. For instance, in three schools, a parental representative sat on school development-plan committees. Governor involvement in sub-committees and working parties was commonplace in the Newcastle schools. Given the close and supportive relations between heads and governors and board members, it would not be unreasonable to see their involvement as further enhancing the position of the head in the running of schools.

Conclusion

This chapter has explored the development of managerialism in the Scottish and English education systems. The evidence offered from the case-study schools, of course, is not representative of developments across Scotland and England, but, taken together with other research studies, it is possible to shed some light upon experiences in the two countries. Across the education systems of the United Kingdom, Conservative governments introduced policies which, if successfully implemented, would restructure roles and relationships along consumerist and managerial lines. Bureaucrats and professionals could not be left to 'administer' the welfare state. Such thinking has strong ideological undertones.

The ideological nature of school governance reforms meant that there would be common themes and objectives to the policies pursued in Scotland and England. Shared themes included the emphasis placed upon the culture of performance management, restructuring the external regulation of the teaching profession and encouraging lay participation in school decision-making. However, whilst these aspects of managerialism are evident both north and south of the border, there are important differences of emphasis. The culture of performance management has been advanced in both systems, but arguably in Scotland, because of the nature of curriculum and assessment reform, it has taken a milder form. Also, attempts to restructure the external regulation of the teaching profession have not gone as far in Scotland as England. It is here arguably that we see the greatest difference between managerialism in the two systems. In Scotland, the educational professionals have been able to retain considerable influence over the external regulation of their profession. An initial reading of policy developments concerning lay involvement in school decision-making might imply that the professionals in Scottish schools have retained much more power over the day-to-day running of schools than their English counterparts. However, school boards and governing bodies appeared to be using their new role to enhance the position of the head.

It is in the changing role of the head that we have witnessed perhaps the clearest signs of a new managerial framework. As a consequence of LMS and DSM, heads have increasing responsibility for financial and staffing matters. Though the government's intention was to replace bureaucratic and professional modes of co-ordination in the education system with managerial and market-based modes, in reality what has happened is that the post-war forms of co-ordination exist alongside the new modes of governance. The style of headship plays a crucial role in shaping the way that these changes to governance impact at school level.

Notes

1 This chapter draws upon findings from, and papers written within, the ESRC-supported project on Devolved Management of Schools (Grant No. R000233653) and the Scottish Office Education and Industry Department-supported project on Devolved School Management, including Raab *et al.* (1995), Adler *et al.* (1996), Arnott *et al.* (1996) and Raab *et al.* (1997).

References

Adler, M. (1997) 'Looking Backwards to the Future: Parental Choice and Education Policy', *British Educational Research Journal*, **23**(3): 297–314.
Adler, M., Arnott, M., Bailey, L., McAvoy, L., Munn, P. and Raab, C. (1996) *Devolved School Management in Secondary Schools in Scotland*, A Report to the Scottish Office Education and Industry Department, University of Edinburgh, Department of Politics: SOEID.
Angus, L. (1989) 'New Leadership and the Possibility of Educational Reform', in Smyth, J. (ed.) *Critical Perspectives on Educational Leadership*, London: Falmer.
Arnott, M. (1993) 'Thatcherism in Scotland: an Exploration of Education Policy in the Secondary Sector', Ph.D. thesis, University of Strathclyde.
Arnott, M., Raab, C. and Munn, P. (1996) 'Devolved Management: Variations of Response in Scottish School Boards', in Pole, C. and Chawla-Duggan, R. (eds) *Reshaping Education in the 1990s: Perspectives on Secondary Schooling*, London: Falmer.
Ball, S. (1994) *Education Reform: a Critical and Post Structural Approach*, Buckingham: Open University Press.
Bottery, M. (1992) *The Ethics of Educational Management*, London: Cassell.
Bowe, R. and Ball, S. with Gold, A. (1992) *Reforming Education and Changing Schools: Case Studies in Policy Sociology*, London: Routledge.
Boyne, G. (1998) *Public Choice Theory and Local Government: a Comparative Analysis of the UK and the USA*, London: Macmillan.
Brown, A., McCrone, D. and Paterson, L. (1998) *Politics and Society in Scotland*, London: Macmillan.
Brown, S. (1994) '5–14: Assessment and Testing', in Kirk, G. and Glaister, R. (eds) *5–14 Scotland's National Curriculum*, Edinburgh: Scottish Academic Press.

74   Margaret A. Arnott

Busher, H. and Saran, R. (1995) 'Introduction: Schools for the Future', in Busher, H. and Saran, R. (eds) *Managing Teachers as Professionals in Schools*, London: Kogan Page.

Caldwell, B. and Spinks, J. (1992) *Leading the Self-Managing School*, London: Falmer.

Chitty, C. (1989) *Towards A New Education System: the Victory of the New Right*, London: Falmer.

Chitty, C. (1992) *The Education System Transformed*, Manchester: Baseline.

Chitty, C. (1997) 'Privatisation and Marketisation', *Oxford Review of Education*, 23(1): 45–62.

Clarke, J. and Newman, J. (1997) *The Managerial State: Power, Politics and Ideology in the Remaking of Social Welfare*, London: Sage.

Deem, R., Brehony, K. and Heath, S. (1995) *Active Citizenship and the Governing of Schools*, Buckingham: Open University Press.

Denham, A. (1996) *Think Tanks of the New Right*, Aldershot: Darmouth.

Eliassen, K. and Kooiman, J. (1993) 'Introduction', in Eliassen, K. and Kooiman, J. (eds) *Managing Public Organisations: Lessons from Contemporary European Experience*, 2nd edn, London: Sage.

Fairley, J. and Paterson, L. (1991) 'The Reform of Vocational Education and Training in Scotland', *Scottish Educational Review*, 23: 68–77.

Fairley, J. and Paterson, L. (1995) 'Scottish Education and New Managerialism', *Scottish Educational Review*, 27: 13–36.

Gallagher, N. (1999) 'The Scottish Inspectorate and their Operation', in Bryce, T. and Humes, W. (eds) *Scottish Education*, Edinburgh: Edinburgh University Press.

Gewirtz, S., Ball, S. J. and Bowe, R. (1995) *Markets, Choice and Equality in Education*, Buckingham: Open University Press.

Grace, G. (1995) *School Leadership: Beyond Education Management. An Essay in Policy Scholarship*, London: Falmer.

Hargreaves, A. and Evans, R. (1997) 'Teachers and Educational Reform', in Hargreaves, A. and Evans, R. (eds) *Beyond Educational Reform: Bringing Teachers Back In*, Buckingham: Open University Press.

Hartley, D. and Rodger, A. (1990) *Curriculum and Assessment in Scotland: a Policy for the 90s*, Edinburgh: Scottish Academic Press.

Hatcher, R. (1994) 'Market Relationships and the Management of Teachers', *British Journal of Sociology of Education*, 15(1): 41–61.

Holliday, I. (1992) 'Scottish Limits to Thatcherism', *Parliamentary Affairs* 63: 448–59.

Hood, C. (1998) *The Art of the State: Culture, Rhetoric and Public Management*, Oxford: Clarendon.

Hoyle, E. and John, P. (1998) 'School Teaching', in Laffin, M. (ed.) *Beyond Bureaucracy? The Professions in the Contemporary Public Sector*, Aldershot: Ashgate.

Hughes, M. (1997) 'The National Curriculum in England and Wales: a Lesson in Externally Imposed Reform?', *Education Administration Quarterly*, 33(2): 183–97.

Johnston, H. and Riley, K. (1995) 'The Impact of Quangos and New Government Agencies on Education', *Parliamentary Affairs*, **48(2)**: 284–96.

Laffin, M. (1998) 'The Professions in the Contemporary Public Sector', in Laffin, M. (ed.) *Beyond Bureaucracy? The Professions in the Contemporary Public Sector*, Aldershot: Ashgate.

Levacic, R. (1995) *Local Management of Schools: Analysis and Practice*, Buckingham: Open University Press.

McCrone, D. (1992) *Understanding Scotland: a Sociology of a Stateless Nation*, London: Routledge.

McPherson, A. and Raab, C. (1988) *Governing Education: a Sociology of Policy Since 1945*, Edinburgh: Edinburgh University Press.

Ozga, J. (1995) 'Deskilling a Profession: Professionalism, Deprofessionalism and the New Managerialism', in Busher, H. and Saran, R. (eds) *Managing Teachers as Professionals in Schools*, London: Kogan Page.

Paterson, L. (1994) *The Autonomy of Scotland*, Edinburgh: Edinburgh University Press.

Pierson, C. (1998) 'The New Governance of Education: the Conservatives and Education 1988–1997', *Oxford Review of Education*, **24(1)**: 131–43.

Pollitt, C. (1993) *Managerialism and the Public Services: Cuts or Cultural Change in the 1990s*, 2nd edn, Oxford: Blackwell.

Pyper, R. and Stoker, G. (1997) 'Editorial: Understanding Governance', *Public Policy and Administration*, **12(2)**: 1–3.

Raab, C. (1982) 'The Quasi-Government of Scottish Education', in Barker, A. (ed.) *Quangos in Britain: Government and the Networks of Policy-Making*, London: Macmillan

Raab, C. (1993) 'Education and the Impact of the New Right', in Jordan, G. and Ashford, N. (eds) *Public Policy and the Impact of the New Right*, London: Pinter.

Raab, C., Arnott, M., Adler, M., Bailey, L. and Munn, P. (1995) 'Devolved School Management and the New Governance of Education: Preliminary Findings', Working Paper prepared for the ESRC Invitational Seminar, Edinburgh, 6 October.

Raab, C., Munn, P., McAvoy, L., Bailey, L., Arnott, M. and Adler, M. (1997) 'Devolving the Management of Schools in Britain', *Educational Administration Quarterly*, **33(2)**: 140–57.

Raffe, D. (1998) '"Home International" Comparisons in UK Policy-Making', *Journal of Education Policy*, **13(5)**: 591–602.

Ranson, S. and Stewart, J. (1994) *Management for the Public Domain: Enabling the Learning Society*, London: Macmillan.

Rhodes, R. A. W. (1997) *Understanding Governance: Policy Networks, Governance, Reflexivity and Accountability*, Buckingham: Open University Press.

Riley, K. (1998) *Whose School Is It Anyway?*, London: Falmer.

SOEID (1993) *Devolved School Management: Guidelines for Schemes*, Circular No. **6/93**, Edinburgh: Scottish Office Education Department.

Stewart, J. (1995) 'Appointed Bodies and Local Government', *Parliamentary Affairs*, **48(2)**.

Stoker, G. (ed.) (1999) *The New Management of British Local Governance*, Basingstoke: Macmillan.

Whitty, G., Power, S. and Halpin, D. (1998) *Devolution and Choice in Education: the School, the State and the Market*, Buckingham: Open University Press.

3 Of myths and management

Listening to teachers talk about their work

Lucy Bailey

Introduction

Concern that welfare services have been 'captured' by professionals to serve their own interests has motivated an interest in reform across the political spectrum, and has led to a questioning of the role of public service professionals both north and south of the border (Munn 1993). The new governance of education, with its emphasis on quasi-market concerns such as value for money, competition and consumer responsiveness, may be offering a new role to education professionals. This chapter draws on research evidence to investigate classroom teachers' changing position as employees in the education system. It critically examines changes in the labour process and in the relationships between teachers, with teacher and head teacher interviews forming the empirical basis of the account. Comparisons are drawn between the evidence from Scottish data, and that from research in England. For reasons of space, only the most salient of the local authority-level differences are highlighted. Overall, the argument that teachers were being 'deskilled' and their work 'intensified' is contrasted with the more complex world that emerges from the empirical data about the way that professional values mediated the pressures of devolved management. It is argued that a mythological 'other', who challenged their philosophy of education, was constructed by the teachers in their accounts of educational change. This was then used both to affirm a particular professional orientation and to create a sense of community between colleagues who work independently for much of the time.

It is impossible to separate the effect of schemes of devolved management – Devolved School Management in Scotland and Local Management of Schools in England – from the impact of the full gamut of changes that have occurred in Scottish and English education in recent years. The teachers themselves spoke of the difficulty of distinguishing one item from the web of reforms in which they had been caught. Devolved management was not a major priority in the day-to-day lives of teachers, with curricular and assessment changes being more immediate concerns. In addition, in some schools a change of head teacher was seen as having had at least as significant an impact on their work. This chapter will not, then, make claims about the impact of new systems of devolved management in isolation, but instead examine the discourse of teachers concerning their work with reference to a number of related changes which have occurred.

This is not, of course, the first study to look at the implications of devolved management on teachers' work. Smyth (1995), in his study of teachers' work in Australia, argues that whilst decentralisation has a 'superficial appeal' (Smyth 1995: 196) to teachers, it actually conceals a process whereby their work is intensified and they are subject to a number of controls. In the English context, Bullock and Thomas (1997) have pointed to heightened job insecurity in both primary and secondary schools, a worsening of pupil–teacher ratios, and an increasing tendency to view teachers in terms of financial cost. Alongside this bleak picture, they set an international comparison of the effects of decentralisation on teacher professionalism, suggesting that a high degree of marketisation tends to deprofessionalisation, whereas delegation in other contexts may actually enhance professionalism. This work reminds us of the utility of comparative analysis in directing attention to the cultural context of educational change. Whilst the main focus in this chapter is on the Scottish context, data from the English component of the study are useful in sensitising the researcher to particular themes and in offering key moments of contrast.

Hatcher (1994) also focuses on the impact of recent English changes. His meta-analysis of previous studies echoes this one in focusing on changes in the labour process and conceptions of professionalism. He argues that new forms of management have had their effects on three elements of teachers' work. First, the work process has been reconstructed, with intensification and increased regulation as key themes. Hatcher argues that teachers are being proletarianised, but that elements of reskilling as well as deskilling are taking place. Second, teachers have been affected by new employment conditions and by an offensive on trade-union rights. Third, a new organisational culture has developed in schools, and different groups of teachers have started to develop different conceptions of professionalism. Hatcher takes an overly deterministic approach, linking changes in teachers' work to capitalism, which can obscure a less unitary interpretation of change. However, his call for further research is in part being answered by the data presented here.

The present study looks at how changes in the labour process (Braverman 1974) both affect and are affected by conceptions of professionalism, without suggesting that one can be reduced to the other. It is not helpful simply to undertake an analysis of the tasks that teachers perform, and then compare them to criteria for the assignation of 'professionalism' to an occupation; neither can 'professionalism' be related simply to the social functions performed by an occupation (Johnson 1972). Following Troman (1996), professionalism is seen as 'a socially constructed, contextually variable and contested concept' (Troman 1996: 476). For example, the emphasis on individualistic market behaviour in recent reforms may be seen as sitting uneasily with the collective tradition of Scottish education (McPherson 1983), and therefore may be more consistent with teachers' professional culture in England. Similarly, skill and expertise are culturally constructed; what is important is for the researcher not to try and analyse the skill level involved in various tasks, but to examine how such changing tasks are represented discursively.

Therefore, in investigating teacher professionalism, the ideal starting place is teachers' own perceptions of this, and how they interpret change and construct a discourse around it. This chapter is divided into three main sections. First, the teachers' discourses of professionalism are charted. Second, a study is made of teachers' day-to-day experience of work, with particular attention being paid to the intensification and deskilling hypotheses, and the implications of this for professionalism are investigated. Third, the contextual conditions of such work are examined, showing how a professional ethos mediated the effects of reform on school hierarchies and the relationships between teachers. In concluding, some speculations are made about the future of teachers' work.

Conceptions of professionalism

Hatcher (1994) has pointed out that the basis for claims to professionalism has varied historically. In the past, in England, it was based on the idea of teacher autonomy; more recently, a 'market-driven technical–rationalist ideology' (Hatcher 1994: 55) has moved to the fore. It would be simplistic to assume that there is homogeneity amongst teachers in their interpretation of professionalism, as Hatcher's account bears out. Moves towards quasi-markets and the managerial ethos of the private sector offer a potential challenge to traditional public-service values and established conceptions of professionalism; alternatively, decentralisation may enhance professionalism by offering increased autonomy (Sleegers and Wesselingh 1995). The data on which the following analysis is built do not permit comparison between distinct groups of teachers, and neither can claims of representativeness be made. It is possible, however, to delineate the parameters of teachers' discourse concerning their professionalism. The intention here is not to suggest a delineation of this discourse that is particularly novel, but to investigate the degree of resilience of this discourse in the face of recent reforms.

It was found that the economic concerns of the market had not yet permeated teachers' discourse about their work. Teachers retained a strong sense that they were engaged in a moral project. Teaching was presented discursively as a 'vocation', which served to privilege the accounts of teachers over the accounts of those who have not received this call. Teachers' discourse of professionalism continued to accord primacy to immediate classroom concerns; less urgent managerial matters were accorded lower priority, and defined as 'distractions'. There were thus a number of elements to this discourse which could be drawn on by teachers to assert their own perspective on their work. A Principal Teacher of Chemistry disagreed with the use of performance indicators by the education authority to monitor teachers' work:

> I think the administration would not view it as a vocation and therefore they don't have the right philosophy. I think a lot of resources and time and effort and money tend to go into that side of it, rather than into the education.

Thus it would be far too simplistic, and somewhat patronising, to dismiss the discourse of professionalism as no more than false consciousness. It is a discourse which can be drawn on by competing groups and for a variety of purposes, but it is inherently neither empowering nor repressive. There are two sides to professionalism; it has been used as a controlling ideology, but it has also operated as a self-defence strategy on the part of teachers (Ozga and Lawn 1981; Grace 1978). Teachers themselves were often aware of this tension; the Principal Teacher of English at another school acknowledged that he was sceptical about the direction in which recent reforms are taking teachers, and yet:

> I can give you situations whereby our minimum non-contact agreement is breached because teachers are approached by the senior management and [they say], 'Look, you've got this cover for the rest of the week; can you just tide it over? It's going to save us a wee bit [of] dosh.' 'No problem.' And a lot of people will do it. I can see myself doing it in that situation because it will always be presented as for the benefit of the pupils.

Teachers' work was conceptualised both as enjoyable and fulfilling, and also as part of the moral project in which teachers were engaged. Teachers did not necessarily actively resist or reject the philosophy behind current educational reforms; they differed in the extent to which they engage in critiques of this form. Rather, the Principal Teacher of English just quoted felt that 'everything seems to be conspiring to drive us into our own little hidey holes'. Moreover, many of them welcomed elements of the new educational settlement, and valued the 'flexibility' and 'freedom' which they felt devolved management had brought. However, their own construction of work did not position teachers simply as players for economic gain in the education market. Hence, the outcome for the education system may be rather different from what policy-makers intended.

Rather than simply seeing teaching as a job, teachers retained a vision of their lives in terms of an educational philosophy. As the Principal Teacher of Mathematics at one school said, 'That is the real world of teaching. We're talking about human beings. We're talking about children.' Similarly, the Principal Teacher of Biology at another school emphasised, 'Education is what I am interested in. That is always my concern; what are you doing for the pupils?'

Teachers' discourse operated to endorse a particular educational vision which was implied to be under threat from some unidentified other, sometimes personified by the government or by a hidden political agenda. The Principal Teacher of Chemistry quoted earlier was typical in asserting that 'I still believe that education is for the kids', implicitly suggesting that others did not. Such statements seemed to operate as rallying cries for a sense of common purpose as a profession, though in practice they offered no real content for differentiating this group from others external to it. The hero of this tale was the classroom teacher, beset by villains who offered a challenge to the fulfilment of the teacher's task, and who presumably thought that education was for someone other than the children. The mythical interpretations thereby placed on policy change operated discursively to give a sense of common purpose. By enabling the teachers to conceive of a mythical 'other' who threatened such statements, these reforms may have actually drawn teachers together as much as they divided them, by engendering a sense of a common enemy against whom varied educational visions could be united. As another Principal Teacher of English said:

> All of these things we are talking about are kind of peripheral to the main thing, the kids in class. So I think, although you might feel the odds are stacked against you, [we] still … feel that we just have to

struggle for it for the sake of [the pupils]. That sounds altruistic, but I think it's true.

This finding is important in the light of predictions made by other researchers that we may see an end of the 'commitment to care' (Wallace *et al.* 1995: 113) in the public services as a consequence of managerial change. Whilst these predictions may still come to pass, in Scotland, at any rate, that situation has not yet been reached. This echoes the finding by Woods (1994) that his two case-study English primary schools 'appropriated' educational change; whilst teachers' work had been intensified, each of his schools had been able to retain its own distinctive ethos.

The mythological 'other' of their discourse provided a target of opposition, but by establishing teachers as moral victims it did not position them as combatants in institutionalised politics. Instead, the discourse suggested that the teacher might need to remain aloof from political engagement (Grace 1987). Hence, the philosophies that this mythology enabled teachers to assert were rarely controversial. A Principal Teacher of Guidance criticised other Principal Teachers:

> The big picture, for a lot of them, isn't in it, so long as they can get in there, teach their youngsters, have a good pass rate, and everything is fine in their garden.

Teachers' confrontation with change was sometimes real, but it is important not to overstate it by overlooking these limits to their discourse.

Scottish educational and wider culture has traditionally emphasised collective values more strongly than the English tradition (McPherson 1983). The teaching profession has also been regulated differently north and south of the border; for example, in Scotland, the General Teaching Council plays an important role in giving the profession some autonomy from the state, whilst no equivalent body existed in England. Moreover, day-to-day work is experienced differently in the two contexts through, for example, class size regulations in Scotland. It is not surprising, then, that it was the Scottish data which produced the strongest pronouncements by teachers of an education philosophy which sat uneasily with recent reforms. A Principal Teacher of Business Studies thought that it would be against 'the Scottish tradition' for schools to 'opt out' of local-authority control, in contrast to the educational culture in England, where:

> a large number of teachers in selective schools, grammar schools, that size of school, still see themselves as a lesser version of Eton.

To summarise, the data from this project can be counterposed to theories (e.g. Beynon 1994) of value shifts among professionals (or, indeed, of the erosion of an ethos of professionalism) in the public sector as a response to marketisation. However, it equally does not suggest that the teachers' world view has been left unchanged. Before finishing this section, it should be noted that some cases were encountered where teachers appeared to be renegotiating their conception of professionalism in response to the emerging educational settlement, and utilising a more 'managerial' discourse to describe their tasks. The research findings suggest that such renegotiation was limited, but the nature and size of the sample of schools precludes the drawing of firm conclusions on the extent of change.

Teachers' work

With the background of marketisation, one might expect to discover a considerable impact on teachers' work. Sinclair, Ironside and Seifert (1996) have argued that substitution, whereby cheaper labour is used to replace the more expensive, may be predicted to accompany intensification and deskilling as part of moves to import the exigencies of the private sector into education. Yet, whilst there was evidence of some intensification and a degree of deskilling of teachers' work, there had also been elements of reskilling, and the professional culture meant that substitution has been limited, especially in Scotland. Professional values had mediated the impact of market reforms, though, in time, conceptions of professionalism may be affected in their turn. Campbell and Neill (1994) have called for greater precision in the formulation of the intensification and deskilling hypotheses. They point out that there is considerable ambiguity as to what can be counted as evidence for each. The analysis here focuses on teachers' own interpretation of their skill and of the management of their time, rather than attempting to establish 'objective' measures for interpreting such claims.

The thesis of intensification (Larson 1980) receives extensive support from the data. Intensification refers to moves by 'capital' to extract additional 'surplus value' from workers. In the case of public sector workers, such as teachers, this may be hard to identify, but can be thought of in terms of the state's expecting more work out of teachers (Apple 1986), although an increased workload may paradoxically overload teachers and make them less productive. Time after time, teachers spoke of feeling 'overwhelmed' by the pressures upon them. There was far more to this than devolved management, with curricular and assessment changes being seen as the worst culprits. However, devolved management committees and paperwork could add to the problem. Time – and its limitations – was a recurrent theme from the interviews (Hargreaves 1994), and this was slowly changing the nature of teaching for some teachers. They spoke about their enjoyment of teaching being eroded, of no longer feeling at ease in the school and in the classroom. One Principal Teacher of Mathematics argued:

> I've been a Head of Department now for 10 years. When I started I was a teacher with extra responsibilities. Now I'm an administrator, a team leader, who has to teach Maths as a hobby, whenever I can get a moment of brain space to think about it. The most distressing thing about the job [is] now that I have almost no satisfaction from teaching Maths, which potentially is the job that I would love. Tremendously fulfilling and satisfying job – I can't get that satisfaction any more because I have to do other things.

In addition, a shift was gradually taking place in the sorts of tasks which were seen as legitimately the work of individual teachers – particularly promoted teachers – such as keeping an eye on repairs and maintenance, responding to curricular consultations, and so on. Nevertheless, many, like this same Principal Teacher, held this reconceptualisation of the role at arm's length

> My workload has greatly increased. Every year there's more than before. A lot of my daily work is … whatever today's silly question is. Somewhere around 4 p.m. I get round to being a schoolteacher again, and get my jotters corrected and my work prepared.

Devolved management was seen as having increased the number of administrative tasks that Principal Teachers had to undertake. Hence, there was considerable evidence of intensification from both the English and Scottish schools. Whilst the systems of governance being introduced contained important differences in the two contexts, a common theme was that of teachers feeling overworked and unable to draw breath. Consequently, teachers had been unable to reap some of the theoretical rewards of devolved management. For example, whilst there was the potential for more involvement in decision-making, many teachers outside of Senior Management Teams were reluctant to get involved in more committees and meetings in an already overcrowded week. It is an oversimplification, however, to describe the changes in teachers' work as 'deskilling' across the different levels of school management. Many Principal Teachers welcomed the ability to make more resource allocation decisions; now that they could order supplies they felt that their sense of responsibility and their ability to respond flexibly to demands had been enhanced. However, others felt that they had always had to make some financial decisions; this was especially so where a school had managed a community school budget in the past. Moreover, some were sceptical about how much real power they had been given; one Principal Teacher of English argued, 'Having to do the budget does not equal freedom to choose.'

In all three Scottish education authorities studied, there was little evidence to substantiate the substitution thesis; fixed-term contracts, voluntary redundancies and early retirement had been used to obviate or reduce the need for compulsory redundancies. Schools did not always follow financial logic in making their decisions, since the work of teachers was not conceptualised exclusively in these terms. At one school, teachers on fixed contracts were retained during the examination period because it was felt to be the morally right thing to do. However, the incentive to employ cheaper teachers, particularly newly qualified teachers, had bitten south of the border, where only the average and not the actual salary costs were devolved.

Although little evidence was found of substitution taking place in Scottish schools, England was seen as a salutary warning for the future, and this coloured attitudes further north. The discourse of 'flexibility' could also engender feelings of job insecurity; at one school, a proposed merger with another school was causing concern amongst temporary and supply staff. At another school in a different education authority, a large supply budget had initially been viewed with suspicion by the trade union, and it had taken time and effort on the part of management to set such fears at rest. These fears in themselves might have acted as a disciplining mechanism on teachers.

Moreover, some teachers felt that their work was being reconceptualised in financial terms. The Rector (head teacher) at one school had caused resentment by asking staff to make a big effort to come into school whenever possible so that the supply-teaching budget could be saved. In the words of the Principal Teacher of Physics at that school:

> That, to me, although said very professionally and as one colleague to another, sends the wrong message completely [about] the value that people put on teachers.

It was feared that teachers were becoming just another factor of production rather than the human dimension of an important educational process, yet teachers were reluctant to reconceptualise their role in these terms.

It is insufficient to note evidence of intensification without considering the relationship between time and professionalism. First, the ability to allocate time autonomously is often integral to a sense of professionalism; and, second, the choice to give extra time voluntarily is important to the feeling of commitment that makes teaching seem like more than just a job. The changes described above arguably deprive teachers of both these claims to professionalism, and hence may alter their perception of their role. Teachers may have always worked long hours and been restricted to some degree in the use of their time through the all-pervasive timetable; however, now they feel forced to spend additional parts of their week in particular ways to meet the arduous demands of administration. Though they may be working no harder than before, they are thereby deprived of the exercise of discretion which is central to a sense of professionalism. In so far as teaching was seen as a 'moral' project, the increased workload decreased the opportunity for demonstrations of commitment, and therefore may in the longer term undermine teachers' sense of vocation whilst extracting little, if any, extra work.

Nevertheless, predictions of change have a tendency to outstrip the ensuing reality. It is important not to lose sight of the fact that, even with so many changes, teachers were to a large extent the same people doing essentially the same job that they had done before. This fact was important, possibly as reassurance, to many teachers. The teacher representative on one school board explained why he thought that the impact of devolved management would be limited:

> There is also the inertia that exists within any institution. Things are there because they are there. Radical change means that there are so many knock-on effects, a large institution like this must contain an element of inertia. Particularly with teachers who tend to be individualistic, who don't necessarily fit very well into bureaucratic machines at all. That is not the way we work. I don't work with other adults most of the time. I don't spend my time with my colleagues. When I am in school, I am with the kids. I am working as part of a team in everything I do, but the fact remains that is not where I am all day every day ... A school is very different from most other institutions. It produces a different type of person – me!

Changing professional relationships

The structures in which teachers operate, and their links with – or isolation from – their colleagues are two contextual dimensions of particular importance to their working lives. In this section, we examine how the new governance impacted on each of these. Other discussions of managerialism and markets in this volume complement the comments made here.

The new education settlement potentially both individualises and regroups teachers. It individualises by inviting comparisons about the cost-effectiveness of different members of staff. 'Effectiveness' becomes measured by examination performance, and league tables encourage the comparison of results. At the same time, new forms of collegiality are encouraged; for example, financial allocations become an outcome of school-based negotiations. It can be seen, therefore, that devolved management and other quasi-market changes potentially revolutionise the basis of the teaching sub-culture. In this section, we explore whether and how this potential has been realised.

The way in which an occupation is managed is central to any claims which it makes to professionalism, and to its members' experience of their work. Self-management and a degree of autonomy for an occupation boost claims to professional standing. The perception of the head teacher's role, therefore, was central. Promotion and career mobility have long been perceived by teachers as taking them 'away' from the classroom. The research data suggest that this divide has been accentuated by recent reforms, although many of the teachers' comments on this area involved speculation about the future rather than observations on current events. A Principal Teacher of Biology was reluctant to seek further promotion because the increased administration which had been brought to senior posts had already, in his opinion, reduced their educational involvement. A Principal Teacher of English articulated the divide that was supposed by many to exist between 'teachers' and 'management':

> I see DSM as a managers' scheme that one or two manic managers want and I don't see many teachers wanting. And I separate them – managers from teachers – because that is what they are doing with themselves. And I see it as a scheme ... [This] sort of management culture is growing. I think there are one or two people who once they leave the classroom forget what it is all about.

Hence, the findings confirm the claim by researchers of the English system that many teachers thought devolved management had actually increased, or threatened to increase, the divide between senior managerial staff and the rest of the teachers (Bowe and Ball with Gold 1992). Yet, whilst senior staff had become the 'management', their derivation from the ranks of teachers was seen as important and as enabling them to empathise with those they managed. Some teachers described a dismal future in which senior staff were drawn from the ranks of industry, and contrasted this with the current situation. Self-management continued to operate as a symbol of professional claims.

Trust in the head teacher was a recurrent element of the teachers' discourse, which implicitly affirmed a belief in some professional code of conduct, and suggested that the judgement of a fellow teacher would have a sounder basis than that of an education authority bureaucrat. Across the authorities, there was a large dose of scepticism about the real decision-making involvement that was consequent upon any supposed consultation. Such a response was not simply jaded cynicism in the wake of the numerous reforms they had experienced; many teachers, voicing trust in their head teachers, expressed the view that it should not be any other way. There was, however, concern that head teachers' role was changing, as they became caught up in financial decision-making rather than leading the development of the curriculum. Whether or not the view of the head teacher as an erstwhile curriculum leader ever really held true, it performed an important role in establishing a norm of teaching as involving purer issues of pupil need than those which surfaced in a regime dominated by finance.

Examination performance tables opened up the possibility of new forms of worker surveillance by management, and there was some evidence of Principal Teachers becoming accountable for examination results to the senior management team, in a way that had not previously existed. Yet, the unpromoted teacher interviewed in one school, for instance, did not feel threatened by the possibility of evaluations being made on the basis of the examination performance of a class. Whilst exam results were analysed in departmental meetings, there was much laughter over the various scores; after all, he continued, each class is so different that you cannot say that one teacher has done better or worse than another. There, and in many other schools, it was not felt that decisions were made, or actions taken, on the basis of different scores. Nevertheless, even when comparisons are not drawn by management, such moves may still encourage self-surveillance and so can operate as a form of indirect control.

References to trade unions and to other forms of teacher collectivity were an important feature of the Scottish findings. Hence, relations between teacher and management, and between one teacher and another, had not become individualised in the way that might have been predicted. For example, at two schools in different education authorities, the teacher representatives on the school board were nominees of the

Educational Institute of Scotland, the main teachers' union. In a third school, school board elections were contested on a trade-union basis. Again, there was a contrast with the individualisation which seemed more characteristic of the English schools.

The relationships that teachers have with one another, and not only those which they have with their managers may, nevertheless, be affected by the new forms of governance, as Woods (1994) found in his study of English primary schools. The new structures could open up possibilities for co-operation. A Principal Teacher of Mathematics said that, whilst there was little history of co-operative teaching in his school, under devolved management there had been the opportunity to bid for learning-support resources to facilitate co-operative teaching. Moreover, the committee structures set up to administer devolved management could engender interdepartmental links. However, it was found that intra-school collegiality could be undermined in at least two ways by financial pressures. First, devolved management had in some cases intensified the internecine conflict between departments as they competed for pupils and the attendant funds. In one school, resentment had been caused when the English department received slightly less in its departmental budget than did the Mathematics department. Similarly, at another school there had been competition between departments in order to attract pupils. Second, financial constraints encouraged the use of temporary contracts by the education authority. A teacher of Business Education reported consequent animosity between staff in his school, as there was concern and rivalry concerning who would be awarded a permanent position.

To summarise, it would not be valid to see the new forms of governance as definitely leading to hierarchical and controlling forms of management, or to rivalry between teachers, although these are potential tendencies consequent upon the change. It was evident that such pressures were being mediated by teachers' conceptions of their role as professionals, and by countervailing tendencies in those very same reforms. Whilst there is a temptation to see policy as pointing education in a single direction, the empirical data have required the construction of a far more complex map of change.

Conclusion

This chapter has emphasised that, without examining the cultural dimension of teaching, the impact of specific policy changes cannot be understood. The long-term impact of devolved management will not be seen by looking at its effect on work patterns alone, but also through the more fundamental challenge that it may pose to how the task of teaching is conceptualised in schools. Caveats are given at other places in this volume concerning the generalisability of research findings. Whilst reiterating this caution, it is worth highlighting some of this chapter's central points.

There have been changes in the work process of teachers; devolved management and attendant reforms have introduced certain pressures to change, and in both England and Scotland there is some evidence of intensification and a degree of deskilling, along with shifting relationships between teachers in schools. But change has been moderated by the way that teachers conceptualise their work and their professionalism, which differs between the two contexts. Several teachers, both Principal and unpromoted teachers, described themselves as having been too busy to work out what the impact of devolved management might be; they constructed their work as focused on the classroom itself, and ignored as far as possible the context in which they were operating. That is not to say that they were unaffected; much has altered for teachers. Yet, again and again, unprompted expressions of strongly held educational philosophies would pepper the interviews. Teaching remains an area of work where the sense of vocation is strong.

It is scarcely new to argue that teachers do not simply fall into line when the next policy calls. However, the processes by which they fail to do so deserve careful exploration. Whilst some teachers, especially in Scotland, were actively rejecting what they interpreted as the agenda of policy changes through their everyday practice in the classroom, others were simply getting by as best they could, simultaneously trying to meet external demands and internal norms. Exploring the discourse of teachers concerning their work, school hierarchies and their professionalism have enabled us to see that a myth of the 'heroic' teacher was being contrasted with a new set of pressures which had come to bear upon teachers' lives. The myth itself continued to motivate teachers, and was central to their claims to see teaching as a moral project. In describing this as a 'myth', it is not being implied that it had no basis in fact, but rather that it was a simplified abstraction that provided the measure against which the current reforms, sometimes favourably and sometimes unfavourably, were compared.

Looking to the future, teacher professionalism may, however, be evolving in the new educational climate, as a technicisation of teaching and an erosion of knowledge hierarchies occurs. Teaching has always had its jargon: for example, the specialist vocabulary of child-centred education. However, curricular changes, financial devolution and other reforms, both north and south of the border, have introduced a detailed technical language to the world of teaching, a gamut of procedures and acronyms.

This has not always been welcomed; a Principal Teacher of English described as 'crazy' the fact that members of the public could no longer easily understand what was being discussed. However, sharing that language may offer teachers opportunities to build up a new sub-culture and so impact on the social construction of teaching skill. This would operate in a context of other, possibly competing, tendencies in contemporary culture; for instance, Nixon and his colleagues (1997) suggest that via postmodernity's deconstruction of knowledge and authority, in consequence, the conception of professionalism of the post-war settlement, which is based on subject expertise and specialist knowledge, is thrown into doubt.

It has been argued here that devolved management is seen more usefully as part of a cultural change rather than as a specific reform. Its impact on the social construction of the skill and role of the teacher is therefore gradual and evolving. Elements of teachers' discourse concerning these changes have been identified above, and it has been claimed that these conceptions of professionalism are both the mediators of change and themselves affected by change. It would be premature, therefore, to see the situation described as the final outcome of the reform process; contestation, transformation and temporary resettlement can be expected to be a continued feature of teachers' lives.

References

Apple, M. (1986) *Teachers and Texts*, New York: Routledge & Kegan Paul.

Beynon, H. (1994) 'Changes in the Experience of Work', in Bryson, A. and McKay, S. (eds) *Is it Worth Working? Factors Affecting Labour Supply*, London: Policy Studies Institute.

Bowe, R. and Ball, S. with Gold, A. (1992) *Reforming Education and Changing Schools: Case Studies in Policy Sociology*, London: Routledge.

Braverman, H. (1974) *Labour and Monopoly Capital: the Degradation of Work in the Twentieth Century*, New York: Monthly Review Press.

Bullock, A. and Thomas, H. (1997) *Schools at the Centre? A Study of Decentralisation*, London: Routledge.

Campbell, R. and Neill, S. (1994) *Secondary Teachers at Work*, London: Routledge.

Grace, G. (1978) *Teachers, Ideology and Control*, London: Routledge & Kegan Paul.

Grace, G. (1987) 'Teachers and the State in Britain: a Changing Relation', in Lawn, M. and Grace, G. (eds) *Teachers: the Culture and Politics of Work*, London: Falmer.

Hargreaves, A. (1994) *Changing Teachers, Changing Times: Teachers' Work and Culture in the Postmodern Age*, London: Cassell.

Hatcher, R. (1994) 'Market Relationships and the Management of Teachers', *British Journal of Sociology of Education*, **15**(1): 41–61.

Johnson, T. (1972) *Professions and Power*, London: Macmillan.

Larson, S. (1980) 'Proletarianisation and Educated Labour', *Theory and Society*, 9(1): 131–75.

McPherson, A. (1983) 'An Angle on the Geist: Persistence and Change in the Scottish Educational Tradition', in Humes, W. and Paterson, H. (eds) *Scottish Culture and Scottish Education 1800–1980*, Edinburgh: John Donald.

Munn, P. (ed.) (1993) *Parents and Schools: Customers, Managers or Partners?*, London: Routledge.

Nixon, J., Martin, J., McKeown, P. and Ranson, S. (1997) 'Towards a Learning Profession: Changing Codes of Occupational Practice Within the New Management of Education', *British Journal of Sociology of Education*, 21(1): 5–28.

Ozga, J. and Lawn, M. (1981) *Teachers, Professionalism and Class: a Study of Organized Teachers*, London: Falmer.

Sinclair, J., Ironside, M. and Seifert, R. (1996) 'Classroom Struggle? Market Oriented Education Reforms and their Impact on the Teacher Labour Process', *Work, Employment and Society*, 10(4): 641–61.

Sleegers, P. and Wesselingh, A. (1995) 'Dutch Dilemmas: Decentralisation, School Autonomy and Professionalisation of Teachers', *Educational Review*, 47(2): 199–207.

Smyth, J. (1995) 'What's Happening to Teachers' Work in Australia?', *Educational Review*, 47(2): 189–98.

Troman, G. (1996) 'The Rise of the New Professionals? The Restructuring of Primary Teachers' Work and Professionalism', *British Journal of Sociology of Education*, 17(4): 473–87.

Wallace, G., McCulloch, G. and Evans, J. (1995) 'Review of *Changing Teachers, Changing Times*', *British Journal of Sociology of Education*, 16(1): 109–13.

Woods, P. (1994) 'Teachers under Siege: Resistance and Appropriation in English Primary Schools', *Anthropology and Education Quarterly*, 25(3): 250–65.

4 School boards and governing bodies

A vehicle for parental participation in decision-making about schools?

Pamela Munn

Introduction

In the past twenty years, policy initiatives in the United Kingdom have been introduced with the intention of redefining the individual's relationship with the welfare state. In many areas of public policy, such as health, housing and education, the intention has been to readjust the relationship by transferring powers from 'producers' or providers of public services to 'consumers' or users of services, and establish quasi-markets in these services (Le Grand and Bartlett 1993). There have also been changes in the nature of accountability of public services, with an increasing use of performance targets or outcome measures to indicate their efficiency, effectiveness and value for money. At the same time there has been an attempt to increase the collective influence of consumers by developing structures to give them a locus in decision-making about public services. The similarity of initiatives across policy sectors, and indeed across countries, is striking. A description of the common features and an explanation of their convergence lie outside the scope of this chapter. Yet, as Raab (Chapter 1) has pointed out, it is important to note that education is one among many areas of public policy in which new approaches to governance have featured; therefore education reforms have to be seen against a backcloth of changes in social policy in general.

This chapter focuses on one sector of education, secondary schools. It explores parental involvement in decision-making through school boards in Scotland and governing bodies in England and Wales. Its concern is primarily with the success or otherwise of these particular mechanisms in giving the 'consumers' of secondary-school service – parents, pupils and members of the local community – collective influence over decisions about the schools. In considering the nature and extent of this influence, this chapter necessarily makes reference to the other influences on public services mentioned above, namely performance targets and individual consumer power.[1]

Traditionally, parental involvement in schooling has been individualistic, concerning the academic progress and general well-being of the parent's own child. An ideal parent from a school's point of view is one who supports and encourages the child's school work, ensures that school rules and regulations are adhered to, and generally upholds the values of the school. Parents who do not conform to this role and who challenge the school's way of doing things are generally typified as 'problems', in much the same way as pupils who do not conform. The familiar ways in which parents can demonstrate their support for the school include regular attendance at parents' evenings, helping on school outings, field trips and sports, and helping in the classroom. Many schools make strenuous efforts to enlist the support of parents and, increasingly, curriculum innovations such as those promoting children's reading skills, feature some structured parental help in encouraging their child's learning. Thus, the focus for much parental involvement is on the learning, progress and attainment of their own child. Increasingly, too, schools are opening their doors to parents as learners, both in daytime classes and in the more traditional evening classes. Again, however, the focus is individualistic, with the school and teacher in a powerful position in terms of learners' progress and attainment. Therefore, notions of schools' partnership with parents typically see the parents as junior partners helping the school to pursue successfully its key activities of teaching and learning.

Opportunities for parents to express a *collective* rather than an *individual* view on school matters have been rare. Parents' or parent–teacher associations exist in many schools. Their role has tended to be one of fund-raising or organising events where information can be transmitted about curriculum developments, particularly in the non-academic areas such as drugs education, where parents are seen as having an important role to play. More recently, where parents' views on school quality have been sought by the school itself, by the (local) education authority, by Her Majesty's Inspectorate (HMI) in Scotland or by the Office for Standards in Education (OFSTED) in England and Wales, an individualistic approach has tended to be adopted, using the efficient and cheap approach of questionnaires to parents, rather than discussion groups or larger-scale meetings, although views have also been sought from governing bodies and school boards. In brief then, there are three aspects to traditional parental involvement:

- it has largely been individualistic;
- it has been to support the largely taken-for-granted values espoused by the school;
- collective action has focused on fund-raising or information sessions.

(Munn 1993a: 1)

Against this backdrop, the transformation of home–school relations embedded in the establishment of school boards in Scotland in 1988 and in the strengthening of governing bodies in England and Wales in the same year (Deem 1990) should not be underestimated. Nothing less than the direct involvement of parents in school governance was intended. To be sure, the nature and extent of the formal powers of these bodies were different (see below), and therefore the scope for direct involvement has varied. Nevertheless, parents collectively were to have a role in running schools. To put this into context, however, it is important to remember that, since 1945 at least, a good deal of power and authority over school has rested with central government. In Scotland, in particular, education-ists typically looked to central government for a lead on curriculum and assessment as well as on issues of school provision and organisation (McPherson and Raab 1988). Simon's (1994) account of the development of comprehensive education in England reveals how much power rested in local authorities and in Westminster, and how little scope there was for individual public-sector schools to be radically experimental in curri-culum, assessment or pedagogy.

Consequently, as we shall see, where school boards and governing bodies have been involved in decision-making, their focus has not been on the grand issues of schooling, such as what is taught and to whom, teaching approaches, assessment policy, the provision and organisation of schooling, and issues of pupils' access and entitlement. These issues have largely been determined by central government. Furthermore, local government has an important role to play in ensuring high-quality school provision at local level. This means that the scope for school boards and governing bodies to have a major influence on, for example, curriculum development or in assessing the quality of schooling has been rather limited, squeezed as they are by both central and local government poli-cies in these and other areas. On the other hand, given the traditions of individualistic parental concerns, school boards and governing bodies have found it difficult, at least in the short term, collectively to have a real influence on decision-making in their schools on a range of routine matters. Much power and authority remains with the head teacher.

Subsequent sections of this chapter outline the powers and responsibilities of school boards and governing bodies, and examine whether these powers and responsibilities have transformed relations in the ways intended.[2] It is argued that the new powers and structures designed to enhance parental involvement in school management have not substantially transformed the culture and working patterns of schools, and it offers some speculations as to why this is the case. This chapter reaffirms the importance of parents' organisations as pressure groups promoting 'consumer' interests in developing school policy. It closes by briefly speculating about the implications for the notion of active citizenship, a theme taken up in Part II by Martin and her colleagues (Chapter 5).

School boards and governing bodies

The 1988 School Boards (Scotland) Act came into force on 1 April 1989. The Act provides for every local-authority school in Scotland (except nursery schools) to have a school board, although their existence is not mandatory. As at May 1994, about 93 per cent of secondary schools had formed school boards (a drop of about 4 per cent from 1990) (Scottish Office 1995).[3] School boards replaced the generally discredited School Councils (Macbeth *et al.* 1980) which had had very limited jurisdiction over a group of schools, rather than over individual schools. The new boards had very few formal powers: for example, the right to veto schools' per capita expenditure, to participate in the selection of senior staff, to set occasional holidays during term time, and to receive advice and reports from the head teacher, including an annual report on the aggregate level of pupil attainment.

The weak formal powers ascribed to boards followed a consultation exercise by the then Education Minister in the Scottish Office, Michael Forsyth MP, distinguishing 'floor' and 'ceiling' powers for the new bodies. There was virtually no support for the proposed ceiling powers, and although the subsequent legislation enables boards to request additional powers and functions, none has done so. Perhaps in recognition of the reluctance of boards to assume greater responsibility for school matters, when school budgets began to be delegated from local authorities to schools in 1994, they were delegated to the head teacher, with boards being informed and consulted (SOEID 1993). This decision may also have been influenced by the continuing power of professional bodies, such as the Head Teachers Association in Scotland, and by evidence about the ways in which school boards were operating. A further consideration may have been the need to legislate to make school boards compulsory for all schools if they had extensive financial power, taking into account the difficulty of finding parliamentary time for new Scottish legislation.

The composition of boards depends on the numbers of pupils on the school roll. Table 4.1 gives details.

Governing bodies of various kinds have long been established in England, but since 1980 there has been parental representation as of right (Deem 1990). They were given a considerable boost in terms of composition and membership by the Conservative government's 1986 (No. 2) and 1988 Education Acts. As a result of these Acts, governing bodies were given some jurisdiction over aspects of curriculum (e.g. the provision of sex education), the internal organisation of schools, financial and resource decisions, staffing priorities, business and community relations, and the hiring and firing of staff. Deem (1990: 169) points out that as a result of the legislation, '[g]overnors now have the power, in theory, to run the school'. The membership of governing bodies consists of parents, local education authority-appointed members, foundation members in the case of voluntary-aided schools, teachers (including the head teacher), and co-opted members. They vary in size according to the number of pupils enrolled. Table 4.2 gives details.

Different rules apply to voluntary-aided and special-agreement schools. For such schools there must be:

- one LEA-appointed member;
- one (at least) parent;
- one or two teachers (depending on whether there are more or fewer than 300 pupils);
- one head (unless he or she chooses not to be a governor);
- plus enough foundation governors to ensure that they outnumber the rest by two, in a governing body of fewer than eighteen, and by three, in the case of a larger body. One of the foundation governors must also be a parent. In the case of primary schools serving an area in which there is a minor local authority, the minor authority can appoint one governor.

In summary, school boards and governing bodies vary in terms of their composition, powers and history. Parents constitute a majority of the membership of school boards in Scotland, whereas in England they have no such majority on school governing bodies. Teachers are represented on both governing bodies and school boards, but local-authority nominees can only sit on the former. Head teachers are the principal professional advisers to school boards in Scotland, but are members of governing bodies in England. Whereas in England, the governing bodies have been

Table 4.1   Composition of Scottish school boards

	Number of pupils			
	1–500	*501–1,000*	*1,001–1,500*	*1,501+*
Parent members	4	5	6	7
Staff members	1	2	2	3
Co-opted members	2	2	3	3

Note: Single-teacher schools will have three parents and two co-opted members, but no staff members because the single teacher is the head teacher.

Table 4.2   Composition of new governing bodies in England (for county, voluntary Controlled and Maintained special schools)

Size of school	Composition of governing body
Schools with fewer than 100 pupils	• 2 parents • 2 LEA-appointed • 1 teacher • 1 head (unless he or she chooses not to be a governor) *and either* • 2 foundation governors (in the case of a voluntary school) and • 1 co-opted member *or* • 3 co-opted
Schools with 100–299 pupils	• 3 parents • 3 LEA-appointed • 1 teacher • 1 head (unless he or she chooses not to be a governor) *and either* • 3 foundation governors and 1 co-opted *or* • 4 co-opted
Schools with 300–599 pupils	• 4 parents • 4 LEA-appointed • 2 teachers • 1 head (unless he or she chooses not to be a governor)

and either

- 4 foundation governors and 1 co-opted

or

- 5 co-opted

- 5 parents
- 5 LEA-appointed
- 2 teachers
- 1 head (unless he or she choses not to be governor)

and either

- 4 foundation governors and 2 co-opted

or

- 6 co-opted

Note: Different rules apply to voluntary-aided and special-agreement schools. For such schools there must be:

- 1 LEA-appointed
- 1 (at least) parent
- 1 or 2 teachers (depending on whether there are more or fewer than 300 pupils)
- 1 head (unless he or she chooses not to be governor)

given statutory powers on a range of matters including staffing, curriculum and discipline, in Scotland, school boards have a largely consultative role, and broadly analogous powers have been devolved to the head teacher. School budgets are delegated to the governing body in England, but to the head teacher in Scotland. Deem and Brehony (1993) warn against attributing too much influence to the legislation. As we shall see, despite the rather different legislative provisions for school boards and governing bodies, they have acted in rather similar ways.

Power to the people?

A clear policy aim underpinning much of the education legislation in the late 1980s and 1990s was to encourage schools to be more responsive to 'consumer', particularly parents', demands. There were, and continue to be, two main ways of putting this aim into practice. First, there was an emphasis on the individual actions of parents, by giving them the right to choose the school their children would attend. Legislation to this effect was enacted in 1981 in Scotland, and provision was made in the Education Act of 1988 for England and Wales. Since school funding depended on pupil numbers, it was anticipated that schools would be responsive to parental concerns rather than risk declining rolls and closure. As argued elsewhere (Munn 1998), parental choice, together with published information about secondary schools – such as pupils' examination results and attendance rates – encouraged some schools to move beyond a concern with effective *presentation* and explanation of figures to propose *substantive developments* in curriculum organisation (setting and streaming) and in curriculum provision (special classes for the more able, more emphasis on technology). Schools hoped that these developments would retain their current pupil population and attract new pupils who would boost their ratings on various performance measures. Parental choice has undoubtedly empowered some parents by enabling them to select schools which conform to their criteria of 'good'. Others, living in small towns in remote areas, did not have a choice beyond the local secondary school, and others again were ill-informed both about the process of choice and the nature of the choices available; Adler (1997) discusses this more fully. The point to emphasise, however, is that schools were intended to respond to the actual or potential individual actions of parents choosing schools for their children.

The second way, as an alternative or, indeed, an addition to choice, is that of voice. Hirschman (1970: 30) defines voice as follows:

> To resort to voice, rather than exit, is for the customer or member to make an attempt at changing the practices, policies and outputs of the firm from which one buys or the organisation to which one belongs. Voice is here defined as any attempt to change, rather than escape from an objectionable state of affairs whether through individual or collective petition.

Before considering whether and how governors and board members exercised collective voice options, it is worth remembering the severe limitations on their power. The 1980s and 1990s have seen a very rapid centralisation of control over schooling. This is particularly evident in the areas of curriculum and assessment, with the introduction of the National Curriculum in England and Wales via the 1988 Education Act and, in 1989, Scotland's rough equivalent in the shape of the 5–14 programme. The recent reform of upper secondary education in Scotland, *Higher Still*, confirms this trend. Kirk (1995), as quoted by Fairley (1998), tartly observes:

> We have moved from a time when ministers prided themselves in knowing nothing about the curriculum to a context in which ministers provide a detailed framework covering practically every area of the school's work.

Neither did a change of government from Conservative to Labour in 1997 signal a retreat in centralised curriculum control. Recent developments in specifying a literacy and numeracy curriculum in the early years of primary schooling – introducing the idea of a literacy hour each day and detailing how it should be spent – leave very little space for teachers' judgement and autonomy. Furthermore, the specification of attainment targets for schools in respect of their pupils' achievements at various stages in their school career suggests a continuation of tight central control. The targets are negotiated between local authorities and schools, but Ministers have let it be known that they are unhappy with any reductions in target levels (*Times Educational Supplement (Scotland)* 1998).

Many other areas of schooling are centrally controlled too, reflecting the increasing control of local by central government, most notably through central-government control of local government's income and expenditure. Since education is the largest single service provided by local government, these controls are significant. Thus, the current system of school governance is one in which there is strong central control of funding, curriculum, assessment and, in Scotland, of class sizes: the administration of these matters is delegated to local government, which in turn delegates to school governors and boards. As a result, the issues over which parent representativeness on these bodies has real discretion and control are extremely limited. Parents certainly have no power over the 'big issues' such as curriculum and assessment policy or school expansion in terms of pupil numbers.

Therefore, it can be argued that the overriding policy aim of both the Conservative and Labour governments has been to raise school standards through the central control of curriculum, assessment and quality-assurance mechanisms. Standards are conceived of primarily in terms of pupils' cognitive attainments as measured by national tests and public examination results. Parental involvement has primarily been seen as a means to that end, and has three main policy strands. One strand has been to stimulate schools to do more and to be more effective in encouraging individual parents to support their child's school learning. This is evident in the development of home–school partnerships of various kinds. Second, parents have been given consumer rights of choice of school, and hence of exit from a school which is failing to meet the needs of their child. These rights were intended to make schools responsive to the policy agenda of raising standards of attainment, by threatening that underachieving, and hence unpopular schools, might be closed. It was assumed that parents would choose schools primarily on their track-record of pupils' attainments. Third, through collective voice options, it was assumed that parents would keep schools up to the mark by interrogating the head teacher and others about pupils' attainments and about plans for school development and improvement.

Underlying the 'standards' agenda, there has thus been 'a permanent and unresolved tension' between the theme of parent participation in school matters and a consumerist approach which is rather more oriented towards satisfaction or exit (Vincent and Tomlinson 1997: 363). Furthermore, the nature of parent participation is both individualistic, in helping to develop their own child's learning, and collective, in the context of school boards' and governing bodies' concern with whole-school policy and practice. Parents on school boards and governing bodies may therefore have something of an identity crisis. They have power and authority, at least potentially, over some school developments, and influence over others. They retain the option of exit; indeed, the Chair of one school board reminded his fellow members and head teacher of his intention to use this option if results did not improve (Arnott *et al*. 1996). In addition, parents are typically involved in schemes to support their child's learning, which puts them in an inferior position *vis-à-vis* expert teachers. An article by a parent, a former governor of a primary school, sums up the situation.

> Even the involved ones among us don't know how to be real partners in our children's education ... We worry about legitimate worries being rebuffed.
>
> (Welford 1998)

She goes on to give a number of examples of how home–school power relationships work:

> For me it was a big deal to go into school to say that my (then) 13 year old daughter cried every night [due to bullying]. When I finally went I was extremely nervous. I was not reassured by the year head telling me this behaviour was normal ... [On teaching methods] my natural impulse was to remain deferential and say nothing. I had sweating palms and had to remind myself to stay calm.
>
> (Welford 1998)

If parents' instincts are indeed to be deferential to teachers and to wish to avoid being branded as the 'parent from hell' because of too much 'interference', then exit can seem a much easier option than individual or collective voice, especially if individual parent deference about their child's learning is replicated in collective deference about the running of schools. Thus, unless larger steps are taken to make schools more participative, schools risk becoming increasingly detached from the communities they serve, with citizenship being conceived of only as the exercise of consumer rights, as under the Citizen's Charter introduced by the Conservative government in the 1990s. What does the experience of school boards and governing bodies tell us about parental participation in decision-making?

School boards and governing bodies at work

School boards and governing bodies are a mechanism through which a collective petition could be organised, or through which the petition of an individual parent could be mediated. Have things worked out this way? What does research evidence suggest? Observations of boards and governing bodies and interviews with a sample of members of these bodies revealed striking similarities in their general operation. They shared the following four features:

- their main role was to support the school and its teachers;
- there was little desire for greater lay participation in decision-making either by parents or by teachers;
- there was strong parental trust in the head teacher's professional expertise and judgement;
- school boards and governing bodies were used by the head teacher to put pressure on the education authority regarding matters such as admissions limits, refurbishment and budgetary allocation.

A key feature of the work of school boards and governing bodies was the reluctance of board members or governors to challenge the head teacher. Head teachers typically presented reports on various aspects of school life and these were discussed to varying degrees, but head teachers were never seriously thwarted in their plans for school development, even where these plans concerned matters of curriculum organisation and provision. Therefore, although some boards and governing bodies discussed and debated issues more than others, the head teachers were able to pursue their policies without serious let or hindrance from the 'lay' body. Comments have been made elsewhere (Arnott *et al.* 1996) on differences among school boards in the way they handled information: some receiving it with no discussion, others discussing it, and still others discussing and acting upon it. Action, however, was largely determined by the advice of the head teacher.

There seem to be four main reasons for this. First, as mentioned above, the principal function of boards and governing bodies was perceived by all concerned as being to support the school. Moreover, 'support' tended to be construed as 'doing what the head teacher thinks is best'. This is a theme in many studies (e.g. Golby 1993; Munn 1993b; Deem *et al.* 1995; Grace 1995; Levacic 1995). Indeed Grace's account of the 'good governor' bears a striking similarity to the concept of the good board member, namely that they gave no trouble. Compare just two of many examples:

> The governing body are very good; they have never disagreed with me up to this point in time.
> > (Female, Infant School Head, quoted in Grace 1995: 78)

and

> [The board is] very supportive ... [It is] a pleasure and a privilege to work with them.
> > (Secondary Head teacher, quoted in Adler *et al.* 1996: 62)

We may note in passing that teachers' constructions of a 'good pupil' typically mean those who do not challenge the school's way of doing things. These constructions pose deeper questions about the purposes of education, as between liberation or control, which are mentioned at the end of this chapter. But, for the moment, we may infer that members of boards and governing bodies either did not see themselves as being in Hirschman's 'objectionable state of affairs' which they wished to change, or that they wholeheartedly agreed with and approved the head teacher's plans for change.

Second, governors and board members referred to their lack of knowledge about issues under discussion and a lack of time to become more informed. The comment by two parent members of a board that:

> there is so much jargon around ... that parents are baffled by many of the discussions at meetings they attend

was typical. This lack of knowledge and time was evident in the conduct of most meetings observed during the course of research. Head teachers, sometimes in consultation with Chairs of boards or governing bodies, set the agenda for meetings. The structure of the formal agenda did not vary much, and always included matters arising from the previous meeting, as well as correspondence and items for information. These items were under the control of the Chair, but it was usually the head teacher who determined the substantive agenda, that is, what was actually discussed. Even where the Chair or members suggested substantive items for discussion, such as the school examination results or curriculum innovations, the head teacher appeared to have a free hand in deciding how to deal with them. The power of head teachers was buttressed by the common practice of tabling papers or giving oral reports and then answering questions. Although head teachers often gave very full accounts and encouraged the asking of questions, this procedure did not give members much opportunity to prepare for meetings. However, it would be wrong to see this in conspiratorial terms, because few examples were observed of requests to the head teacher to produce or circulate papers in advance.

Third, especially in Scotland, there was suspicion about the political motives behind the establishment of school boards. Some members saw boards as part of a complex jigsaw of innovation designed to undermine comprehensive education rather than to enhance parental involvement in school matters. Thus there was a reluctance to do anything which would make life more difficult for the head teacher, who was seen to embody the values of comprehensive education. The following extract from an interview with a parent member conveys the flavour of this point of view:

> How did school boards come about in the first place? Is it to do with parental choice or is it to do with political ideology? My own view is that school boards could be abolished tomorrow and I don't think the education of our children would be compromised particularly.

It was rare for parent members to initiate policy development, particularly in the area of teaching and learning. Very few schools had parent representation on school-development planning groups, where the opportunity to take such initiatives might have arisen. Where the head teacher had solicited parent membership of such groups, this tended to reflect a commitment to an open and consultative management style rather than to the existence of boards or governing bodies as such. These head teachers typically talked about the need to involve staff actively in decision-making through setting up working groups on topics such as improving or using new technology, or developing teaching strategies for ages 12–14 (in Scotland). Thus their recruitment of parents to such groups was facilitated by the existence of boards and governing bodies, rather than determined by their existence. It was often difficult for parents to attend development-planning meetings, as they were held during the school day or immediately afterwards. Furthermore, it would be surprising if parents exerted real influence in that context, given their well-documented reluctance to become involved in decision-making about teaching and learning (Deem *et al.* 1995; Arnott *et al.* 1996; Bullock and Thomas 1994; Golby 1993). Although school-board members, unlike governors, had no formal power over the curriculum, they were free to debate and discuss it. Their lack of involvement may be explained by lack of knowledge and expertise as much as by lack of legislative provision.

Fourth, the language of performance management in education makes it very difficult for parents to play an active role in school decision-making. Schools are increasingly accountable for meeting targets that are expressed, for example, in terms of a specified percentage of pupils achieving success in public examinations or standardised attainment tests, or on attendance or exclusion rates. With the best will in the world, it can be difficult for head teachers to convey such information concisely and to explain reasons for performance measures being met or not. At some meetings, head teachers spent an hour or more going through performance tables in what seemed to be genuine attempts to inform governors or board members about pupils' current academic performance as contrasted with previous years and with other local schools, and also placing the results in a national context. This information was difficult for experienced education researchers to follow. It was confusing even for board members and governors used to dealing with statistical information. Therefore, although school boards and governing bodies may well ask for information about the achievement of targets or outcomes, it is doubtful whether they are really in command of the information with which they are presented.

Furthermore, performance-management systems tend to be less concerned about the detail of *process*, that is about how outcomes are achieved, than about the *outcomes* themselves. In so far as there are concerns about process, they tend to be with the existence and efficiency of quality-assurance systems to ensure that outcomes are being monitored. These aspects are typically a concern of local and central government inspectors rather than of parents who, again, are likely to lack expertise in quality-assurance systems. Hence, performance management might well be seen as severely limiting the agency of the individual citizen or parent, as well as their collective voice. Their role can, but need not, be that of a passive recipient of services that are more efficiently managed and more publicly accountable through performance measures than in the past.

Output systems can easily mystify groups of parents charged with school governance. A numerate head teacher can present output data in all kinds of ways. Intentionally or not, these systems distract attention from the processes by which the school operates, even where there is an interest in it. If we accept that the quality of relationships between teachers and pupils and among pupils is of interest to board members and governors, then ways need to be found of reporting on this, as well as on performance measures such as attainment. Many commentators (e.g.

Rutter *et al*. 1979; Sammons *et al*. 1997; Stoll and Fink 1996; Pring 1997) would argue that positive relationships, high expectations of pupils, and valuing pupils, all contribute to improvements in attainment. This kind of information about relationships, a key aspect of process and the lived reality of schools for pupils and teachers, is difficult to quantify and can be neglected in performance-management reports. Yet, for school boards and governing bodies concerned with improving school quality, these 'process areas' are the very ones about which they need to seek information.

Although head teachers have the dominant influence on school boards and governing bodies, they cannot afford to disregard their existence. Several members mentioned that head teachers would wish to 'take the [board or governing body] with them' in any major policy development. Furthermore, boards and governing bodies often acted as pressure groups in relation to local authorities, to try to obtain resources for the school. These ranged from replacing an unpleasantly noisy fire alarm, to sustaining pressure on a large refurbishment programme when the budget for the second phase seemed under threat. They felt comfortable in this role, supporting the school against a more distant local authority. Again, as might be expected, school boards and governing bodies varied in their effectiveness in this role (Arnott *et al*. 1996). Those which were well connected to the world outside the immediate confines of the school and had significant collective cultural capital – such as their knowledge of educational developments, how to exert influence and self-confidence in making a point – tended to be used by head teachers as pressure groups. Where pressure on a local education authority was seen as necessary by the head teacher, the well-connected board or governing body played a key role. Local officials could be subject to robust questioning by board members or governors, in marked contrast to their relations with the head teacher.

This is illustrated by the following extract from observation notes, relating to the governing body's challenge to a local education authority official about admissions policy. The head teacher had brought it to the governors' attention that several pupils, who had placed the school second on their preference form, were being allocated to the school in preference to 'first choice' pupils:

> The LEA official stresses that admissions is a complex system and by no means easy to organise. The parent governor says loudly, 'rubbish!' The LEA official looks to the Chair and asks if he could finish what he is saying. He adds that, with growth in the primary schools, this secondary school's four feeder primaries will be full in two to three years' time. The Head says that feeder primaries only mean anything

when the school is full. The Chair says that the LEA needs to understand the geography of the area. The LEA official again pleads with the Chair to hear him through.

In contrast, boards and governing bodies with weak networks tended not to act as supportive pressure groups for their head teachers, who may have perceived little gain in securing their support.

The evidence suggests, however, that even in the pressure-group role, well-connected boards and governing bodies looked to the head teacher for advice on the issues to pursue and sometimes on the tactics to adopt. For example, when Lothian Region schools' budgets were cut and cash reduction targets imposed, one school board asked the head teacher whether it should lobby at both local and national level (a senior Cabinet member was the local MP), and whether it should focus on the issue of the particular cash reduction target or broaden the debate to issues of school funding in general, class sizes, and other matters. The head teacher and the Chair of the board jointly worked out a plan of action.

An issue which can constrain the effectiveness of school boards and governing bodies is that of the extent to which they represent parents in general. Research on the membership of governing bodies shows that the white middle-class male is in the ascendant (Keys and Fernandes 1990; Golby 1993). This state of affairs obviously raises questions about the ability of governing bodies adequately to represent parental opinion. Similar questions arise in Scotland, where some boards have ceased to exist because insufficient numbers of parents have put themselves forward as candidates. Some head teachers have talked of the need to encourage parents to stand for election. This was seen to be a problem in several schools, but especially for some schools in 'mixed' or 'deprived' catchment areas. For example, one head teacher described the parent members of the board as

> definitely not representative of the catchment area but of a small group of very caring parents.

At another school in a 'deprived' area, parent members were described as being 'active, interested parents' and as 'good parents who come from two areas of owner-occupied housing', while their lack of representativeness was referred to as 'a farce'.

Many boards in Scotland have attempted to counter the charge of unrepresentativeness by making strenuous efforts to canvass parental opinion on particular topics by, for example, using questionnaires, organising social events, and setting up stalls at parent-consultation evenings. They have largely been disappointed by low response rates and turnouts.

Parents' organisations

If school boards and governing bodies provide, in practice, a very limited vehicle for the collective voice of parents, are there other organisations which can promote this? National and local parent organisations are a relatively neglected area of study in terms of education policy-making (Vincent 1997). We know little about how parent groups operate, the networks that they use and the role and influence of their members on national and local committees on which they are increasingly represented. A small-scale study investigating the aims, strategies and success of two national and four local parents' organisations was undertaken in Scotland in 1994–96. It involved semi-structured interviews with executive members of the groups, and with established actors in the policy arena such as local and national politicians, officials, and teacher-union representatives. An analysis of the organisation's records and minutes of meetings was also undertaken (Munn 1998).

The study does not provide a basis for generalisation, partly because of the research design and sample size but also because of the key role which education plays in Scotland as a feature of Scottish identity (see e.g. Davie 1961; Gray *et al.* 1983; McCrone 1992). The symbolic importance of education as a distinctive feature of national identity is unlikely to operate so powerfully in other countries, where devolved powers to local constituent elements of the larger state exist. Thus, Scottish parents' groups (and others) are likely to be activated by – and resistant to – policy changes which are seen as attempts to diminish or 'anglicise' distinctive features of the school system in Scotland. Perhaps the most notable example of this was the campaign mounted by national groups. In the early 1990s, the Scottish Parent Teacher Council and the Scottish School Board Association worked with others to form the Parents' Coalition to contest the Conservative government's plans to introduce the national testing of all pupils in primary schools. With the support of local authorities and of the teachers' unions, the Coalition prevailed upon the government to change its policy. As a consequence, there are no 'league tables' of primary schools in Scotland featuring pupils' test results. There was thus the situation in which government – having given enhanced legitimacy to parental voice in education policy through the introduction of school boards – had to live with that voice being raised in opposition to its own policies.

Local organisations could also provide a forum for the collective voice of parents on particular issues. The Dyslexia Association could point to successes in terms of keeping the issue of dyslexia as a specific learning difficulty high on the agenda of local councils, and of securing recognition of the need for teachers to undertake specific training in the diagnosis of and strategies for coping with dyslexia. Similarly, the parents of traveller children have succeeded in having their patterns of irregular attendance at school considered sympathetically, and parents of children with severe and profound learning difficulties have been working with a local college of further education to secure educational provision at age 16+ for their children.

Parents' organisations, then, can be influential in education policy-making on the 'big issues' of schooling. Furthermore, although the Parents' Coalition worked in harmony with teacher organisations to campaign against national testing, it resisted being 'captured' by teachers. It did not support continued action against tests once the government had backed down, despite the teacher unions' wish to campaign against all forms of national assessment (Munn 1995). Indeed the independence and integrity of parents' groups was highlighted as an important issue by a local politician:

> I think the parents' groups have grown in influence and I think it's been connected to just two or three individuals who have really taken on the professionals ... and have shown that they are as competent as anyone else about understanding and making points ...
> I think the importance of the national groups is that they have refused to be hijacked by teachers or local authorities or by government. They have walked a very independent path and that's been important for their integrity [to] all the players [in the policy community].
>
> (Munn 1998: 390)

Collective parental voice can be heard clearly when a major policy development such as national testing is contested. It is less easy to detect in the initiation of policy or in the development of policy. This may be partly because of the lack of research in the operation of parent networks, but the local politicians talked of the need to inform and consult parents groups, rather than seeing them as critical in policy-making. None could point to a recent significant policy issue where parents' organisations were key players. Nonetheless, parent representatives are increasingly found in important committees, alongside representatives of teacher unions and local councils, in what can be seen as an attempt by government to manage consensus about policy developments initiated by the Scottish Office. The role that these parents adopt – and whether they are as deferential as they are on school boards and governing bodies, now that they have been brought in to policy-making circles – remains a matter of speculation.

Conclusion

The devolved management of schools in Britain has featured a number of policy themes. The key theme for the purpose of this chapter is that of promoting lay, especially parental, participation in school decision-making, through establishing school boards in Scotland, and enhancing the power of governing bodies in England. The policy aim was to raise standards by making schools more responsive to parents' concerns, and hence to change the nature of the relationship between parents and schools. Schools were to be more accountable to parents as a constituency, and school boards and governing bodies were the key vehicle for this new process of accountability.

The changed relationship intended through the establishment of school boards and the enhancement of the powers of governing bodies was a major one: nothing less than a reversal of the balance of power between teachers and parents. It is hardly surprising that such a change has not taken place in the schools studied, particularly in Scotland where there is substantial evidence of parental trust in the professional expertise of teachers and support for schools (Munn 1993b; SOED 1990; MacBeath and Weir 1991). Therefore, providing opportunities for a more participative role for parents at school level, through mechanisms such as school boards and governing bodies, is no guarantee that they will be taken up or used. Similarly, mechanisms such as the annual parents' meeting, where governors report to the generality of parents, seem to have been poorly attended (Martin *et al.* 1997). This chapter has suggested a number of reasons why school boards and governing bodies defer to head teachers' judgements and plans. These include: the language of performance management; lack of time for parents to get to grips with matters of concern to the school; lack of knowledge; and, in Scotland, suspicion about the political motives underlying the introduction of boards from a Conservative government which was popularly conceived as lacking legitimacy in Scotland.

A rather different speculation on the way that school boards and governing bodies defer to the head teacher would be that schools, as organisations, do not encourage active participation in decision-making by their own staff and pupils. Traditionally, head teachers have exercised enormous power over the day-to-day running of 'their' schools (e.g. Grace 1995; Hendrie 1997), and secondary schools especially have tended to have hierarchical management structures, evident in the levels of promoted posts (e.g. in Scotland, Assistant Principal Teacher, Principal Teacher, Assistant Head Teacher, Deputy Head Teacher, Head Teacher). Commentators point to this hierarchical organisation as signalling to pupils the importance of respect for authority, particularly in the operation of discipline systems (e.g. Munn *et al.* 1992; Galloway *et al.* 1985) but in the business of learning as well. Traditional teaching presupposes deference on the part of the learner, whose task it is to soak up the superior skills and knowledge of the teacher (see Paterson 1998 for an elaboration of this point).

Smout (1987: 229), writing about schools in Scotland in the first half of the twentieth century, comments acidly:

> Perhaps, then, it is in the history of the school more than in any other aspect of recent social history that the key lies to some of the more depressing aspects of modern Scotland. If there are in this country too many people who fear what is new, believe the difficult to be impossible, draw back from responsibility and afford established authority and tradition an exaggerated respect, we can reasonably look for an explanation in the institutions that moulded them.

Pupil–teacher and parent–teacher relations are changing slowly, but old habits die hard. Members of school boards and governing bodies have important powers to seek information, to discuss school matters, and to ask for explanations of why things turn out the way they do. Governing bodies have greater powers than this, should they choose to use them. Perhaps we will see more vigorous debate and a willingness to accept greater responsibility for school affairs in the context of the constitutional changes that are bringing greater devolution to Scotland and Wales and directly elected mayors and provosts in cities. If these changes are genuinely devolutionary, locating power away from the centre, then reinvigorated local participation in decision-making may result. If so, school boards and governing bodies may, in turn, become more vigorous and less deferential, and begin to take decisions over the real work of schools: teaching and learning.

However, a rather different scenario is that in Scotland a Parliament would lead to the strengthening of central Scottish government, even possibly at the expense of local civic bodies. This is because there would be no guarantee that a Scottish Parliament would necessarily reflect the same political ideology and composition as that in Westminster. In developing this point, Paterson (1998) argues that increasing Scottish centralisation would be put forward in terms of reflecting the view of the majority of Scottish people. For education, this would mean sustaining central control of the curriculum and assessment and a strengthened HMI to monitor standards. In such circumstances, the scope of local authorities or of school-board members to put their own stamp on schools would be severely constrained. Indeed, their role might well be seen as that of monitoring the implementation of centrally driven policies, in itself a rather impoverished notion of local democracy. Developments in Wales may be similarly centralist.

At a time of significant constitutional change in the UK and the possibilities arising of some kind of federal system of government, it is impossible to predict the consequences for that part of civil society that is encapsulated in school boards and governing bodies. A reinvigorated interest in active participation and the emergence of flexibility and diversity in the school curriculum may result. Given the current centralist approach to such matters, however, this seems some way off. In the meantime, parents' organisations working at national and local level remain an important vehicle for ensuring that the collective voice of parents is heard on important matters of school policy.

Notes

1   I am grateful to Lindsay Paterson and to the editors for their comments on earlier drafts of this chapter.
2   Descriptions of the data on which the chapter draws are to be found in its Introduction.
3   About 64 per cent of schools had formed boards after a first parental election, and almost one-third of these were contested, while 24 per cent formed a board after a subsequent by-election to fill remaining vacancies (SOEID 1995). Thus, although almost all secondary schools have boards, the statistics tend to confirm head teachers' reports about the difficulties of finding people prepared to serve on them.

References

Adler, M. (1997) 'Looking Backwards to the Future: Parental Choice and Education Policy', *British Educational Research Journal*, 23(3): 197–313.
Adler, M., Arnott, M., Bailey, L., McAvoy, L., Munn, P. and Raab, C. (1996) *Devolved School Management in Secondary Schools in Scotland: a Report to the Scottish Office Education and Industry Department*, Edinburgh University: Department of Politics.
Arnott, M., Raab, C. and Munn, P. (1996) 'Devolved Management: Variations of Response in Scottish School Boards', in Pole, C. and Chawla-Duggan, R. (eds)

Reshaping Education in the 1990s: Perspectives on Secondary Schooling, London: Falmer.

Bullock, A. and Thomas, H. (1994) 'Context, Complexity and the Impact of Local Management of Schools', Paper presented at the Annual Conference of the British Educational Research Association, St Anne's College, Oxford, 8–11 September.

Davie, G. E. (1961) *The Democratic Intellect: Scotland and her Universities in the Nineteenth Century*, Edinburgh: Edinburgh University Press.

Deem, R. (1990) 'The Reform of School Governing Bodies: the Power of the Consumer over the Producer?' in Flude, M. and Hammer, M. (eds) *The 1988 Education Reform Act: Its Origins and Implications*, London: Falmer.

Deem, R. and Brehony, K. (1993) 'Consumers and Education Professionals in the Organisation and Administration of Schools: Partnership or Conflict?', *Educational Studies*, **19(3)**: 339–55.

Deem, R., Brehony, K. and Heath, S. (1995) *Active Citizenship and the Governing of Schools*, Buckingham: Open University Press.

Fairley, J. (1998) 'Local Authority Education in a Democratic Scotland'. Paper presented at the Education, Local Government and the Scottish Parliament Conference, Stirling, 18 February 1998.

Galloway, D., Martin, R. and Wilcox, B. (1985) 'Persistent Absence and Exclusion from School: the Predictive Power of School and Community Variables', *British Educational Research Journal*, **11(1)**: 51–61.

Golby, M. (1993) 'Parents as School Governors', in Munn, P. (ed.) *Parents and Schools: Customers, Managers or Partners?*, London: Routledge.

Grace, G. (1995) *School Leadership*, London: Falmer.

Gray, J., McPherson, A. and Raffe, D. (1983) *Reconstructions of Secondary Education: Theory, Myth and Practice Since the War*, London: Routledge & Kegan Paul.

Hendrie, W. F. (1997) *The Dominie: a Profile of the Scottish Headmaster*, Edinburgh: John Donald.

Hirschman A. (1970) *Exit, Voice and Loyalty*, Cambridge, MA: Harvard University Press.

Keys, W. and Fernandes, C. (1990) *A Survey of School Governing Bodies*, Slough: NFER.

Le Grand, J. and Bartlett, W. (eds) (1993) *Quasi Markets and Social Policy*, London: Macmillan.

Levacic, R. (1995) *Local Management of Schools: Analysis and Practice*, Buckingham: Open University Press.

MacBeath, J. and Weir, D. (1991) *Attitudes to School*, Glasgow: Jordanhill College.

Macbeth, A., McKenzie, M. and Breckenridge, I. (1980) *Scottish Schools Councils: Policy Making, Participation or Irrelevance?*, Edinburgh: HMSO.

McCrone, D. (1992) *Understanding Scotland: the Sociology of a Stateless Nation*, London: Routledge.

McPherson, A. and Raab, C. (1988) *Governing Education: a Sociology of Policy Since 1945*, Edinburgh: Edinburgh University Press.

Martin, J., Ranson, S. and Tall, G. (1997) 'Parents as Partners in Assuring the Quality of Schools', *Scottish Educational Review*, **29(1)**: 39–55.

Munn, P. (1993a) 'Introduction', in Munn, P. (ed.) *Parents and Schools: Customers, Managers or Partners?*, London: Routledge.

Munn, P. (1993b) 'Parents as School Board Members: School Managers and Friends?', in Munn, P. (ed.) *Parents and Schools: Customers, Managers or Partners?*, London: Routledge.

Munn, P. (1995) 'Teacher Involvement in Curriculum Policy in Scotland', *Education Review*, **47(2)**: 209–17.

Munn, P. (1998) 'Parental Influence on School Policy: Some Evidence from Research', *Journal of Education Policy*, **13(3)**: 379–94.

Munn, P., Johnstone, M. and Chalmers, V. (1992) *Effective Discipline in Secondary Schools and Classrooms*, London: Paul Chapman.

Paterson, L. (1998) *Education, Democracy and the Scottish Parliament*, Scottish Local Government Information Unit, Discussion Paper 8.

Pring, R. (1997) 'Educating Persons', in Pring, R. and Walford, G. (eds) *Affirming the Comprehensive Ideal*, London: Falmer.

Rutter, M., Maungham, B., Mortimore, P. and Ouston, J. (1979) *Fifteen Thousand Hours: Secondary Schools and Their Effects on Children*, London: Paul Chapman.

Sammons, P., Thomas, S. and Mortimore, P. (1997) *Forging Links: Effective Schools and Effective Departments*, London: Paul Chapman.

Simon, B. (1994) 'The Politics of Comprehensive Reorganisation: a Retrospective Analysis', in Simon, B., *The State of Educational Change: Essays in the History of Education and Pedagogy*, London: Lawrence & Wishart.

Smout, T. C. (1987) *A Century of the Scottish People*, London: Fontana.

SOED (1990) *Talking about Schools: Surveys of Parents' Views on Schools and Education in Scotland*, Edinburgh: HMSO.

SOEID (1993) *Devolved School Management: Guidelines for Schemes*, Circular **6/93**, Edinburgh: Scottish Office Education Department.

SOEID (1995) *Statistical Bulletin: School Boards in Scottish Schools: May 1994* Edn/BB/1995/11.

Stoll, L. and Fink, D. (1996) *Changing Our Schools: Linking School Effectiveness and Improvement*, Buckingham: Open University Press.

Times Educational Supplement (Scotland) (1998) 'Secondary Scores Inquiry', 11 September.

Vincent, C. (1997) 'Community and Collectivism: the Role of Parents' Organisations in the Education System', *British Journal of Sociology of Education*, **18(2)**: 271–83.

Vincent, C. and Tomlinson, S. (1997) 'Home–School Relationships: the Swarming of Disciplinary Mechanism?', *British Educational Research Journal*, **23(3)**: 361–77.

Welford, H. (1998) 'Try to Speak Before You're Spoken to', *Independent*, 12 November.

Part II

The governance of schooling

Studies in other countries

5 Community-active management and governance of schools in England and Wales[1]

Jane Martin, Penny McKeown, Jon Nixon and Stewart Ranson

Introduction

The radical reconstruction of education, by the Conservative government, from the mid-1980s was designed not only to improve 'a service' but also to play a central role in the wider reform of a polity constituted in the post-war era on social democratic principles of justice to ameliorate class disadvantage. Public goods were conceived as requiring collective choice and redistribution. The Conservatives strove to create a new political order of neo-liberal consumer democracy based upon different principles of rights and choice designed to enhance the agency of the individual. The public (as consumer) would be empowered at the expense of the (professional) provider. Public goods, to achieve equity rather than equality, were conceived as aggregated private choices (Ranson 1994; 1995).

This programme of reforms to restructure power and responsibility in education emphasised school self-management and governance at the same time as national regulation of the curriculum. The central idea of the reforms was that of market formation, the objective of which was to increase public choice through two means:

- 1 *Empowering active consumer participation* by providing parents with information for accountability, the right to choose, appeal and register complaints, and the opportunity to play a leading role in initiating and running new grant-maintained schools (Gewirtz *et al.*, 1995; Ball *et al.* 1994, 1995).
- 2 *Differentiating the governance of education* by deregulating local government. The governance of education was no longer exclusively in the hands of local education authorities who formerly had the responsibility for administering the system; under the

reformed system each school was granted statutory responsibility for the governance of the institution in partnership with the LEA. The establishment of grant-maintained schools and city technology colleges was designed to foster competition by increasing the diversity of institutional types within an internal educational market.

This context was designed to constitute the self-managing institution. Under new formula funding that eliminated traditions of privileged funding for schools in disadvantaged areas, schools became resourced according to the numbers of pupils, based upon principles of equity. Devolved management sought to encourage schools to use this autonomy and be flexible in the way they deployed resources and staff in the development of their distinctive identities (Levacic 1995; Deem *et al.* 1995; Deem 1997).

The organising assumption was that placing schools under the pressure of competition would improve their performance, and that 'good' schools could achieve results whatever the contexts in which they are located. Schools in contexts of disadvantage, therefore, would not need to be privileged with additional resources because of their less fortunate circumstances. Though, for others, these policies '[could] easily discriminate against schools serving disadvantaged communities' (Hillman 1996). The study of the National Commission on Education of schools in contexts of disadvantage argued, nevertheless, that some schools can defy all expectations and achieve 'success against the odds' (National Commission on Education 1996).

This chapter draws upon a study of schools, located across the United Kingdom in some of the most disadvantaged areas, facing severe levels of unemployment, poverty and social fragmentation (Ranson *et al.* 1997a; Nixon *et al.* 1997a). The discussion will examine how schools in England and Wales have developed their responsibilities for devolved management in striving to improve educational achievement in these contexts of disadvantage.[2] This chapter will argue that those schools in our study which were most successful at renewing themselves were those which placed active involvement of the community at the centre of their strategies of management and governance. This can best be explained and understood through an analysis of the key actors and the discourses and practices which make up the dominant regimes of governance in the school which will shape the approaches adopted towards devolved management.

The chapter considers the layers of devolved management before developing case-study analysis of three community-active regimes of governance which highlight the importance of partnership for schools. We shall conclude with consideration of the implications of the system of devolved management for such regimes in England and Wales.[3]

Contested concepts of devolved management

'Local management' and 'devolved governance' are abstractions, empty conceptual vessels awaiting substantive interpretation and definition. For the purposes of this discussion, we will define *management* as a process of decision-making about the strategic choices (purposes, tasks and conditions) which face an organisation or institution; and *governance* as a system of rule which constitutes the form and process of the public sphere. This understanding recognises that they are 'essentially contested' concepts and that 'management' and 'governance' will, in practice, not be neutral but driven by the values of the dominant institutional or political order. This was clearly the case with the policy developments of devolved management and governance, though the government of the day proceeded in this field as if their values reflected objective knowledge.

The early experiments in devolved management, for example in Cambridge and Solihull, or in Strathclyde, emphasised the financial aspects of the 'local or devolved management of *resources*' (Ranson *et al.* 1997a, 1999). The ideas embodied in the reform legislation, however, reflected the developing ascendancy of the new managerialism (Coopers & Lybrand 1988). Schools, it was argued, would flourish if they developed models of management which, purportedly, had proved themselves in the private sector. Institutions were encouraged to develop the new management – valuing the customer, strategic planning, targeting resources, delegation and quality assurance. Better performance depended upon better management: there was one model of management and it was private. Schools were businesses no different from any others, needing to manage resources flexibly to achieve efficiency. They were supported by a frame of devolved governance which emphasised consumer choice and 'accountability' (Bullock and Thomas 1997).

Whilst the case-study schools in our study were apprehensive, justifiably, about the impact of the legislation on their resources, anticipating cuts and loss of staff, nevertheless they valued the opportunity presented to shape the development of their institutions. They developed their understanding of devolved management at a number of levels:

- 1 *Flexible resource management:* they learned to switch resources within their schools to respond to their most pressing needs, and they became skilled entrepreneurs in preparing bids to win new resources from external sponsors to replenish the resources they lost from traditional sources in a shrinking local government.

- 2 *Strategic institutional management:* they learned to value the processes of school-development planning, to clarify strategic priorities in ways which enabled them to focus on planning, target resources, shape staff development and monitor their progress.

But for the purposes of this paper we wish to argue that what was distinctive about all the case-study institutions was that these processes of devolved management were driven by different values and purposes to those which informed the legislation. The values which informed the management were of a different value order to the dominant paradigm of the Conservative legislation:

- 3 *Value management:* substantive, intrinsic values of education as learning, as the unfolding of human potential, informed the purposes of institutional management rather than the preoccupation with the instrumental rationalities of efficiency or 'outputs' as credential accumulation. The schools had a clear conception of who comprised their stakeholder groups, and they had an understanding of their needs. They had also clarified the purposes they were pursuing, and the processes that they were following, in an entirely different language of public values to those of the dominant order (Table 5.1).

The purposes of and opportunities presented by devolved management and governance were often interpreted by schools in our study in very different ways from those intended by the drafters of the neo-liberal education reform. The kinds of value which informed the challenge to underachievement and the purposes of institutional renewal sometimes reflected a new professionalism, sometimes an emergent community oriented public management (Nixon *et al* 1997b; Nixon and Ranson 1997). Table 5.1 contrasts a system of local education devolved according to the principles of community governance as against those of the market. In place of management concerned with resource efficiency for self-interested aggrandisement in the education market-place, was an understanding of management as being preoccupied with values of educational purpose which demanded for their fulfilment co-operative action with parent communities as well as other institutions. Governance, as a system of rule, presupposed reaching shared understanding and agreement with those communities in ways which presupposed their active participation and partnership.

Table 5.1 Organising principles of governance and management

	Market	*Community*
Management	*Self-management*	*Value management*
	• autonomy	• local system
	• flexible resource management	• enabling learning
	• efficiency	• effective process
	• instrumental rationality	• value rationality
Governance	*Consumer democracy*	*Local democracy*
	• individuals/consumers	• citizens and their communities
	• competition	• collaborative
	• equity based on numbers	• equality based on need
	• 'exit'	• participation and 'voice'
	• answerability	• consent and agreement

To understand why the values which informed the interpretation and development of devolved management and governance varied between schools, as well as between these educational institutions and the dominant paradigm presented by a Conservative government, we need to develop an understanding of the 'regimes' which control the schools.

Devolved management and dominant regimes

Schools in our study could be described as 'losers' under the reformed system of devolved management, in the sense that they had lost resources, and were in danger of losing the support of the local families who would have been the school's natural client group, and at the same time the public consent for the authority of the school as an educational institution. In a market system, this is synonymous with 'failure'. This is not just a question of image or perception – although both are important. It required these schools to make a fundamental re-examination of the

impact of social and economic disadvantage upon learning and the experience it caused – of exclusion and alienation. If under-achievement was
to be addressed, it required the schools to reach out to their parent
communities and to renew their institutions from the outside in, rather
than inside out.[4] Only by acknowledging the complex, cultural aspects of
'failure', and by working with the community to rebuild a strong sense of
cultural identity and personal agency, could schools hope to 'succeed'.

But schools varied in how they interpreted 'failure' and in which
parties they believed would offer a material base for this institutional
renewal. The construction that a particular school puts on 'failure' – the
extent to which it acknowledges 'failure' and takes responsibility for it –
affects not only what kind of school it is but whether or not it is likely to
survive as an institution. In outlining the range of institutional responses
to 'failure', we are seeking, therefore, to distinguish the kind of response
that, from the evidence of the schools we have studied, is most likely to
lead to institutional survival and educational improvement. In so doing,
we hope to develop an explanatory framework within which to discuss our
initial finding: that 'agreement' regarding the purposes of education, based
on a shared understanding between school and community, is a necessary
condition of school survival.

Two important respects in which the case-study schools differ is in the
extent of their restructuring and the level of their support from parents
and community. The latter is partly defined by the former, but other
factors also come into play: for example, the history of the school, local
demographic change and the relative popularity of competing schools.
These contingent factors render any programme of restructuring vulnerable. However, on the evidence of our research, those schools that
conceive of restructuring as community-based and that seek to involve
parents as complementary educators are more likely to withstand the
negative impact of these contingent factors.

These two dimensions, the extent of restructuring and the level of
parent support, highlight the importance within our analysis of the notion
of 'regimes' of power. 'Regime' theory is a useful tool for our purposes,
since it maps the close relationship, particularly within urban environments, between development on the one hand and political alliance and
coalition on the other. (See Elkin 1987; Fainstein and Fainstein 1986;
Stoker 1995; Stoker and Mossberger 1994; Stone 1989, 1993, 1995.)
'Regimes' develop, according to 'regime' theory, in order to deal with the
complex concentration of 'difference' within urban politics and to create
co-operation between disparate factions. 'Regimes' are, thus, 'co-ordinating devices which provide the opportunities for bargaining with the
different sides in controversies and, importantly, establish the parameters

of the bargaining game for all the participants' (Dowding 1996: 83). 'Regime' theory insists that, while the distribution of power can usefully be described in terms of structures *of* power, it is not the structures themselves that *have* power. Only people have power, which they then deploy through the structure of relationships (alliances, coalitions, confederations, etc.) that they develop. This is a useful insight to bring to bear on our analysis of the schools we have studied and the particular survival strategies they have adopted.

School 'regimes'

An analysis of the dominant 'regimes' within our nine case-study schools enables us to highlight significant differences between them in terms of institutional response to 'failure' within a system of devolved management and governance:

Non-reforming 'regimes'

In two of the schools there is very little evidence of any restructuring. One of these schools is able to survive because of the community support it receives, while the other is in a more vulnerable position since it lacks this support. In both of these schools, 'failure' is seen as located 'out there' in the locality: the school either pulls up the drawbridge and adopts a siege mentality, or presents itself as an 'oasis' from which young people can temporarily escape the deprivations and deficiencies of their own social and cultural backgrounds. Some parents share the view of the school as 'refuge', and of their own culture as in some way deficient; in the case of one of the schools this shared view provides the basis of parental support for the school. Nevertheless, both schools are locked into routines of accommodation that render structural change not only inoperable but, from the school's perspective, undesirable. The defining purpose of these institutions is simply to be there, and, in being there, to offer, if not an alternative, then at least a 'sanctuary' from the conditions that prevail outside; conditions that are assumed to be intractable and beyond the expertise of the teacher: 'haven', 'refuge' and 'sanctuary' are terms commonly used by parents and teachers to describe what they value about these schools. Such institutions place a high premium on 'care' and on the 'caring' aspects of teacher professionalism; and yet the 'carers' make no assumption that this 'care' will bring about significant changes in the conditions of learning. Indeed, the hopelessness of the 'care' helps to lock the school into its own structural stasis.

Community-passive 'regimes'

Three of the schools have been actively restructuring, but have adopted a traditional conception of the restructuring process as profession-led. Of these, one is again particularly vulnerable, given its lack of community support. Where schools are committed to this traditional conception of restructuring, they are more likely to see 'failure' as a breakdown in the 'compact' between student and teacher; particularly as this 'compact' relates to the expectations each has of the other in respect of the student's learning. 'Failure', in other words, focuses upon the problem of student under-achievement and the way in which that problem is compounded by low expectations. Where the schools differ is in their conceptualisation of student capacities: schools that lack community support are more likely to see themselves as compensating for a basic lack in the individual student, while schools that have such support are more likely to see themselves as enabling the student to realise her or his full potential. However, each of the schools is restructuring with reference to professionally defined positions, such that the restructuring is profession-led. We see this traditional conception of restructuring as the dominant response to 'failure' and as providing legitimisation for the 'new' teacher professionalism and many of its associated practices.

Community-active 'regimes'

The remaining four schools of those we have studied are also actively restructuring, but on the basis of a new conceptualisation of partnership, community and the role of parents and professionals in promoting learning. Each of these four schools has the support of the community for the programme of community-based regeneration being undertaken, and in reaching out to the community is creating a power-base from which to achieve legitimisation. 'Failure' is here seen as requiring a shared sense of responsibility, with the school acknowledging its own need for change while also challenging students and parents to make a similar commitment. Within our case-study schools there is no instance of an institution that is restructuring around community-active 'regimes' *and* that lacks the support of parents and community. We would see the more progressive and radical elements of the 'new' professionalism as being intrinsic to this conception of restructuring, based as it is upon 'regimes' of power in which the local community is active in a local democratic framework of governance, and in which learning is acknowledged to be both an entitlement and a shared responsibility of parents and teachers. Schools that view their own institutional restructuring as an aspect of *community-based regeneration* are, on the evidence of this project, more likely both to survive and to succeed as learning institutions.

Community-based regeneration

The key characteristic of community-based regeneration is that it is led by community-active 'regimes'. The altered coalitions and alliances that these 'regimes' denote involve a radical reappraisal of the key elements within devolved management of education:

A redefinition of the role of educational stakeholders

Community-based regeneration requires the active engagement of parents as potential 'complementary educators' and of students as active learners. This requirement assumes a reorientation of the institution towards its public in ways that render that relationship at once more reciprocal and at the same time more potentially 'agonistic' in its recognition of 'difference' – cultural, religious, ethnic or class. Parents and students are agents, not consumers: their actions help constitute education as a public sphere.

A realignment of professional interests

The role of the teacher within community-based regeneration is that of 'agreement-maker', committed to the integration of divergent viewpoints and interests. The cases illuminate the emergence of a 'new' professionalism: evident, for example, in the pedagogies of active learning, the organisation of 'positive' approaches to school discipline, and the reconstruction of the teacher's 'authority' in respect of relationships with students, parents and community, and colleagues.

Value-driven leadership within the school

Schools committed to community-based regeneration are characterised by strong and decisive leadership from the head teacher. So, of course, are very many other schools. What distinguishes the schools that fall into this category are the values upon which leadership is based: values that include (as core principles of 'agreement-making') the recognition of 'difference' and the commitment to decision-making through dialogue and shared understanding regarding the conditions and purposes of learning.

A redefinition of the boundary between schools and parents

Community-based regeneration involves parents and community members as active participants. It requires the development of creative management strategies that seek to ensure cultural 'difference' as a presence in the decision-making structures of schooling through, for example, the empowerment of parent governors, the establishment of public forums that bring parents and community members together, and the development of community action programmes as an integral part of the students' curriculum experience.

Case studies

Three illustrations of practice taken from our case-study schools in England and Wales highlight ways in which more autonomous schools are attempting community-based regeneration.

School A

The context of a vigorous market environment (all but two secondaries in the local authority are grant maintained) and the aftermath of grant-maintained status in April 1992 (before which time the school was threatened with closure) is important for the relationships being forged between School A and its parents. There are four important parameters:

1   The diverse geographical spread of the pupil population – usually described as split between local families, mostly Asian middle-class high aspirational parents, and the predominantly Afro-Caribbean pupils from the estates further afield.
2   The major 'client-group' of the highly aspirational Asian middle-class families – the supportive families who represent a steady supply of high-achieving pupils for the school.
3   The school's recognition of other ethnic communities from which pupils come, including Afro-Caribbean and Somali – a group of pupils described by the deputy head as speaking up to 40 different languages.
4   The apparent falling away of traditional types of parental support (Parent–Teacher Association) after the positive GM ballot, a time when the school recognised the need to retain the support of parents.

The key manifestation of the school's desire to regain the support of parents is through the revival of the PTA in a new format. Described as the Friends of School A Association, Year 7 and Year 8 parents have been invited to form an open forum for the development of links between parents and the governing body. Whilst the traditional concerns such as fund-raising will remain on the agenda, there is a desire on the part of the school to make it clear to parents the responsibility which the governing body has for the school due to grant-maintained status and to emphasise that they have a voice on that body. Such a link would also seem to emphasise the notion of the parent body having representation through parent governors. The new association is in its infancy and we cannot therefore assume too much about its vigorous development. Nevertheless, it is an expression of the school's commitment to empowering parents to collectively contribute to the governance of the institution.

School B

School B has a strong tradition of community links with immigrant communities, and has recently set up a forum for the Somali communities which it serves. School B is situated in a multiracial city where many of the inhabitants are second-generation immigrants from Africa or Asia. More recently, however, the school serves an increasing number of Somali refugees and has a large population (200) of Somali children in the school. The city has become essentially socially segregated and School B serves an area which is predominantly multiracial black and white working class. The market in education would appear to be reinforcing the social boundaries as the aspiring middle classes gravitate towards schools in the north of the city. The context of a Welsh host community – and the Welsh components of the National Curriculum – only serves to contribute to the sense of 'otherness' experienced by School B and its students.

Due to its traditions of communicating with immigrant groups, School B is sensitive to cultural issues which can create unnecessary barriers. A respect for the traditions of the Somali community is illustrative of this. As the community tutor told us: 'Somali parents' main concern is that they get the best for the children – for their sons to do better than they did.' They are concerned, for example, 'to get pupils back to school when there has been an exclusion.' (Community tutor). Usually Somali parents will come to see teachers without an appointment. The school is therefore careful to have an open-door policy which includes a member of staff being able to meet parents on this basis rather than offend and inconvenience parents by turning them away. Supporting children in a refugee situation creates particular difficulties in socialising young people, and the need to mediate cultural difference is acute. Somali students, for example, will tend to grunt in response to communication, which teachers can misconstrue as insolence. The community tutor has to explain to pupils that they are behaving impolitely.

A meeting was facilitated by the school for Somali parents. It was conducted in the Somali mother tongue. Agreement was reached on three representatives. The first invitation to this group was to address all the Somali pupils in school. Since then, the group has dealt with a number of issues which have been raised either by the group representatives or by teaching staff. As a result, the school has improved the environment for Muslim prayers, at the request of the group. The community tutor has mediated with religious leaders over religious objections to pupils drawing the human body – which was causing concern to members of teaching staff. The school has now agreed to amend some of the tasks which children were refusing to do. Incidents which had become confrontational in the classroom have thus been resolved due to an improved understanding of the religious code to which pupils must adhere. A further meeting is planned for the group to meet with the Head of Religious Studies, and other staff are now requesting meetings with the group.

School C

School C currently has over 75 per cent black pupils, predominantly from Asian families, and serves a community with a high proportion of 'outer ring' grant-maintained schools in an area which also has a strong independent school sector. The key forum for negotiating community-active regeneration is the governing body.

A new head teacher has strong personal values about working with the families of students, is a strong supporter of comprehensive education and cares deeply about schools addressing the under-achievement of black students. She is originally from Bangladesh herself, and has an understanding of the cultural tensions between the Bangladeshi and Pakistani communities from which most of the families have come. Her choice to wear traditional dress sends strong signals to families regarding her cultural identity, and her decision to establish an open surgery on Monday evenings underlines her availability for parents. She articulates well her perceptions of the tension between what the school wants to do and what parents will accept, and sees her role as the leading professional able to mediate between the two positions. However, her strong sense of the educational values which the school must uphold clearly direct her strategy in meeting the (culturally defined) wishes of parents. Whilst she acknowledges the need to negotiate, she describes this as 'giving way on the little things' – such as granting parental wishes for organised single-sex PE groups. Her personal understanding of the 'generation gap', the position of girls in Asian families and her ability to see 'both sides' of Western and Asian cultures enhances her position as mediator and negotiator.

With a high proportion of 'outer ring' grant-maintained schools in the area, together with a strong independent sector, awareness of competition is expressed and the school's reputation with parents is an issue. Senior management is aware of what parents like to see in schools – the traditional things – uniform and homework – and are prepared to meet parents half-way. This reveals a motivation for working with parents in order to satisfy a 'client group'. We might speculate at this stage that the school is endeavouring to carve out its niche as a school which promotes high achievement for black pupils, and that the developing understanding of the culturally defined wishes and needs of parents will be a significant factor.

Current practice would indicate that the governing body is the key forum for negotiation on behalf of parents. Parent governors are an extremely supportive group, but will assert their interests. For example, there is the issue of Muslim parents requesting that girls have the opportunity to wear headscarves as part of the school uniform. This request was contested in the governing body, but agreement was reached to accommodate parents' wishes. As a result, it has been felt, the wearing of headscarves is no longer an issue and few girls do so. The governing body is described as 'well-balanced', with Muslim governors and black governors representing parent viewpoints. It appears to be a forum which supports the head teacher's values of raising expectations, but also a body with which the head needs to press certain issues, such as particular instances of the community use of the premises. The head teacher, nevertheless, recognises the importance of the support of the governing body. Elsewhere the governing body is recognised as a negotiating forum to reach shared agreements with parents. The role of the head teacher and her senior management team would seem to have become pivotal in maintaining the balance of power between a reasonably assertive parent voice on the governing body and what could best be described as the interests of the professionals.

Implications for governance

The analysis of markets argues that there are constraints which schools cannot overcome because the conditions for doing so lie beyond their control. This paradox lies in grasping that the market is a public mechanism, which, under the guise of the general interest – the principle of equity – actually works, as we have argued, to reinforce particular social interests against the public, collective choice. In so doing, it alters the nature of public governance: institutions which enter into shared understanding and public agreements with their parent communities – for example to create a multi-ethnic institution which reflects that community – come to realise that they cannot be maintained against the unintended consequences of aggregated individual decisions to search for schools which are believed to possess greater social distinction. But if some parents begin to drift away from a school, this lowers the resources that it will attract and can reduce the quality of the curriculum offered. This can erode the confidence of local communities in the school, its capacity to deliver its 'agreements' and thus accelerate a process of drift and decline.

As a result, the market places collective welfare beyond the reach of public deliberation, choice and action: in other words, democracy. While some are empowered by the market to change their position ('exit'), individuals together are denied the possibility of 'voicing' their views to alter the collective distribution of educational welfare (Hirschman 1970). 'Exit' is used to hold 'voice' at bay, substituting the power of resources in exchange for the power of a better argument in public discourse. In principle, a community is denied the possibility of clarifying its educational needs and priorities as a whole through the processes of practical reason, in which judgements are formed about what is in the public good, based on reasoned argument that leads towards practical collective choices that are monitored, revisable and accountable to the public. In particular, the disadvantaged are denied the possibility of deliberating upon and determining their life chances.

Where the predicaments of a period are collective or public in nature – such as the educational opportunities of all young people – they cannot be resolved by individuals acting in isolation, or by 'exit', because we cannot stand outside them; they require public institutions and public choices to resolve them. The case studies have provided illustrations of the emergent forms of governance needed to support well-managed schools in contexts of disadvantage. Indeed our work suggests the primacy of governance which shapes the purposes, tasks and conditions of school management.

Community-active regimes have an orientation to governance which dissolves the boundaries of social classification by reaching out to, and seeking agreement with, the communities which it serves. This approach to governing with consent 'seeks to increase the scope for collective community choice and to widen the local political process in order to meet the challenges of ... uncertainty' (Stewart and Stoker 1988).

For some schools, the differences between traditions appear so significant that they are creating forums for parent groups to meet – and re-present their educational traditions – in a discussion of the key issues facing the school that can allow shared purposes and policies to emerge for governing-body decision-making. Schools will be more successful when they have the agreement of the parent community. Some institutions are therefore learning that, because such agreement may no longer be taken for granted, they need to constitute new forms of governance which will allow for democratic participation, agreement and consent. Such forums for participation have the potential to create the conditions for public discussion and mutual accountability, in which 'citizens' may take into account each other's needs and claims and, in so doing, learn to create the conditions for each other's development. In this way, learning becomes an intrinsic part of the public discourse. We have argued elsewhere (Martin *et al.* 1996) that such institutional arrangements, which also recognise different interests and accommodate cultural diversity, will help the school to renegotiate the collective agreements required to legitimate its authority as an educational institution with parents and the community and, at the same time, will have the potential to strengthen the public sphere through active democratic discourse.

Our central argument is that schools must, *as a matter of survival*, reach out to the local community in order to establish an alternative power base from which to reclaim their professional legitimacy and authority. This requires both institutional restructuring and professional reorientation – away from school-led change and towards community-based action that points to a new governance of education to counter market forces.

Conclusion

The institutional changes necessary to reach agreements with parents and the community about the purposes and processes of learning are at the same time renewing the authority of the institution. Thus those processes which are central to pedagogy are those which also deepen and reconstitute institutional legitimacy. We have argued (Nixon and Ranson 1997) that such agreements underlie not only the renewal of learning (in schools and the community) but also the reconstitution of governance in civil society.

The analysis of this study, if it is in any way correct, has the most profound implications for education policy, which at present is under the influence of a dominant ideology that schools can be improved merely by addressing internal issues of improvement. Institutional systems and contexts appear residual factors from this position. The argument of this chapter is that, while schools can transcend the constraints they face by internal restructuring, some schools with exemplary management remain vulnerable and are in decline because of constraints which are beyond their control. Structures matter. Many schools will only be able to sustain the strategic changes that they make to their institutions when the appropriate conditions are established locally and indeed nationally (Ranson 1994; Ranson *et al.* 1997a).

While community-based restructuring offers the best possibility of institutional survival for vulnerable schools, the structures that support the new community-active regimes remain 'fragile conquest(s) that need to be defended as well as deepened' (Mouffe 1993). They cannot be taken for granted. In particular, they require two conditions, neither of which is currently in place:

1   *A system of local planning:* Each of the schools committed to community-based restructuring is vulnerable to both local demographic change and competition from neighbouring schools. These two factors put schools at risk. The risk of merger or closure is chronic for the majority of schools that we have studied, and is a measure of the extent to which local planning remains market-led. Our research suggests that the governance of education may need to be rebalanced in such circumstances so that the local education authority reclaims the legal responsibility to regulate the market in order to support community-active schools as part of a coherent, local education system which would remain publicly accountable but less vulnerable to the vagaries of the market.

2   *A national agenda that protects response:* Even in those instances where systems of local planning are in place to support community-active regimes, the lack of a national agenda that favours (or even comprehends) a planned response to need (as opposed to an unplanned response to the outcomes of market forces) still renders these regimes vulnerable. Policy-making at national level needs to arrest both the trend to centralise control and the continuation of market competition between schools, by strengthening the capacity of democratic local governance to shape local education to meet local as well as national needs.

Notes

1   This chapter draws upon the following previous publications from the research team: Martin, J., Ranson, S., McKeown, P. and Nixon, J. (1996); Nixon, J., Martin, J., McKeown, P. and Ranson, S. (1997a); Ranson, S., Martin, J., McKeown, P. and Nixon, J. (1997a) and Ranson, S., Martin, J., McKeown, P. and Nixon, J. (1999).

2   The study was funded by the Economic and Social Research Council Project Ref. L311253003.

3   For the purposes of the case-study work (which forms the basis of this partic-
    ular paper), a sub-set of nine local contexts (three in England; two in Wales;
    two in Scotland; two in Northern Ireland) was created from seventeen that
    were chosen to reflect authorities with high disadvantage and at different
    stages of market formation/institutional differentiation. Two secondary
    schools were chosen in each of the nine local contexts for a first stage of case-
    study work (focusing on senior managers and their strategies). A smaller
    sub-set of nine schools was chosen for intensive fieldwork to reflect different
    types of school (grant-maintained; voluntary-aided; single-sex, etc.); different
    forms of disadvantage (ethnicity, gender, class); and judgements about the
    presenting issues within the schools and about the quality of institutional
    management (three schools in England; two in Wales; two in Northern
    Ireland; two in Scotland). The intensive fieldwork within the smaller sub-set
    of nine schools has involved interviews with the following groups: senior
    managers (regarding contexts, values, strategies and practices relating to the
    management of difference); heads of subject department and pastoral heads
    (regarding the structure of the curriculum and the way that the formal and
    informal assessment systems differentiate students); pupils in Years 8 and 10
    (aged 14 and 16 respectively); the tutors and parents of pupil interviewees (to
    explore the conditions for learning among disadvantaged students); and
    school governors and teaching staff at all levels (to explore strategies for
    managing institutional change). A quantitative survey of patterns of institu-
    tional management and a survey of parents have also been based upon the
    seventeen original contexts.
4   In this respect we take issue with much of the school effectiveness research.
    On this see Nixon *et al* 1996.

References

Ball, S. J., Bowe, R. and Gewirtz, S. (1994) 'Competitive Schooling, Values,
    Ethics and Cultural Engineering', *Journal of Curriculum and Supervision*, **9(4)**:
    350–67.
Ball, S. J., Bowe, R. and Gewirtz, S. (1995) 'Circuits of Schooling: a Sociological
    Explanation of Parental Choice of School in Social Class Contexts', *Sociolog-
    ical Review*, **43(1)**: 52–78.
Bullock, A. and Thomas, H. (1997) *Schools at the Centre: a Study of Decentralisa-
    tion*, London: Routledge.
Coopers & Lybrand (1988) *Local Management in Schools*, London: HMSO.
Deem, R. (1997) 'The School, the Parent, the Banker and the Local Politician:
    What We Can Learn from the English Experience of Involving Lay People in
    the Site Based Management of Schools', in Pole, C. and Chawla-Duggan, R.
    (eds) *Reshaping Education in the 1990s: Perspectives on Secondary Schooling*,
    London: Falmer.
Deem, R., Brehony, K., Heath, S. (1995) *Active Citizenship and the Governing of
    Schools*, Buckingham: Open University Press.
Dowding, K. (1996) *Power*, Buckingham: Open University Press.
Elkin, S. (1987) *City and Regime in the American Republic*, Chicago: University of
    Chicago Press.

Fainstein, N. and Fainstein, S. (1986) 'Regime Strategies, Communal Resistance and Economic Forces', in Fainstein, S., Hill, R. C., Judd, D. and Smith, M. (eds) *Restructuring the City: The Political Economy of Urban Redevelopment*, New York: Longman.

Fitz, J., Halpin, D. and Power, S. (1993) *Grant Maintained Schools: Education in the Market Place*, London: Kogan Page.

Gewirtz, S., Ball, S. J. and Bowe, R. (1995) *Markets, Choice and Equity in Education*, Buckingham: Open University Press.

Glatter, R., Woods, P. and Bagley, C. (eds) (1977) *Choice and Diversity in Schooling: Perspectives and Prospects*, London: Routledge.

Hillman, J. (1996) 'The Challenge of Disadvantage', in National Commission on Education (ed.) *Success Against the Odds*, London: Routledge.

Hirschman, A. O. (1970) *Exit, Voice and Loyalty: Responses to Decline in Firms, Organisations and States*, Cambridge, MA: Harvard University Press.

Levacic, R. (1995) *Local Management of Schools: Analysis and Practice*, Buckingham: Open University Press.

Martin, J., Ranson, S., McKeown, P. and Nixon, J. (1996) 'School Governance for the Civil Society: Redefining the Boundary between Schools and Parents', *Local Government Studies*, 22(4): 210–28.

Mouffe, C. (1993) *The Return of the Political*, London: Verso.

National Commission on Education (1996) *Success Against the Odds: Effective Schools in Contexts of Disadvantage*, London: Routledge.

Nixon, J. and Ranson, S. (1997) 'Theorising "Agreement": the Bases of a New Professional Ethic', *Discourse: Studies in the Cultural Politics of Education*, 18(2): 5–28.

Nixon, J., Martin, J., McKeown, P. and Ranson, S. (1996) *Encouraging Learning: Towards a Theory of the Learning School*, Buckingham: Open University Press.

Nixon, J., Martin, J., McKeown, P. and Ranson, S. (1997a) 'Confronting "Failure": Towards a Pedagogy of Recognition', *International Journal of Inclusive Education*, 1(2).

Nixon, J., Martin, J., McKeown, P. and Ranson, S. (1997b) 'Towards a Learning Profession: Changing Codes of Occupational Practice Within the New Management of Education', *British Journal of Sociology of Education*, 21(1): 5–28.

Power, S., Halpin, D., and Fitz, J. (1997) 'The Grant Maintained Schools Policy: the English Experience of Self-governance', in Pole, C. and Chawla-Duggan, R. (eds) *Reshaping Education in the 1990s: Perspectives on Secondary Schooling*, London: Falmer.

Ranson, S. (1992) *The Role of Local Government in Education*, Harlow: Longman.

Ranson, S. (1994) *Towards the Learning Society*, London: Cassell.

Ranson, S. (1995) 'From Reforming to Restructuring Education', in Stewart, J. and Stoker, G. (eds) *Local Government in the 1990s*, London: Macmillan.

Ranson, S., Martin, J., McKeown, P. and Nixon, J. (1996) 'Towards a Theory of Learning', *British Journal of Educational Studies*, 44(1): 9–26.

Ranson, S., Martin, J., McKeown, P. and Nixon, J. (1997a) 'The New Management and Governance of Education', Final Report to ESRC, Project Ref. L311253003.

Ranson, S., Martin, J. and Nixon, J. (1997b) 'A Learning Democracy for Co-operative Action', *Oxford Review of Education*, **23(1)**: 117–31.

Ranson, S., Martin, J., McKeown, P. and Nixon, J. (1999) 'The New Management and Governance of Education', in Stoker, G. (ed.) *The New Management of British Local Governance*, London : Macmillan.

Stewart, J. D. and Stoker, G. (1988) *From Local Administration to Community Government*, London: Fabian Society (Series 351).

Stoker, G. (1995) 'Regime Theory and Urban Politics', in Judge, D. and Wolman, H. (eds) *Theories of Urban Politics*, London: Sage.

Stoker, G. and Mossberger, K. (1994) 'Urban Regime Theory in Comparative Perspective', *Government and Policy*, **12**: 195–212.

Stone, C. (1989) *Regime Politics: Governing Atlanta 1946–88*, Lawrence, KS: University of Kansas Press.

Stone, C. (1993) 'Urban Regimes and the Capacity to Govern: a Political Economy Approach', *Journal of Urban Affairs*, **15**: 1–28.

Stone, C. (1995) 'Political Leadership and Urban Politics', in Judge, D., Stoker, G. and Wolman, H. (eds) *Theories of Urban Politics*, London: Sage.

6 Schools in competition

Open enrolment in an academically selective school system

Penny McKeown and Grainne Byrne

Introduction

Using data from a project commissioned by the Department of Education for Northern Ireland (DENI) (McKeown *et al.* 1997), the intention of this chapter is to consider, with respect to the operation of the market and schools' relationships with their parents, the ways in which a policy that is common to all the UK, but differs in the manner in which it has been implemented, has impacted on the post-primary school system in Northern Ireland.

Bash and Coulby (1989: 1) suggested that the 1988 Education Reform Act 'has fundamentally and probably irreversibly transformed the nature of state education' in England and Wales. The education system in Northern Ireland was also made subject to similar provisions. These were brought together under the Education Reform (NI) Order, enacted in 1989.

Although each of the reform provisions can be examined separately, their significance is better appreciated when they are considered together. As Ball (1990: 60) indicated:

> [The ERA] is not in its conception or its purpose a bits and pieces Act. At the heart of the Act is an attempt to establish the basis of an education market.

These changes, and subsequent ones, have had far-reaching implications for schools' relationships with their wider contexts. In particular, the government's wish to drive up the quality of education provision by increasing schools' accountability has created, across the United Kingdom, a climate of inter-school competition. In this competition for pupils (and thereby funding) schools have had to reconsider the relationships established with their parent communities. For example, as well as the statutory requirements to provide a range of information to parents of existing and prospective pupils, the quest to persuade parent 'customers' to choose their 'product', has persuaded many schools to try to become more open to, and inclusive of parents.

Open enrolment provisions in Northern Ireland

The Northern Ireland reform legislation relating to the creation of a 'market' for pupils is similar to that in England and Wales, but with some differences of terminology. Enrolment and admissions numbers for each school, set by DENI, determine the maximum number of pupils in each institution. A school must admit applicants up to this limit. Parents are free to express a preference for a particular school, and, in the event of an over-subscription of applicants, published admissions criteria must be applied by the school to determine which pupils will be admitted. Provisions exist for parental appeal against a decision to refuse admission.

The information to be provided to parents is also similar. Governors must publish a report to parents at an annual parents' meeting. Parents have rights to regular information about the progress of their child, and DENI publishes school performance tables every January.

There have also been some differences in the content of the education reform package as it related to the market. In particular, the categories of new school created in Great Britain were not imposed in Northern Ireland. Following the pre-reform consultation exercises, the proposal to create a category of grant-maintained (GM) schools was removed. No City Technology Colleges or Technology schools have been created. Instead, a new category of Grant-Maintained Integrated school (GMI) has allowed interested parents to inaugurate a religiously mixed school, or to vote to change the status of an existing school.

The school system in Northern Ireland

This largely similar legislation has been applied to a school system which is very different in some important ways from the systems in the rest of the United Kingdom. First, in spite of attempts at change in the 1960s and 1970s, the education system in Northern Ireland is almost completely an academically selective one: most children in Primary 7 take a transfer test to compete for a grammar-school place. Those who do not achieve the highest grades, and those who opt out of the test, are placed in secondary schools. Second, the majority of schools (both primary and post-primary) are segregated according to religion: the state (Controlled) sector is attended mainly by Protestant children; Catholic children are provided for in separate (Maintained) schools. The GMI sector caters for only approximately 2 per cent of the school population. Third, there is no substantial independent sector: only a handful of schools are not grant-aided by DENI.

There is also still a strong tradition of single-sex education. One effect of this proliferation of types of school is that, compared with England and Wales, mean school size is small, and even small communities may have up to five or six post-primary schools.

Such variety has been underpinned by the arrangements for the provision of free home-to-school transport. Until September 1997 this was provided by Education and Library Boards (ELBs) to all primary and post-primary pupils who travelled more than two, or three miles, respectively, to school. This facility permitted children to bypass local schools and to travel long distances daily.

In combination, these distinguishing features of the Northern Ireland school system create a very different context in which the education market has to operate. As a result, competition between schools for pupils is undertaken within a number of 'markets'. Basically, these are:

- between Catholic grammar schools;
- between Catholic secondary schools;
- between non-Catholic grammar schools;
- between non-Catholic secondary schools; and,
- between integrated and secondary schools.

These 'markets' are not completely distinct. About 4 per cent of children cross the sectarian divide to go to school. In a few districts there are comprehensive schools which serve the needs of the whole ability range of pupils. The growing integrated sector also draws pupils from both communities.

The complexity generated by this variety of provision, especially in the greater Belfast area, is illustrated by two quotations from heads. A Principal of a co-educational secondary school near a town on the fringe of greater Belfast analysed the nature of competition for pupils in his area and the difficulties confronting his own school:

> Well, there is spare capacity in [the town] ... you have School X which is a girls' school with a good reputation but even it is not achieving its intake at present. So what chance have we got with girls? ... School Y, their intake has just been decimated these last 2 or 3 years; their intake has gone to hell altogether. School Z had a new Principal, and it has just bulged and bulged, it is a new school with

new housing around it; ... and it is full and more than full. There is plenty of space in School Y, plenty of space in School X for all the local townspeople now. So, and if this integrated school opens in this area, where they are closing down schools, which does not seem just quite so sensible – but they are talking about opening an integrated school this time next year.

A grammar-school Principal, just outside greater Belfast, painted a picture of similar complexity in that sector:

The (district) is a minefield ... we're in competition then with School X and School Y in Belfast and interfacing round about Castletown for School Z, and interface about the Glenhill area for School W. Not so much School V.

Outside the main urban areas, geography provides some constraints on options available for post-primary schooling. In some rural areas, only one school of each type (Catholic, non-Catholic, grammar and secondary), may serve a widely dispersed rural population.

These markets do not, of course, operate on a basis of parity of academic or social esteem. Structural inequalities within the education system in Northern Ireland are well established (Gallagher *et al.* 1997). Patterns of social and educational disadvantage are embedded within the selective system and the hierarchy of schools. McGill (1995), using free school meals' data, has described one aspect of this:

the picture is one of rigid strata in Northern society. At the top come Protestant grammar schools, where only 4 per cent of pupils (on average) are entitled to free school meals, followed by Catholic grammar, where the figure is 16.5 per cent. Next is the small integrated sector on 23 per cent, ahead of Protestant secondary schools with 26 per cent. Well down the list are Catholic secondary schools, where no fewer than 45 per cent of children can get free school meals.

Access to grammar schools is also related to socio-economic background. Indeed, DENI's Statistical Bulletin (June 1996) indicates that the historically strong association between social deprivation and the performance of pupils in the transfer test has become more pronounced since 1993/94 when the transfer tests were changed from the verbal reasoning format to a curriculum-oriented format.

In 1995/96 pupils in those (primary) schools with the lowest proportions of pupils entitled to free school meals (FSM) were more than 3 times as likely to achieve a Grade A as those in the highest FSM schools ... [Further] in 1995/96, opt out rates were highest in high FSM schools ... A substantially larger proportion of Catholic pupils attend schools in the high FSM category.

(DENI, 1996b)

These inequalities are summed up by Gallagher *et al.* (1997: 74). They state that:

Entrance to grammar school is not random by social class or location (as might be expected in a meritocratic system). The observed inequalities reflect ... social class differences in exam performance in the test at age 11 that determines grammar school entrance.

The research

This project was commissioned by DENI and was undertaken between 1994 and 1996. Its aim was to identify the impact of LMS on schools with fully delegated budgets. Both primary and post-primary schools were included. However, this chapter relates only to findings from the post-primary sector.

The main methods of data collection were:

- a postal questionnaire to all schools in Northern Ireland with fully delegated budgets (since 1993); this included the majority of primary schools and all post-primary schools. There was a response rate of 68%, not skewed heavily in any one sector.
- interviews with Principals, governors and teachers in 48 schools identified through a stratified sample, by education and library board area, school sector (primary, post-primary), school management type (Controlled, Maintained, Integrated and Voluntary Grammar) and size of school.

Responses to competition

As Ball (1994) has indicated, schools are not simply the passive victims of parental preference. The research confirms that they view themselves as agents in the new situation. Although some Principals and governors of small, declining secondary schools seemed to feel overwhelmed at times by the strength of their 'opposition', even these interviewees were taking steps to try to retrieve their situations.

Bagley (1994) has described the ways in which schools in England have responded substantively to competition and parental preference: by attracting pupils from a wide geographical area, by increasing their 'share' of the market, by securing a particular section of the market, by restructuring financially (normally through a change of status) or by struggling simply to survive. These are likely responses with or without an academically selective system of schooling. This chapter seeks to establish the extent to which these and other actions to protect and promote their enrolment are undertaken differentially by grammar and secondary schools in Northern Ireland, and to explore the impact of these strategies on the two sectors.

The bases of competition between schools

Schools were asked to record, in order of priority, the five aspects of school life that they emphasised in promoting their schools. Overall, the factors identified by most schools as being among the five most important in promoting themselves were:

- Caring atmosphere – 94.5 per cent of schools
- General academic success – 84.2 per cent
- Good discipline – 81.1 per cent.

However, there was some difference in emphasis between secondary and grammar schools: while 50 per cent of all schools emphasised academic success as their first priority, this group represented almost 75 per cent of grammar schools, but only 40 per cent of secondary schools. Conversely, approximately one-third of schools indicated that their main promotional emphasis was their caring atmosphere. These included fewer than 20 per cent of grammar schools, but 85 per cent of secondary schools.

Furthermore, a number of emphases were identified only by secondary schools. These included their (varying) pupil grouping arrangements, and the fact that they regarded themselves as a community-oriented, or a neighbourhood, school. In interviews, heads referred to other aspects of school life used to promote the school. Schools' policies of retaining small class sizes (as far as possible) were mentioned frequently.

One aspect of school activity, which may be related to issues of school image within the wider community, is that of the stricter enforcement of school discipline policies. Figures for England and Wales (Williams, 1994) have shown a large increase in the numbers of pupils suspended or excluded from school for breaches of discipline. Research studies have also indicated a growing trend towards stricter discipline within some schools, partly in order to reassure parents about good discipline within the school and to protect the learning environment within schools (Gewirtz *et al.* 1995; Woods 1993). Our questionnaire asked schools to indicate the extent to which their practices relating to the suspension and exclusion of pupils had changed in the period since 1991. As Table 6.1 indicates, differences in practice were significantly related to school sector.

In the secondary sector, much higher percentages of schools reported an increased usage of both of these modes of discipline. Supplementary evidence, emerging from a study of suspensions from school in 1996–97 in Northern Ireland (Kilpatrick *et al.* 1998), throws light on interesting aspects of these differences. In that year, almost 80 per cent of the post-primary pupils suspended came from secondary schools (2,086 pupils, who received a total of 3,031 suspensions) compared with 293 grammar-school pupils, who accounted for 341 suspensions. Rates of suspension also varied inversely by school sector (see Table 6.2).

Table 6.1 Trends in the suspension and exclusion of pupils, by school sector

	Suspensions			Exclusions		
	Increase	No change	Decrease	Increase	No change	Decrease
Secondary	57% of schools	40%	3%	35%	61%	4%
Grammar	12%	81%	7%	5%	87%	8%

Table 6.2 Rates of suspension in 1996–97, by school sector

	Secondary schools	Grammar schools
No suspensions	14% of schools	52%
Low rate of suspensions (i.e. <1 per 100 pupils)	24%	38%
Moderate rate (i.e. <3 per 100 pupils)	31%	8%
High rate (i.e. >2 per 100 pupils)	35%	2%

Schools gave different emphases to different types of misbehaviour, according to school sector. Secondary-school pupils were most likely to be suspended for offences within school, such as disruptive behaviour (15 per cent), attacks on other pupils (12 per cent) and abusive language towards each other and teachers (11 per cent). However, the most common reasons for grammar-school suspensions were criminal activities (possession of illegal substances, vandalism or theft) (18 per cent), persistent misbehaviour (17 per cent) and truancy (11 per cent). Many of these problems involve indiscipline beyond the school's boundaries, which might be thought by the school to affect its image within the wider community.

Encouraging parents of potential pupils

Schools were also asked about their strategies for establishing contact with parents of potential pupils. Just over half of the schools reported that they had organised opportunities for the parents of potential pupils to become involved with the school. Similar percentages of grammar and secondary schools employed these strategies, which included formal/semi-formal meetings, and interviews/visits to school, induction days, sports' days, meetings and half-day sessions on transfer procedures.

Almost one-third of grammar and secondary schools invited such parents to social events, including PTA functions, fêtes and fairs, and schools' dramatic or musical productions. In addition, a small group of secondary schools (ten schools) also offered school facilities for use by prospective pupils and their parents. Some facilities that were mentioned were libraries, homework centres and two parents' centres. No grammar school mentioned any such strategy.

Fostering positive and productive links with parents of existing pupils

In acknowledgement of schools' growing understanding of the importance of parental support, both for the school as a whole in a competitive environment, and for the enhancement of children's learning (Hannon, 1995), the survey asked schools to indicate the nature of existing links with their parent bodies, beyond those required by the legislation. The results show some similarity of practice between the secondary and grammar sectors, but also some significant differences.

Similar percentages of secondary and grammar schools held curriculum meetings for parents (about one-third of schools); used parents to raise funds for the school (about 60 per cent); and involved parents, other than parent governors, in formal decision-making (about 6 per cent). However, significant differences were recorded in a large number of areas of practice.

Table 6.3 provides clear evidence of much higher levels of engagement with parents by schools in the secondary sector, compared with grammar schools, even in the more 'traditional' areas of parent–teacher meetings and home visits by members of school staff. Both in the areas of direct support for children's learning and in the more school-wide aspects of information exchange between schools and parents, secondary schools were deploying much more energy to involve their parent communities with a range of aspects of school life.

How schools promote themselves

Principals, governors and teachers in interview recognised the continuing importance of the school's reputation in protecting its enrolment. However, they indicated that, since the introduction of open enrolment, they had begun to attempt explicitly to shape this reputation, through various means. Among the most important of these was local positive publicity about school life and about the successes of pupils. There was very little difference between the sectors as regards their means of promotion. Similar percentages of schools (in declining levels of frequency) used: a school handbook, local press publicity and advertisements, a promotional video and publicity on local radio and television. One secondary school had employed a marketing consultant.

Organising external links and promotional activities

The strategies adopted by some schools to protect and increase enrolment are likely to have resource implications. Important among these is the

Table 6.3 Aspects of parental involvement in schools – percentages of schools responding

	Secondary (%)	Grammar (%)
Home–school reading scheme	47	2
Form-group/year-group parent–teacher meetings	87	70
Parents assisting in class	11	—
Parental involvement in assessment of pupil work	6	—
Home visits by teachers	40	24
Newsletter for parents	81	19
Surveys of parent opinion	50	27

need to deploy teacher time in supporting and fostering links with important stakeholders. Schools were therefore asked if they had, since 1991, created any internal promoted posts with responsibility in areas linked to promotion of the school. Ninety-seven per cent of schools responded to these questions; significantly different responses were obtained from secondary and grammar schools:

Table 6.4 presents a striking picture of greater activity by secondary schools in almost all of these areas. They are three times as likely as grammar schools to have created posts for marketing the school, and approximately twice as likely to have done so in the areas of links with Further Education colleges and fostering links with parents.

This widespread incidence of attempts to strengthen vertical integration between primary and post-primary schools was confirmed in the school interviews. In particular, primary-school Principals described much more frequent and regular contact initiated by local post-primary schools. In addition to customary visits by Primary 7 pupils to local post-primary schools, these heads now reported Year 8/Primary 7 teacher contact to plan curriculum transitions and Year 8 induction, visits by hitherto-unfamiliar grammar-school Principals, and many more personal invitations to attend functions in the secondary and grammar schools.

Attracting pupils from a wider geographical area

The introduction of open enrolment in Northern Ireland in 1991 ended defined catchment areas for schools. The availability of free home-to-school transport (until 1997) for pupils travelling more than three miles to school created an opportunity for post-primary schools to recruit more widely than traditionally had been the case. The strategies used have been described above. Our survey therefore asked schools to indicate, in

Table 6.4   New posts created, by school sector – percentages of schools responding

Type of posts created	Secondary (%)	Grammar (%)
Marketing	28.4	9.1
Public relations	50.8	36.4
Links with industry	31.2	31.8
Links with FE colleges	28.1	11.4
Links with primary schools	49.1	43.2
Links with parents	32.5	18.2

very general terms, whether they were recruiting pupils from the same, or from different geographical areas from those they had done in 1991. They were asked to record changes in the percentages of their pupils who lived within one mile, one to five miles, and over five miles, from their schools. Comparison of the responses, by school sector, revealed some differences between schools (Table 6.5).

The responses demonstrate very well the extent to which secondary schools are more 'local', in general, than grammar schools. While over 40 per cent of grammar-school pupils travel more than five miles to school, almost 80 per cent of secondary-school pupils live within five miles of school; the differences are most marked at the very local level.

However, perhaps unexpectedly, while the overall location of pupil domicile has not altered greatly since the introduction of open enrolment, it is in the secondary sector that most change has occurred, probably as a result of the initiatives described above. Slightly fewer secondary-school pupils live very close to school, and the numbers travelling further has increased somewhat. In the grammar-school sector, the responses indicate that there has been almost no change in traditional patterns of enrolment.

New regulations, with effect from September 1997 limit free home–school transport to those pupils who must travel more than three miles to attend their nearest suitable school. 'Suitable', in this case, does not permit a preference for a co-educational school, but does allow choice based on religious denomination. Although full information on the changes is not yet available, the Belfast ELB was able to indicate the number of bus passes issued to new admissions in both grammar and

Table 6.5 Domicile of pupils in relation to school – mean percentages 1991/92 and 1994/95 – by school sector

School sector	Percentage of pupils living within 1 mile of school	Percentage of pupils living within 1–5 miles of school	Percentage of pupils living >5 miles from school
Secondary schools			
1991/92	37.1	44.2	20.4
1994/95	35.4	43.8	22.1
Grammar schools			
1991/92	16.1	39.8	43.6
1994/95	15.9	40.0	44.4

secondary schools in 1997/98, and the comparable figures for 1996/97 (Table 6.6).

These figures show a dramatic (and proportionately similar) decrease in the numbers of pupils entitled to free home–school transport. Given the higher levels of FSM entitlement in the secondary sector, fewer families in this sector may be able to fund transport costs to more distant schools. Thus, this change in regulations may be expected to have the most adverse impact on secondary schools trying to draw in pupils from a wider area.

Securing a particular section of the 'market'

Selection by specialist abilities

Increasingly, practices of pupil selection by schools in England and Wales are not entirely based on academic ability. City Technology Colleges, Technology Schools and others select according to a range of pupil capacities and suitabilities. In Northern Ireland schools, however, there is, as yet, no evidence of selection according to anything other than academic criteria. However, survey responses indicated that 36 per cent of schools had changed their admissions criteria since 1991/92.

A disproportionate number of these were over-subscribed grammar schools (71 per cent) which had introduced a criterion of family or staff links with the school.

Changing patterns of intake

Research suggests that, as a result of the exercise of parental preference, in conjunction with open enrolment, two major modifications of traditional practice are developing. One of these has been some blurring of the traditional dividing-line of 'suitability for an academic education'. Interview data revealed a picture of changing patterns of intake between the secondary- and grammar-school sectors. The Transfer Procedure

Table 6.6   Belfast Education and Library Board area: numbers of post-primary pupils entitled to free home-to-school transport

Type of pupil	September 1996	September 1997
Secondary-school pupils	853	145
Grammar-school pupils	450	75

regulations also changed at the time of the introduction of open enrolment. Historically, grammar schools could only admit approximately 30
per cent of children in the age cohort – those deemed academically 'suitable' for a grammar-school education. However, under the new
regulations they must admit pupils up to their physical capacity. Also,
within their admissions criteria, they must admit pupils in descending
order of Transfer Procedure grades – all pupils with grade A must be
admitted before any B grade applicants, and so on. In some cases, where
such schools (often smaller ones) have not filled up with A and B grade
applicants, they have had to admit pupils with grades C and below.
Figures supplied by DENI in 1997 indicate that in 1995 approximately 6
per cent of Year 8 admissions to grammar schools were pupils who had not
attained Grades A or B in the Transfer tests. These pupils are not spread
uniformly across the sector.

This practice has had a considerable impact on the intake of some
secondary schools, removing all of their more 'academic' pupils. The
consequences of this practice were clearly indicated by the Principal of a
Maintained secondary school:

> in this area the creation of a further grammar school is going to take
> more pupils away from the secondary sector. And when I say 'more
> pupils', I am not worried about bodies; I am worried about the stretch
> of ability. It will remove effectively the top ability range which we
> have, which is the only group succeeding academically. So the
> grammar school will have the range of ability which reaches from the
> very best at 100 per cent, down to round about 60 per cent ... The
> new grammar school ... will take our 'A' stream totally out altogether.
> And for us, our 'A' stream at the minute are the (Transfer grade) Ds.
> Our 'A' stream are the Ds, you know.

Conversely, a few grammar schools with growing numbers of less
'academic' pupils report having to provide remedial help for those unable
to cope with their curriculum, and, in some cases, according to secondary-
school Principals, have asked such pupils to leave before Year 11 (Form 4)
and the beginning of General Certificate of Secondary Education (GCSE)
studies.

Sixth-form selection and competition

The other area of change has occurred in the requirements for the
entrance to sixth form. The survey showed that a number of schools had
begun to specify minimum GCSE grades for entry to the sixth form. There

were significant differences between secondary and grammar schools: an increased standard of GCSE achievement is required in 52 per cent of grammar schools and 10 per cent of secondary schools.

It is not possible to establish from the survey data whether this standard is required of all pupils wishing to enter the sixth form, or whether it is only applied to pupils wishing to enter the school post-GCSE. At interview, however, a number of schools indicated that this minimum requirement is applied to all prospective sixth-form entrants, so that some of their own pupils are obliged to leave the school after GCSE. It does appear, therefore, that, in a context of growing grammar schools, an increasingly important selection point for pupils is that which takes place after GCSE to permit entry to the sixth form. Two main reasons were cited for this change: one was the need to establish objective criteria in the event of an over-subscribed sixth form; the other to ensure as far as possible that only pupils likely to achieve grades A to E at A level would undertake academic studies.

This transfer point at 16+ has, of course, important implications for school budgets and some secondary schools have taken action to create their own sixth forms. The Principals of these schools believed that the introduction of General National Vocational Qualifications (sometimes in combination with A levels) offered parents of prospective pupils the possibility of continuation to a sixth-form education within the school. Growing numbers of pupils are choosing this option instead of transferring to a grammar school. The Principal of a Controlled grammar school emphasised this point:

> the other area we have lost, and it's different kind of competition, is the 16+ where the local secondary schools have established Sixth Form courses and we, I think, had no pupils who transferred from any of the local secondary schools this year, whereas when I first came here, we might have had 20 or 22; 22 × £2,000 is two teachers.

Restructuring financially

Since 1991, schools in England, Wales and Scotland wishing to restructure financially have had the option of becoming grant-maintained. This option is not available to schools in Northern Ireland, except in the more specific form of opting out into GMI status. To date, relatively few existing schools have made this transition. Most GMI schools are those which were founded as integrated schools. These are mainly in the primary sector, but in any case, fewer than 2 per cent of all children of school age in Northern Ireland are being educated in integrated schools.

The impact of competition: Changing 'market share'

This research suggests that the introduction of open enrolment has been beneficial for grammar schools, in general, at the expense of secondary schools. In interviews, Principals and governors of schools in both sectors confirmed this finding. The extent of this benefit can be demonstrated in a number of ways.

School size

Although the mean size of secondary schools has grown slightly (from 528 to 547 pupils) since 1991, grammar schools have grown relatively more (from 774 to 857). These figures need to be contextualised: a number of secondary schools have been closed under rationalisation arrangements or amalgamation during the period in question, and two new Catholic grammar schools have opened. Also, in spite of the growing numbers of pupils in the post-primary sector as a whole, secondary schools, as a group, have accounted for a declining proportion of the age cohort over the period 1991 to 1997.

The figures in Table 6.7 vary somewhat according to geographical area: in the Belfast ELB area, grammar schools now admit more than 50 per cent of the age group.

Table 6.7 Secondary-school enrolment in Northern Ireland, as a proportion of the post-primary-level age cohort (1991–97)

Month	Percentage of post-primary-level cohort in secondary schools	Number of pupils in all post-primary schools
January 1991	61.4	141,146
October 1992	60.7	145,012
October 1993	60.1	148,264
October 1994	59.8	150,036
October 1995	59.7	151,597
October 1996	59.6	152,743
October 1997	59.3	153,095

Source: DENI (1999)

Trends in enrolment

More than half of Northern Irish grammar schools reported stable enrolments during the period of the research, but just 40 per cent of secondary schools were in this category. No grammar schools had lost more than 10 per cent of their 1991/92 enrolment by 1994/95, but 20 per cent of secondary schools had suffered in this way (Table 6.8).

The impact of changes in enrolments

Since 1991, schools' maximum enrolment has been limited by the imposition of an enrolment number. An important aspect of the analysis, therefore, was to compare, for each responding school, the number of pupils on-roll with the school's enrolment number. This permitted an assessment of the extent to which schools are at capacity or not. In our analysis, levels of enrolment were banded by a variable 'Subscription Level'.

Table 6.9 gives probably the clearest picture of the extent to which 'market share' is now skewed to the advantage of grammar schools in Northern Ireland.

Table 6.8 Breakdown of schools by sector and enrolment trend

School sector	Enrolment increase >20%	Enrolment increase >10%	Little change	Enrolment decrease >10%	Enrolment Decrease >20%	N
Secondary	17.2% of schools	22.4% of schools	40.5% of schools	13.8% of schools	6.0% of schools	116
Grammar	11.4	36.4	52.3	—	—	44

Table 6.9 Breakdown of schools by sector and subscription level

School sector	Percentage that are full	Percentage that are at 99–95% capacity	Percentage that are at 94–75% capacity	Percentage that are at <75% capacity
Secondary	21	13	36	30
Grammar	57	39	4	—

Struggling to survive

It is evident that the introduction of open enrolment in Northern Ireland has, in general, benefited grammar schools at the expense of secondary schools. In trying to establish which schools may be struggling, one step in the analysis has been to compare the relative sizes of responding schools in each sector. Using size bands supplied by DENI, a breakdown by school type and size revealed the clear distinctions between the sectors (Table 6.10).

Taken in conjunction with the information already provided about enrolment trends and the extent to which schools in each sector are at or near capacity, the picture revealed is one of large, over-subscribed and relatively well-funded grammar schools. This contrasts sharply with a secondary sector in which almost half the schools have fewer than 450 pupils, and in which 30 per cent of schools are at less than three-quarters of their capacity. Financial stringency is common in this sector, yet levels of pupil social and educational disadvantage (measured according to formula criteria) are generally much higher than in grammar schools.

For some of these secondary schools, interview data confirmed that they are struggling to survive. For example, in terms of the pressure to retain their numbers, the Principal of a Maintained secondary school suggested that, 'another grammar school, opening next year, will kill us off entirely'. A Principal of a Controlled secondary school, which had falling rolls and a large number of educationally disadvantaged pupils, also spoke of the school's acute and continuing financial difficulties:

> I am not living within what I am given under the formula … It is only this prop up money (i.e., transitional and curriculum reserve funding) that has kept this school afloat.

Issues arising from competition: The schools' analysis

A number of recurring themes about the impact of competition emerged from the discussions with Principals, governors and teachers.

Table 6.10 Breakdown of responding schools by type and size

School sector	Small (%)	Medium (%)	Large (%)
Secondary	43.5	36.7	20.8
Grammar	10.5	28.9	60.6

Open enrolment/demographic change

Changes in enrolment could not be simplistically attributed to success in competition under open enrolment. Demographic change, the rationalisation or amalgamation of neighbouring schools, and the requirement introduced in 1991 – that schools admit up to their physical capacity – have affected school enrolments, without necessarily any changes in individual school policies. Grammar schools, as a group, have benefited considerably from the latter.

Localised markets

The extent and nature of competition for pupils varies widely, according to the school's local context. Markets, except in the major urban areas (Belfast and Derry), seem to be localised. In large areas of rural Northern Ireland, population sparsity creates a situation of little choice for many parents; the particular school attended is determined by the child's Transfer grade, religion and gender.

Impact of integrated schools

Especially in areas where surplus school capacity already exists, the creation of integrated schools was considered to be having an impact on traditional enrolment patterns. This was identified as a concern by secondary- and grammar-school Principals of all management types. Some secondary-school Principals believed that integrated secondary schools, like grammar schools, were perceived by parents as more 'socially acceptable' than secondary schools, so their own schools were suffering more from this new competition than grammar schools. In addition, many Principals, from all sectors, believed that the different funding arrangements for the integrated sector gave those schools an unfair financial and practical advantage in seeking pupils. Recent research (McKeown and Osborne 1997) has confirmed instances of the more generous funding of Integrated, *vis-à-vis* Controlled and Maintained schools.

Ability range

Reference has already been made to many secondary-school Principals' perceptions of a narrowing in the ability range of pupils admitted to their schools. This situation was confirmed by Don Hill, Deputy Secretary of DENI, in his evidence to the Northern Ireland Affairs Committee (1997:

24): 'Open enrolment has meant that there are more (secondary) schools with a significantly higher level of low achievers.'

Principals believe that this situation compounds their schools' existing difficulties in dealing with higher proportions of socially disadvantaged children (as evidenced by FSM entitlement). It is considered likely to affect the longer-term capacity of these schools to attract pupils and to deal effectively with their problems. Conversely, in a number of grammar schools, the ability range has broadened beyond those pupils achieving Transfer Grades A and B. This development has implications for resourcing the curriculum in both grammar and secondary sectors, and it may impact eventually on the levels of attainment at GCSE by pupils in each sector.

Financial difficulties

The favourable enrolment situation of grammar schools at the expense of secondary schools has already been demonstrated. Loss of enrolment will obviously have budgetary consequences for a school, especially at a time of financial stringency. Many secondary-school Principals and governors spoke of extreme pressure on budgets, leading to teacher redundancies, economies in spending on special-needs provision and on essential books and equipment. End-of-year budget deficits were often the result of these pressures.

Developing wider links with primary schools

The growing scramble in the post-primary sectors to protect pupil numbers has also meant that schools are casting their recruitment nets more widely. Although geography preserves traditional catchment areas in some rural areas, in urban districts post-primary schools are drawing pupils from an increasing range of primary schools. The head of a Maintained primary school spoke of local post-primary schools 'selling their wares' more energetically each year, and the Principal of an Integrated secondary school reported drawing pupils from 35 primary schools.

Other issues

Among grammar-school Principals there was a view that it was becoming more difficult to predict the level and quality of applications for Year 8 admissions as parents became more adept at playing the market 'game' in trying to ensure the admission of their child to a grammar school. Thus, even schools which traditionally had accepted only children with the highest grades might find themselves under-subscribed with higher grade applicants. This situation was illustrated by the Principal of a Controlled grammar school:

> we had the reputation of not taking any B grade children at all, and then last year people with grade Bs didn't bother applying. Second preference Bs took a lot of our places, and we were down to C grades. Whether this year will be different, I don't know.

Conclusions: An assessment of the impact of the education market in Northern Ireland

The evidence presented here has painted a vivid picture of the impact of linking open enrolment with formula funding in an academically and socially divided school system. Several issues have emerged about the nature of competition and its effects in practice.

There appear to be significant differences between the sectors, in terms of the ethos which they try to 'sell' and the nature of their relationships with parents. Although very sensitive to their image in the wider community and to the views of individual parents, grammar schools appear to be much less willing than secondary schools to engage with their parental constituencies as a whole, or to involve individual parents in aspects of learning support for their children. This may be a result of the fact that they are routinely over-subscribed and, within limits, take their choice of pupils.

Competition exists on a very uneven playing field, and its effects have been felt differentially within the sectors. The evidence suggests that the advantages traditionally enjoyed by grammar schools have been reinforced in the post-primary 'market' system. As they are routinely over-subscribed for reasons which are not always educationally based, they now admit, under open enrolment, a growing number of pupils whose strengths may not be academic and who may not be suitable for that type of schooling. There is an issue as to whether these pupils should have been accepted by those schools in the first instance. However, current legislation and their financial value to the schools mean that they will continue to be admitted into Year 8. This may have resource and performance implications for the grammar schools which they attend.

There are also heavy transaction costs to schools of trying to cope with a market system. Especially in secondary schools, the vigorous promotion of enrolment, through the means described above, uses up considerable percentages of managers' and teachers' time and requires the deployment of monetary and physical resources. These transaction costs may be worthwhile for those schools that are successful in attracting pupils, but place a heavy burden on others, for very little reward.

It is difficult to predict the future distribution of enrolment. The recent opening of two Catholic grammar schools will add some capacity to that sector over the next six years. Otherwise, almost all grammar schools are now at capacity, and cannot expand further without DENI permission and capital investment. The Department's figures (DENI 1995) for projected school populations suggest growth in the post-primary sector until at least 2001/02. If grammar schools are not permitted to expand, the growth in pupil numbers may well slightly redress the balance of enrolments in favour of the secondary schools, during this period.

There are major consequences for many secondary schools of this system of enrolment. Problems of educational and social disadvantage have become more concentrated in some of the smallest, most under-subscribed secondary schools, and the reduction in pupil numbers – due to competition from both grammar and integrated schools – has caused growing financial difficulties for them. Increasingly, because their intake is skewed towards the lower ability range, and because even more of their pupils are also socially disadvantaged, these secondary schools have had to deploy an increasing proportion of scarce resources to address not only learning difficulties, but also to create mechanisms to tackle a range of additional emotional and behavioural problems.

Many of the secondary-school Principals interviewed considered that their schools were under threat, either in the short or medium term. This situation has probably been made more difficult by the net monetary transfer away from secondary schools since the introduction of formula funding, reported by the Northern Ireland Audit Office (1995).

The major significance of these developments lies in their effects on the learning opportunities and outcomes for pupils in these schools. Gallagher *et al.* (1997: 72) have examined the differential levels of pupil attainment at 16+ in secondary and grammar schools, and conclude that, 'Who you are and the type of school attended seem to be the key determinant of educational outcomes (at GCSE) in Northern Ireland.' They also argue that

> the clear and measurable link between educational achievement and social disadvantage … may be exacerbated by social and spatial differentiation between grammar and secondary schools … The net effect is that the lowest level of achievement is found among young people (who) are most likely to live in socially disadvantaged areas, come from socially disadvantaged households and attend secondary schools where many of their peers share the same background.
>
> Gallagher *et al.* (1997: 92)

It seems clear that, in Northern Ireland, the introduction of open enrolment in combination with formula funding into an academically selective school system has exacerbated the inequalities which existed before 1991. Competition is leading to a growing concentration of pupil social disadvantage and educational under-achievement in a number of small, declining and under-capacity schools, which are increasingly unable to make ends meet. It is hard, therefore, to disagree with the conclusion of the Northern Ireland Economic Council that,

> every attempt should be made to determine to what extent the current educational system can be modified to remove the adverse effects of open enrolment/parental choice, together with selection, on the problem of underachievement.
>
> Gallagher *et al.* (1997: xxxii)

These findings and recommendations must also throw into question any initiatives in the other Great Britain school systems to extend selection based on academic criteria.

References

Bagley, C. (1994) 'Life in the Marketplace', *Managing Schools Today*, **3(9)**, July, 3–4.

Ball, S. (1990) *Politics and Policy Making in Education: Explorations in Policy Sociology*, London: Routledge.

Ball, S. (1994) *Education Reform: a Critical and Post-Structural Approach*, Buckingham, Open University Press.

Bash, L. and Coulby, D. (1989) *The Education Reform Act: Competition and Control*, London: Cassell Educational.

Department of Education, Northern Ireland (1993) *Learning for Life: School Performance Information 1991/92*, Bangor: DENI.

Department of Education, Northern Ireland (1995) *School Population Projections 1995/96–2001/02*, Statistical Bulletin SB4/1995, Bangor: DENI.

Department of Education, Northern Ireland (1996a) *Learning for Life: School Performance Information 1994/95*, Bangor: DENI.

Department of Education, Northern Ireland (1996b) *Transfer Procedure Test Results, 1989/90 – 1995/96*, Statistical Bulletin 1/96, June, Bangor: DENI.

Department of Education, Northern Ireland (1997) *Learning for Life: School Performance Information 1995/96*, Bangor: DENI.

Department of Education, Northern Ireland (1999) *Enrolments at Schools in Northern Ireland*, Statistical Press Release, March, Bangor: DENI.

Gallagher, A., Shuttleworth, I. and Gray, C. (1997) *Educational Achievement in Northern Ireland: Patterns and Prospects*, Research Monograph 4, Belfast: Northern Ireland Economic Council.

Gewirtz, S., Ball, S. and Bowe, R. (1995) *Markets, Choice and Equity in Education*, Buckingham: Open University Press.

Hannon, P. (1995) *Literacy, Home and School: Research and Practice in Teaching Literacy with Parents*, Lewes: Falmer.

Kilpatrick, R., Barr, A. and Wylie, C. (1998) *Report of the 1996/97 Northern Ireland Suspension and Expulsion Study*, Belfast: School of Education, Queen's University.

McGill, P. (1995) 'Far More Catholic Children in North Live in Poverty', *The Irish Times*, 28 December, Dublin.

McKeown, P. and Osborne, R. (1997) 'Issues of Equity in School Funding: School Budgets in Northern Ireland under Formula Funding Arrangements', Paper read at conference on 'Public Dimensions of Public Services: Issues of Equity, Accountability and the Role of the Profession', University of Wales, Cardiff Business School, April.

McKeown, P., Byrne, G. and Barnett, R. (1997) *An Initial Analysis of the Impact of Formula Funding and Local Management of Schools on the Management of Northern Ireland Schools*. Research Report Series, No. 5, Bangor: Department of Education for Northern Ireland.

Northern Ireland Affairs Committee (1997) *Underachievement in Northern Ireland Secondary Schools*, Second Report, Session 1996–97, London: HMSO.

Northern Ireland Audit Office (1995) *Local Management of Schools*, Report by the Comptroller and Auditor General for Northern Ireland, Belfast: HMSO.

Williams, E. (1994) 'The Exclusion Zone', *Search*, **21**, Winter.

Woods, P. (1993) 'Responding to the Consumer: Parental Choice and School Effectiveness', *School Effectiveness and School Improvement*, **4(3)**: 205–29.

7 School-based management in the United States

*Priscilla Wohlstetter and
Penny Bender Sebring*

Introduction

School-based management (SBM) is a popular education reform that has been adopted by many states and school districts in the United States as a way to improve the performance of the education system. SBM allows people who work in schools to make decisions about how money is spent, who is hired and how students are taught. Thus, while state and local school boards (as in traditionally managed schools) set goals and standards, under SBM the decisions and processes used to meet those outcomes are made at the school level.

Widespread interest in SBM stems from a belief that the public education system is not working, partly because decisions are made by a bureaucracy – the district office – that is too large, unwieldy and distant from students. Proponents of SBM argue that the education system must devolve decision-making authority in order for school performance to improve. They argue that educators in schools are closest to students, and therefore are in the best position to assess student needs and to design educational programmes to meet those needs. At the same time, teachers and others will gain greater ownership of school improvements, having made the decisions themselves. Proponents of SBM have also argued that devolved decision-making will promote a more effective use of dwindling resources. According to this argument, schools can designate resources more wisely, such as funds for staff development and classroom supplies, to meet local needs and priorities, than can district formulas for resource allocation that may be disconnected from the local context.

In recent years, thousands of districts across the United States have experimented with some form of SBM, and similar efforts have been adopted by Australia, Canada, France, New Zealand, Scandinavia, Spain and the United Kingdom (Peck 1997). Devolved management also has been popular in the business world as a tool for improving productivity.

Since the 1970s, companies in the United States faced with increasing competition from other countries, such as Japan, created employee work teams to deal with issues of setting production goals, managing product quality, and determining work methods. Many such companies experienced improvements in employee satisfaction, commitment and productivity, and saw decreases in employee turnover and absenteeism rates (Mohrman 1994).

Drawing on results from several large-scale assessments of SBM by the Center on Educational Governance (CEG) and the Consortium on Chicago School Research (CCSR),[1] this chapter examines school governance and organisation under SBM, as well as strategies that hold the most promise for raising student achievement. The first section offers a brief overview of the history of SBM reforms in the United States, highlighting the variety of approaches that have been taken in implementing SBM. The next section examines the consequences of SBM reforms, asking the question 'what difference does SBM make in school operations?' Emphasis is given to the new roles and relationships for educators and parents within SBM schools. This section also points to factors that explain differences between 'improving' and 'struggling' schools. The improving schools have moved beyond the hard work of implementing SBM to foster school organisational change and to strengthen the practices that are essential to student learning: effective school leadership, parent and community partnerships, professional capacity and community among the teachers and staff, a student-centred learning environment and high-quality teaching. They have also succeeded in improving student performance. Struggling schools, on the other hand, have adopted SBM, but have not been able to garner the full involvement of teachers and parents in concrete and systematic efforts to restructure the school organisation and improve teaching and learning. Unlike most other chapters in this volume, we draw from research on both elementary and high schools.

Data sources

The Center on Educational Governance conducted assessments of SBM in a range of school districts, while the Consortium focused exclusively on the Chicago Public Schools. The focus of CEG's research on SBM was to identify the organisational conditions that helped schools use SBM to bring about changes in teaching and learning. The sample included 44 schools in the United States, Canada and Australia.[2] The research focused primarily on large, urban school districts with student populations of more than 60,000. Most of these schools were working hard to meet the needs of their changing populations and had been operating under SBM for at least four years, with some of them operating for much longer than that. CEG researchers conducted site visits over a two-year period (1993 and 1994) and interviewed more than 500 people, from school-board members, superintendents and associate superintendents in district offices to Principals, teachers, parents and students in schools (Wohlstetter *et al.* 1997a; Wohlstetter *et al.* 1997b; Wohlstetter and Mohrman 1996; Robertson *et al.* 1995; and Wohlstetter *et al.* 1994).

Since its inception in 1990, the Consortium has conducted numerous studies to understand the impact of democratic participation, at the school level, on school organisation and instructional practices. Recent studies have shifted attention to specific initiatives of school district leaders who, under a 1995 reform law, were appointed by the mayor (local schools retained most of their powers). Thousands of students and teachers in elementary and high schools have participated in surveys, along with Principals and local school-council members. A longitudinal analysis of standardised test scores, using value-added methods, was conducted for the years 1990–96. Consortium researchers also have carried out in-depth studies (Bryk *et al.* 1998a; Bryk *et al.* 1998c; Ryan *et al.* 1997; Sebring *et al.* 1995; Sebring *et al.* 1996).

Overview of SBM reforms in the United States and their origins

In SBM schools, many decisions about budget, staffing and curriculum are made at the school level by Principals, teachers, and often parents and community members. SBM schools usually receive a lump-sum budget to cover most of their operating expenses. With this budget, individual schools are responsible for deciding how to allocate their own resources, and many also have the power to decide whom to hire. One school, for example, might decide to give individual teachers a stipend to buy books for their classrooms by eliminating an assistant librarian position, while another school may choose to hire a part-time teacher instead of a custodian. SBM schools also typically have the power to define their own educational mission and how they will achieve it. One SBM high school in Rochester, New York, focused its mission on helping students become responsible and effective citizens, and, to accomplish this goal, rescheduled the school day so that students could volunteer in the community.

Despite current interest, SBM is not a new phenomenon in the history of American education reform, and elements of SBM can be traced back to the early 1900s (Murphy and Beck 1995). Some observers have noted that SBM seems to surface in times of crisis or periods of intense stress, such as during a teachers' strike or following a world war. The stress apparently produces a sense of urgency to change the existing system to better meet new demands. Further evidence suggests that the way in which the system is changed – that is, how power is redistributed under SBM – reflects the balance of power at different points in history.

The use of SBM to respond to crisis first emerged during the Teacher Council Movement (1909–29), when teacher representatives were elected to serve on teacher councils and empowered to make policy recommendations for individual schools. This movement was strongly influenced by the labour movement under way at that time and the strife that resulted led to the realisation that teachers needed more say in how schools were run. The power of teachers at this time is reflected in the model of SBM that was adopted, which featured teacher-dominated councils.

The Great Depression and World War II prompted the Democratic Administration Movement (1930–50), during which time SBM recurred, and attempts were made to increase teacher, student, parent and community member participation in school decisions. Influencing many public agencies, this movement tried to improve organisations by making them more democratic; and consequently, school councils were structured to represent a range of perspectives and interests.

In the mid-1960s, SBM became popular once again during the Community Control Movement (1965–75), which stemmed from a concern that the needs of the poor were not being addressed by public agencies. During this movement, a wide range of constituents became involved in making school policy, including leaders of community groups and minority parents. Unlike the previous two movements which originated within the educational setting, the Community Control Movement started with leaders outside the schools who demanded more voice in school policy decisions (Murphy and Beck 1995).

The unifying theme of all of these attempts at SBM was a sense of crisis. At the same time, the model of SBM that was adopted reflected the interests of various groups pushing for decentralisation. Once the crisis was perceived to be over and demands for empowerment were satisfied, the system centralised once again. Recent interest in SBM is following this pattern – SBM was proposed as a remedy to meet the intense criticism levied at American schools during the 1980s.

Current SBM plans are adopted most often by the local school board and the district superintendent, who oversee the management of all schools in the district. Sometimes the impetus for SBM comes from a teachers' union that is interested in expanding the role and professionalism of teachers. In such cases, provisions governing SBM plans – who has decision-making power and areas of decision-making authority – are usually hammered out through the collective bargaining process, along with the more traditional 'bread and butter' issues of salary and tenure. In other instances, local school boards vote to adopt SBM, and plans are implemented under the direction of the district superintendent. In several states, notably Kentucky, Illinois and Texas, SBM has been mandated at the state level by the legislature (in Illinois, it applies only to the Chicago Public Schools). Thus, the decision to adopt SBM is typically made by policy-makers outside the school or even the district (Wohlstetter and McCurdy 1991). Sometimes there is resistance to such mandates by individual schools or local boards, and implementation has been slow to start and poorly executed.

At least three different forms of SBM have been implemented throughout the 1980s and 1990s. One approach is Principal control, where the school Principal is empowered to make decisions and is held accountable by the district for results. Parents and teachers may serve in an advisory capacity to the Principal, and a site council may or may not exist. A second form of SBM is administrative decentralisation or teacher control, where power is shifted down the professional hierarchy to teachers. In this model, the faculty usually elects a group of teachers to a site council that serves as the school's policy-making body. Parents and administrators sometimes serve on the council. Lastly, power and accountability shift to parents and community members under community control, the third form of SBM. The rationale behind this approach is that these groups are the chief consumers of education: parents care most about what happens to their children, and community businesses are concerned about the competencies of future employees.

Regardless of the form of SBM that is adopted, there are some common characteristics across SBM schools. First, SBM schools typically have site councils that are composed of some combination of administrators, teachers, parents, community members and occasionally students (in high schools). Members of councils are elected either by their own constituency or by the school community at large, and serve for fixed terms. In terms of power, the council may only advise the Principal, or it may be empowered to make all the major decisions at the school in the areas of budget, staffing and curriculum. Often, the Principal serves as chair of the council. Another commonality across SBM schools is the network of sub-committees, work teams, or task forces that are usually created by the school to support the work of the council. Sometimes these groups serve at the discretion of the council and make recommendations to the council for approval; at other times the groups have discretion over certain decision areas, such as student assessment or curriculum and instruction. Thus, a key feature of SBM schools is the variety of forums for discussing ideas that give many school constituents a voice in decision-making.

There is considerable variability in the elements of SBM plans that are centrally prescribed by district offices or state mandates and in those which are locally designed by individual schools. Although the form of SBM is usually prescribed, the size of the council and who chairs it can be local school decisions. High-school councils, for instance, tend to have student representatives and members of the community from local businesses, while councils at elementary schools often feature high levels of parent involvement. The scheduling of council meetings and how decisions are made (i.e. consensus v. majority vote) are also usually the decisions of individual schools. Finally, the extent to which power is transferred to schools varies across SBM plans, with budgeting responsibility devolved most frequently, followed by personnel decisions, and then decisions related to the curriculum.

Consequences of SBM reforms

Changes in how schools are organised and managed

Questions of power – how much is transferred to the school and who wields it – are among the central SBM policy issues. The districts that we studied had devolved significant authority to the schools regarding budget, personnel, and curriculum and instruction decisions. We found meaningful differences, however, in the ways that improving schools and struggling schools responded to that power.

New decision-making structures in schools

The improving schools found it advantageous to disperse power broadly throughout the school organisation and to use site councils to co-ordinate the efforts of various 'stakeholders involved in the decision-making process. This widespread involvement was accomplished through the use of council sub-committees, whose membership was open to interested parents or teachers, and grade-level teacher teams. Thus, improving schools created multiple teacher-led decision-making teams that cut across the school both horizontally (e.g. grade-level) and vertically (e.g. mathematics, science, or other discipline) to involve a broad range of school-level constituents. In addition to being members of grade-level and subject-area teams, teachers also were members of council sub-committees and other school-wide committees addressing a site priority or goal (e.g. student assessment). Interestingly, the networks of sub-committees and work teams were remarkably similar across improving schools, regardless of the particular model of SBM.

In terms of operations, the decision-making groups in improving schools tended to be structured formally, with assigned members and regular meeting times. Meeting agendas were used and sometimes were distributed prior to the meeting time. Often, minutes were taken during meetings and distributed to all teachers. Parents and community members typically were informed of major group decisions through school newsletters.

In addition, the improving schools tended to have a strategic focus. In Chicago, for example, the mandated school improvement plan is a key mechanism for bringing together parents, community members and teachers around a comprehensive, strategic plan for school development. The plan lays out goals and specific strategies for improvements. It also details a monitoring process and benchmarks by which progress will be measured. A strategic orientation helps a school resist fragmentation and incoherence in the planning and implementation of new programmes (Bryk *et al.* 1998a; Sebring and Bryk 2000).

The schools that were most successful in implementing change had a well-defined vision (values and goals regarding student outcomes) – a vision that guided curriculum and instruction reform as well as conversations in decision-making forums. This 'instructional guidance mechanism' served as a constant focus on student learning, and was continuously referred to during the decision-making process (see also David 1996; Gleason *et al.* 1996; Guskey and Peterson 1996; Newmann and Wehlage 1995). In the improving schools, this vision was frequently generated through ongoing dialogue about the school's purpose, vision and model of education. This enabled school participants to develop a common understanding of what they wanted their school to become, so they could collectively work to accomplish it. It served to frame discussions about which changes to introduce and which performance outcomes were important.

In sum, the improving schools established many forums to facilitate discussions among stakeholders about issues of teaching and learning. SBM provided more opportunities for involving a broad group of people, which effectively reduced the workload of council members and expanded the commitment to reform beyond a select few. By contrast, struggling schools tended to concentrate power in the hands of a few – often the Principal and a small group of committed teachers. Furthermore, subcommittees and other decision-making groups (if they existed at all) did not have wide participation, and the committed few often became exhausted and burned out. Worse yet, some struggling schools were embroiled in power and control issues that interfered with any vision-setting or strategic planning. As a result, they became bogged down and could not begin a dialogue about the school's purpose or a common understanding of what the school was to become.

The changing role of Principals

Principals gained considerable authority under SBM. In traditionally managed schools, Principals must accept teachers assigned by the district office (primarily based on seniority), but, under devolved management, Principals often recruited and hired the professional staff that they wanted. Principals carefully recruited competent new teachers who would contribute to the emerging vision of the school. In Chicago, where discretionary monies accompanied local control, new funds were instrumental in hiring additional teachers. Principals also worked to counsel poorly performing teachers.

Effective Principals, regardless of the model of SBM, frequently sought input from various stakeholders, so that at the same time that Principals gained authority, they shared power with a wide range of participants in order to broaden the commitment to reform. So, for example, in schools that operated under Principal-based management, Principals typically consulted with and relied on the advice of a representative council in making their decisions. Thus, Principals at improving SBM schools typically used an inclusive, facilitative approach to management.

Across the various models of SBM, Principals spent increasing amounts of time on managerial responsibilities. Principals at improving schools were viewed by teachers as efficient managers – 'things got done' in these schools. Teachers had the books that they required to start classes. Principals secured academic and social support services for students in need, so that classroom disruptions were minimised. Principals also shielded teachers from issues in which they had little interest or expertise, so they could concentrate on improving teaching and learning. Finally, Principals served as liaisons to the outside world, bringing in new ideas and funding to the school (Sebring and Bryk 2000; Wohlstetter and Briggs 1994). Principals also were personally visible in the community. Their actions ranged from serving on local community/business boards; to giving talks in the community to stem negative perceptions about the school; to stopping a neighbourhood liquor store from marketing products to students (Bryk et al. 1998b: chapter 6).

Principals in improving schools worked to focus the school community on student learning. They set high standards for teaching, and encouraged teachers to take risks and try new methods of teaching. Such Principals regularly visited classrooms to demonstrate their interest and to monitor improvements in instruction. Building on their knowledge of curriculum and instruction, such Principals were skilled at developing and articulating a 'vision in outline' for the school. They worked hard to create opportunities to invite teachers and parents to further elaborate and shape the vision.

By contrast, SBM was less successful when Principals worked from their own agenda rather than helping to develop a common one. This has also been found in other studies of SBM (i.e. Lindle 1996). Many Principals in struggling schools were perceived by their staff as being too autocratic. These Principals often loaded up the council with trivial details, and typically identified, on their own, a vision for the school that presented it as a *fait accompli* to the staff. This often led to a power struggle between teachers and the Principal, and in some schools the faculty simply rejected the Principal's unilateral agenda for change. Teachers frequently referred to 'the Principal's vision' in these schools, and often were not willing to accept guidance and leadership from the Principal because they felt little sense of ownership and accountability to the plan.

New players in school-level decision-making

The SBM schools that have been able to institute changes in teaching and learning have a broad base of leadership that often includes a cadre of teachers and parent/community leaders, in addition to the Principal. Thus, SBM schools tended to focus on developing leadership bases among many stakeholder groups, both within and outside the school community.

Teachers

Involvement of teachers in SBM schools varied widely from advisory roles to decision-making positions. Sometimes the teachers' span of influence was limited to a few issues, while, at other schools, teachers rose to become instructional leaders (formerly the Principal's responsibility), making decisions that affected many areas of school operations. Across most SBM schools, teachers held a majority of seats on the site council, and increasingly were making decisions in non-instruction areas, participating in hiring and other school-management decisions, and helping to establish school policies. This is not the case in Chicago, where parents are in the majority on the local school councils.

In the improving schools, a cadre of teachers took on many of the governance issues surrounding SBM, including responsibilities such as material selection, budget development and professional development schedules (see also Gleason *et al.* 1996). In many cases, for example, these teachers assumed leadership in introducing ideas about new instructional practices. Furthermore, these teacher leaders were effective at ensuring that all stakeholders felt welcome to participate in decisions, particularly those that concerned them directly, and in broadening and sustaining the school's commitment to reform.

As David (1996) found, this cadre of teacher leaders was able to foster shared leadership and accountability to the school-wide programme among a broad range of individuals throughout the school. This picture of broad, participatory leadership differed starkly from that found in the struggling schools, where teachers who introduced new practices often did so only in their own classrooms and played no real leadership role with the rest of the school.

To build internal capacity for change and improvement, Principals made major commitments to the professional development of teachers, especially in the areas of curriculum, instruction and, to a lesser extent, teamwork and budgeting. They created time for this to occur, and allocated school discretionary resources to support it. Building this human resource capacity usually involved entering into relationships with outside agencies, such as universities, non-profit organisations or federal regional educational laboratories, to obtain training and consultation. Moreover, successful professional development was sustained, of high quality, delivered at the school level, and clearly tied to school-wide goals (Kruse *et al.* 1995).

The improving schools also broadened the subject matter of training. In addition to training in teaching, learning, curriculum and assessment, schools offered instruction in interpersonal skills (group decision-making, consensus-building, and conflict-resolution); in management skills (running meetings, budgeting, and interviewing); and in the process of school improvement.

Professional development activities at the improving schools were strategic, in that they were deliberately tied to each school's reform objectives. These activities were often aligned with the school's mission and goals for introducing innovations in curriculum and instruction and improving student performance. The Center on Organization and Restructuring of Schools also found such alignment to be a critical component of effective SBM (Newmann and Wehlage 1995). At many of the schools that were studied, the council or a separate decision-making group assessed professional development needs, and planned and coordinated development activities to meet those needs.

In the improving schools, there was an emerging professional community. This meant that there were regular opportunities for reflective dialogue among educators about practice, pedagogy and student learning.

Teachers opened their classroom doors and shared their work with peers. Rather than just following rules and regulations, teachers were motivated by a growing consensus regarding their beliefs and values about student learning (Sebring *et al.* 1995).

By contrast, there was little evidence of professional community in struggling schools, and they typically viewed professional development as an individual activity rather than a means of creating school-wide capacity for improvement. Often the target group for training was only the small group of individuals who sat on the site council. In these schools, there were found more instances of 'one shot' training of the 'go, sit, and get' variety rather than on-going professional development models. Some teachers were able to opt out of professional development altogether. At one struggling school that was attempting a school-wide focus, more than a quarter of the staff was absent on staff development days.

Parents

SBM usually increased the authority of parents with respect to school policy and their level of involvement in school operations. At the extreme was the community control model of SBM where parents and other community members constituted a majority on the school councils. In Chicago, for example, their mandated duties included selecting a Principal, influencing and approving the school improvement plan, and approving the budget. Indeed, in many SBM schools, councils were a significant resource for building parent involvement and connections to community and social service organisations (Ryan *et al.* 1997; Wohlstetter *et al.* 1997b). In the improving schools, parents were sometimes recruited, specifically for their expertise, to serve on particular work teams (e.g. technology).

The evidence suggests, moreover, that expanded participation by the local community in school decisions provided strong social support for fundamental change in the school. Structures, such as work teams, that encourage interactions among parents, community members and educators, help to crystallise shared concerns and mobilise people to action (Bryk *et al.* 1998b). Nevertheless, schools varied in the intensity of parental involvement, with many schools seeing only marginal involvement of parents in decision-making (e.g. working parents have difficulty attending council meetings). In fact, the number of parents in Chicago running for school councils has been declining.

As David (1996) and Guskey and Peterson (1996) found, extending professional development beyond teachers and including all stakeholders were helpful in encouraging active participation in the decision-making process. The improving elementary schools supported parents in their parental role by offering parent training classes, and by teaching parents ways to monitor homework and reinforce learning at home (see also Epstein 1995). However, in struggling schools there were no such initiatives, and many parents did not feel comfortable coming to the school, especially parents whose first language was not English. Like the teachers, parents who sat on local councils were typically not trained for their new decision-making responsibilities, and so had difficulty participating effectively in educational decisions and school-management decisions unless they arrived on the job already trained (Wohlstetter *et al.* 1994).

An altered role for the district office

Devolving power and authority to local schools necessarily alters the policy orientation and activities of the district office. Without restructuring the district office, schools were unlikely to make changes because of the tensions that arose when expectations and controls under centralised management were left intact. Furthermore, even when power and authority are successfully devolved, schools continue to need assistance with the improvement process. Research suggests that district offices can contribute positively to the success of devolved management in three ways: (1) promoting real autonomy at the local level; (2) supporting schools in building local capacity and stimulating innovation; and (3) establishing an accountability system that serves both the district and local schools (Bryk *et al.* 1998b: chapter 7). In most districts studied, district office administrators were often not prepared for such changes. As in the case of the school-level SBM participants, there was little evidence that district administrators received training to undertake their new roles and responsibilities (Wohlstetter *et al.* 1994).

Promoting autonomy

Earlier research (Wohlstetter and Odden 1992) determined that most school councils created under SBM had little real power, often operating as advisers or endorsers in the decision-making process, rather than as policy-making bodies. After the dust cleared from 'implementing SBM', school administrators and teachers were given little to manage. Thus, school participants found it difficult to influence central issues of curriculum and instruction, and school councils focused instead on peripheral issues, such as building operations (e.g. school schedules, fundraising) and implementing district directives.

When the district had a deliberate policy to promote autonomy at the local level, schools were more likely to use their power to improve teaching and learning. Superintendents and other district office administrators consciously altered their roles to become less mandate-minded and more service-oriented. In Edmonton (Canada), for example, schools had money for professional development and maintenance, and purchased those services from outside the district. District office departments offering such services became school-oriented, as they had to sell their services to schools in order to stay in existence.

Building local capacity and stimulating innovations

School districts often failed to provide struggling schools with the timely information on the management and operation of the school, so that local actors could make informed decisions. Traditionally, corporations and district offices have gathered the aggregate information most useful for making system-wide decisions, but this is insufficient in SBM – where schools need easy access to the information as well (see David 1996 for similar findings). In Australia, Victoria's solution was to install an on-line, interactive computer system in its schools, with data on budgets and personnel, student achievement, electronic invoicing and purchasing, and a master schedule. This computer network was by far the most advanced among the districts that we studied, although several other districts, including Edmonton, Jefferson County (Kentucky) and Chicago, have linked the school sites electronically with the district office.

Salary scales were rarely changed in ways that would provide the incentives necessary for sustained involvement in school-based decision-making and reform. Unfortunately, too many districts mistakenly seemed to assume that no extra energy and commitment were needed to undertake SBM. A common result, over time, was that participation among teachers decreased after a few years; the majority of teachers became disengaged, while a small group of teachers handled most of the responsibilities. The experiences of organisations outside education are instructive with respect to the kinds of incentives necessary to sustain reform (Lawler 1986, 1990). Although options vary, a core element of any plan for SBM participants would include a salary element for the new knowledge and skills that the participants acquire and develop in order to implement reforms in school and classroom practices.

District office restructuring and total quality management efforts in Jefferson County, Prince William County (Virginia) and San Diego (California), promoted the notion of the schools as the customers of district departments. 'You never have to make more than two calls', offered the superintendent of Jefferson County to his Principals. 'Make the first call to the appropriate district department, and if they're not responsive, the next call should be to me.'

Superintendents can also provide schools with support by developing a district-wide culture of risk-taking. The superintendent in Jefferson County encouraged schools 'to go out on a limb' – to try something new either instructionally or with the curriculum – and supported them by offering extra money for professional development to all schools that voted to adopt SBM. In general, schools needed this support from the district office in order to build local commitment for undertaking the massive task of restructuring.

As David (1996) and Newmann and Wehlage (1995) found, the improving schools tended to be in districts that provided schools with resources for professional development. These schools often looked outside the district organisation to private companies, universities, and research institutes for technical assistance and training in management and group decision-making. Struggling schools relied on the district to provide training and, as a result, the subject matter of professional development activities often was restricted to the topics that were identified by the district office.

Establishing a system of accountability

An underlying premise of SBM is that school-level participants trade increased autonomy for increased accountability. Under SBM, schools are empowered to make decisions, while, at the same time, being held accountable by the district and the community for improving student performance. Research to date suggests that the best assurance of accountability is strong professional norms among the teachers, coupled with informed parent and community involvement (Bryk *et al.* 1998b: chapter 7; Wohlstetter and Griffin 1998). At the same time, each school is accountable to district leaders, who need to know that schools are fulfilling their responsibilities to children and using resources effectively. District leaders also need to be vigilant about inequities in educational opportunities that can emerge in a devolved system, as schools with more capable staff and more involved parents surge ahead of others.

One of the more important principles of an accountability system is coherence between the district office and schools, in terms of goals and objectives. There is a real threat that an accountability system under devolved management could undermine the values and strengths of local control. What happens if the district administration imposes standards and timelines that are inconsistent with legitimate goals and objectives of schools? Schools are then caught between multiple and conflicting standards and expectations. Therefore, a key function of the district office in designing an accountability system is to determine what conditions are allowed to vary from school to school, and what conditions must remain the same.

Another aim of an accountability system is to identify low-performing schools, so that corrective action can be taken. In such cases, district administrators have used their authority to place schools on remediation or probation. In a few instances, schools have been reconstituted – the local school council is dissolved, and new teachers are installed at the school.

Besides the obvious need to know about low-performing schools, however, there are two other critical aims of an accountability system. One is to identify sites of exemplary practice, so that other schools can learn from them. The other is to acknowledge the progress that schools are making. In some systems, schools falling in these latter two categories receive rewards or incentives. One important side benefit of such an accountability system is that district offices tend to become increasingly knowledgeable about individual schools and their reform designs. With this information, the district office can serve effectively as a clearinghouse for information – helping to connect schools that are working on similar reforms, and partnering low performers with schools that are more successful.

A system of external accountability that is compatible with the basic rationale of devolved management will also strengthen the knowledge and skills of local participants. To accomplish this requires that the district office report data in a way that is meaningful to various stakeholders, especially to school staff and parents. In the United States, standardised test scores are the primary type of information that is used for accountability. Space does not permit discussion of the complexity of measuring student achievement over time by school, but it demands considerable care. Measuring student achievement over time requires that tests be the same from year to year, but new items will also need to be introduced to reflect new learning objectives and to provide for test security. In addition, researchers have begun to make use of value-added approaches to assessment that take into account students' achievement level when they enter a particular grade (Bryk *et al.* 1998b: chapter 7; Bryk *et al.* 1998c). Other sources of complexity, such as student mobility and comparing schools with different family-income levels, also need to be addressed.

Beyond test scores, evidence is needed regarding the efforts that school staff are making in order to improve teaching and learning. Otherwise it is impossible to understand some of the reasons behind rising, flat or declining test scores. Hence, multiple indicators and in-person observations are also critical elements of an accountability system.

Concluding remarks

Given the range and diversity of the districts, schools and forms of school-based management that were included in the analysis, we believe that these findings are likely to be generalisable to many schools interested in using devolved management to bring about significant improvement in school performance.

The evidence suggests that there are tangible advantages to SBM if it is fully implemented, and if local leaders use their authority and resources to strengthen the essential supports for student learning. School-level participants have shown that they can assess student needs and make changes to improve professional practice and student learning. However, by itself, devolving power and authority to schools will not ensure that they will work to strengthen the essential supports for learning. Schools need the support of the district administration and usually the help of external partners. In addition, schools need to establish the structures, processes and incentives that will more fully involve the various constituents in school improvement efforts.

With greater autonomy, entrepreneurial Principals and teachers can move forward. Yet schools differ with respect to the strength of their human resources, and those with weak Principals, demoralised teachers and apathetic site councils are likely to stagnate. Consequently, under devolved management, variations across schools can become more marked.

Low-performing schools present a serious policy challenge for districts and states. In Chicago, as well as other cities in the United States, superintendents have begun to intervene and put schools on probation or reconstitute the schools. The research has only begun to assess the effectiveness of these policies, but clearly, implementation requires considerable care, based on high-quality information and expert advice. The balance between local and central control is extremely delicate. If there is too much intervention, devolved management becomes meaningless. On the other hand, if there is little monitoring, the central authority forsakes its responsibility for education. One of the keys to managing this balance may be for the central administration to emphasise its role in building local capacity, stimulating innovation and holding schools accountable for student performance.

Notes

1 The Center on Educational Governance, located at the University of Southern California, unites faculties from the Schools of Education, Business and Public Administration to conduct research on educational governance and management, focused on improving the productivity of elementary and secondary schools. The Center, which receives government and foundation support, combines research, aimed at building new theories about what makes schools work, with action research and dissemination activities, in order to spread best practices broadly and deeply. The Consortium on Chicago School Research is an independent federation of Chicago area organisations that conducts research activities designed to advance school improvement in Chicago's public schools and to assess the progress of school reform. Its members include faculties from area universities, leadership from the Chicago Public Schools, the Chicago Teachers' Union, education advocacy groups, and the Illinois State Board of Education. Consortium studies are funded by several private foundations.

2 Sample school districts in the United States included: Bellevue, Washington; Chicago, Illinois; Denver, Colorado; Jefferson County, Kentucky; Milwaukee, Wisconsin; Prince William County, Virginia; Rochester, New York; San Diego, California; and Sweetwater (National City), California. Center researchers also visited 14 schools in Edmonton, Alberta (Canada) and Victoria, Australia.

References

Bryk, A., Sebring, P., Easton, J., Luppescu, S., Thum, Y., Nagaoka, J. and Bilcer, D. (1998a) 'Chicago School Reform: Linkages Between Local Control, Organizational Change, and Student Achievement', Unpublished paper presented at the American Educational Research Association, San Diego.

Bryk, A., Sebring, P., Kerbow, D., Rollow, S. and Easton, J. (1998b) *Charting Chicago School Reform: Democratic Localism as Lever for Change*, Boulder, CO: Westview Press.

Bryk, A., Thum, Y., Easton, J. and Luppescu, S. (1998c) 'Academic Productivity of Chicago Public Elementary Schools', Unpublished paper presented at the Consortium on Chicago School Research, Chicago: University of Chicago.

David, J. (1996) 'The Who, What, and Why of Site-based Management', *Educational Leadership*, **53(4)**: 4–9.

Epstein, J. (1995) 'School/Family/Community Partnership', *Phi Delta Kappan*, **76(5)**: 701–12.

Gleason, S., Donohue, N. and Leader, G. (1996) 'Boston Revisits School-Based Management', *Educational Leadership*, **53(4)**: 24–7.

Guskey, T. and Peterson, K. (1996) 'The Road to Classroom Change', *Educational Leadership*, **53(4)**: 10–14.

Kruse, S., Louis, K. and Bryk, A. (1995) *Professionalism and Community: Perspectives on Reforming Urban Schools*, Thousand Oaks, California: Corwin Press.

Lawler, E. (1986) *High-involvement Management*, San Francisco: Jossey-Bass.

Lawler, E. (1990) *Strategic Pay: Aligning Organizational Strategies and Pay Systems*, San Francisco: Jossey-Bass.

Lindle, J. (1996) 'Lessons from Kentucky About School-based Decision-making', *Educational Leadership*, **53(4)**: 20–3.

Mohrman, S. (1994) 'High-involvement Management in the Private Sector', in Mohrman, S. and Wohlstetter, P. and associates (eds) *School-based Management: Organizing for High Performance*, San Francisco: Jossey-Bass.

Murphy, J. and Beck, L. (1995) *School-based Management as School Reform: Taking Stock*, Thousand Oaks, California: Corwin Press.

Newmann, F. and Wehlage, G. (1995) *Successful School Restructuring: a Report to the Public and Educators*, Madison, WI: University of Wisconsin, Center on Organization and Restructuring of Schools.

Peck, B. (1997) 'Devolution in Decision Making: Some Changes in National Approaches', *Phi Delta Kappan*, **78(7)**: 582–83.

Robertson, P., Wohlstetter, P. and Mohrman, S. (1995) 'Generating Curriculum and Instructional Changes Through School-based Management', *Educational Administration Quarterly*, **31(3)**: 375–404.

Ryan, S., Bryk, A., Lopez, G., Williams, K., Hall, K. and Luppescu, S. (1997) *Charting Reform: LSCs – Local Leadership at Work*, Chicago: University of Chicago, Consortium on Chicago School Research.

Sebring, P. and Bryk, A. (2000) 'Principal Leadership and the Bottom Line in Chicago', *Phi Delta Kappan*, **81(5)**.

Sebring, P., Bryk, A., Easton, J., Luppescu, S., Thum, Y., Lopez, W. and Smith, B. (1995) *Charter Reform: Chicago Teachers Take Stock*, Chicago: University of Chicago, Consortium on Chicago School Research.

Sebring, P., Bryk, A., Roderick, M., Camburn, E., Luppescu, S., Thum, Y., Smith, B. and Kahne, J. (1996) *Charting Chicago School Reform: the Students Speak*, Chicago: University of Chicago, Consortium on Chicago School Research.

Wohlstetter, P. and Briggs, K. (1994) 'The Principal's Role in School-based Management', *Principal*, **74(11)**: 14–17.

Wohlstetter, P. and Griffin, N. (1998) *First Lessons: Charter Schools as Learning Communities*, Pittsburgh: Consortium for Policy Research in Education, University of Pennsylvania.

Wohlstetter, P. and McCurdy, K. (1991) 'The Link Between School Decentralization and School Politics', *Urban Education*, **25(4)**: 391–414.

Wohlstetter, P. and Mohrman, S. (1996) *Studies of Education Reform: Assessment of School-based Management*, Washington, DC: U.S. Department of Education, Office of Educational Research and Improvement.

Wohlstetter, P. and Odden, A. (1992) 'Rethinking School-based Management Policy and Research', *Educational Administration Quarterly*, **28(4)**: 529–49.

Wohlstetter, P., Smyer, R. and Mohrman, S. (1994) 'New Boundaries for School-based Management: the High Involvement Model', *Educational Evaluation and Policy Analysis*, **16(3)**: 268–86.

Wohlstetter, P., Mohrman, S. and Robertson, P. (1997a) 'Successful School-based Management: Lessons for Restructuring Urban Schools', in Ravitch, D. and

Viteritti, J. (eds) *New Schools for a New Century: the Redesign of Urban Education*, New Haven, CT: Yale University Press.

Wohlstetter, P., Van Kirk, A., Robertson, P. and Mohrman, S. (1997b) *Organizing for Successful School-based Management*, Alexandria, VA: Association for Supervision and Curriculum Development.

8 Devolved management in New Zealand schools

Kerry Jacobs

Introduction

Smyth (1993) has argued that, in many countries, educational bureaucracies are being replaced by devolved forms of school-based management. These reforms involve a combination of New Right 'marketisation', community empowerment, new forms of performance measurement and central control. While devolved management involves state withdrawal from direct intervention in the day-to-day operation of schools, in many cases this is accompanied by indirect control or management structures, allowing the state to steer the education process from a distance.

This chapter describes the devolved management reforms in New Zealand and analyses how the new responsibilities were managed at the school level. During the 1980s and 1990s New Zealand was subject to dramatic social and economic restructuring which transformed the country from one of the most protected to an entrepreneurial, free-market economy (Osborne and Gaebler 1992: 330). The operation of the public sector was also substantially restructured, with many of the state trading activities being privatised and the remaining core being subject to private-sector management practices and performance measures. Reform of the education system occurred in the context of these wider structural and economic changes. This chapter provides a description of the nature of the New Zealand education reforms and an assessment of their impact on several schools. A central aspect of the New Zealand education reforms was the devolution of financial and administrative responsibility to the school level.

Devolution of financial responsibility has been significant in the United Kingdom models of devolved management in education. The heart of the Local Management of Schools (LMS) initiative in England and Wales is formula funding and the devolution of budgets and financial responsibilities to schools. Schools are also called to account in financial terms, and the question of markets and market performance can be seen as an extension of the budgetary responsibility, as schools are obliged to attract students in order to balance their budget. However, there is some concern in the British literature about how the financial responsibilities of the schools are balanced with their educational responsibilities (McGovern 1992). Studies of the English 'devolved management of schools' initiative indicate that financial management responsibilities have often been delegated to small groups, allowing the 'real work' of the school to go unhindered (Bowe and Ball 1992; Broadbent *et al.* 1993). Laughlin *et al.* (1994) extended the idea of small groups managing the LMS process within the school, but indicated that the very individuals who intended to 'absorb' change could become a force for change within the organisation, and could redefine the core values of the schools.

The question to be addressed here is whether the issues and patterns observed in the British literature are repeated in the New Zealand context. Is devolved financial management alien to the school environment, or can schools adjust and accommodate the new responsibilities? Do small groups absorb the changes, or do the changes lead to a redefinition of core values within the schools?

The next part of the chapter provides a historical background of the development of the education system in New Zealand. The third part describes the education reform in New Zealand, followed by an exploration of how the specific schools that were studied balanced the new managerial responsibilities with their existing educational obligations, and how they responded to the tension between central control and local autonomy.

The development of the New Zealand education system

The history of formal education in New Zealand is relatively short, as it is linked to European colonisation. In 1840, the British government signed a treaty with the indigenous Maori population, guaranteeing them civil, political and religious rights. This treaty was followed by a flood of immigration, which strengthened the place of the religious organisations that had already been active among the Maori population. The origin of the education system in New Zealand can be found in the work of these religious organisations, particularly the Anglicans, the Methodists and the Roman Catholics (Cummings and Cummings 1978). With the establishment of a representative government in 1853, education became the duty of the provinces, which established school committees and started to levy the local population to pay for schooling.

However, in the 1870s, the central government sought to secure control over education. Their key argument for centralisation was to obtain uniformity of provision throughout the colony. The Education Boards Act 1876 and the Education Act 1877 saw the establishment of a Department of Education, ten regional education boards and individual school committees. The Department represented the central-government interests, while the regional education boards and the school committees were meant to provide a degree of local control. However, the Department of Education effectively dominated the process (Cummings and Cummings 1978: 94). This led to a highly centralised and highly interventionist system of state education:

> New Zealand's education system has been for many years one of the most centralised in the world. Whilst Britain's system relied heavily on the intermediary role of the Local Education Authorities, New Zealand had only a minimal regional level of organisation mainly focusing on the primary schools and playing a servicing rather than a policy role.
>
> (Gordon 1992a: 281)

Between 1877 and 1988, the Department of Education was the primary steering mechanism concerned with the operation of schools. The Department tended to be staffed by teachers and educationists, and was generally seen as supporting staff within the schools. Rather than clashing with the schools, the Department reinforced the 'educational values' that were considered important within schools, particularly concepts of equality within and between schools, and excellence in teaching (Gordon 1992a). The Department of Education allocated funds to the regional education boards, who were responsible for purchasing services on behalf of the individual primary schools. As secondary schools developed, they were not accountable to the local education board, but were run by boards of governors who dealt directly with the local office of the Department of Education. The Department maintained control over funding and teaching within secondary schools. The funding was allocated to the schools along strict budget lines, which gave schools little financial discretion. Teachers' salaries were negotiated annually between the teachers' union – the Post Primary Teachers' Association – and the government. The Department also maintained control over student access to secondary education and over teaching standards. Most of the secondary schools were subject to a zoning system, which required them to accept all student applications from the area specified by the Department as 'their zone'. The Department's inspectorate also inspected secondary schools, although there was no inspection of individual teachers, as there was in primary schools.

The election of the first Labour government, which remained in power between 1935 and 1949, cemented the principle of equal educational opportunity and education as a right of all citizens as the basis of the New Zealand system; therefore, education was a public good to be provided by the State (Grace 1990). However, during the 1980s, many of the fundamental aspects of social and economic policy were challenged by a New Right (Lauder 1987) ideology emanating from the Treasury.

Education reforms

After its election in 1984, the fourth Labour government abandoned the interventionist economic policies that had been in place and adopted a free-market economic policy (Jesson 1989: 66). The Treasury played a significant role in the transformation of economic policy and secured considerable influence over key individuals within the Cabinet (Codd 1993). In their post-election brief to the government, the Treasury paid notable attention to the area of education, devoting one volume of their two-volume briefing to that area. The Treasury (1987) recommended that state intervention in education should be minimised, and that the education should be restructured around markets, contracts and consumer choice, rather than state provision and control. They argued that, where 'government imposition between customer and provider was unavoidable', the institutions should be subject to 'methods of management and accountability'.

Grace (1990) has argued that the Treasury was crucial in creating an education policy crisis in New Zealand. Together with articles from the mass media (du Chateau 1987), it succeeded in creating a state of moral panic, in which the education bureaucracy and the teaching profession were presented as radical and subversive groups which had 'captured' the education process for their own interests. It was therefore necessary that the government seize back control of the education system from these vested interests (Grace 1990: 173). The basis of the crisis was not a concern with falling school performance,[1] but a concern that 'liberal and feminist dominated teacher unions' were corrupting a future generation (du Chateau 1987: 20). The existing systems were also severely criticised for failing to deliver on the fundamental principle of equality, particularly in terms of the Maori population (New Zealand Council for Educational Research 1987: 2). The Treasury presented education reform as the solution to the perceived problems of 'provider capture' and Maori inequality. However, it was evident that the central motive behind the Treasury proposals was a concern about the costs associated with free access and state provision of education (The Treasury 1987: 3).

The then Prime Minister, David Lange, had some reservations about the New Right reforms recommended by the Treasury, but argued that there was a need to respond to the growing public concern with 'provider capture' and state sector spending (Lange 1987: 28). On 21 July 1987, the government announced a Taskforce to Review Education Administration. The terms of reference required the Taskforce to recommend how the functions of the Department of Education could be delegated, and how the powers (and responsibilities) of the schools could be increased, reflecting concerns with both the issue of 'provider capture' and empowering local communities. The composition of the Taskforce also reflected a mix of both business and educationist perspectives (Macpherson 1989: 32).

The Taskforce's Report (Picot *et al.* 1988) was critical of what it saw as 'serious weaknesses' in the existing education system. It argued that the present administrative structure was over-centralised and overly complex, the existing management practices were ineffective, and the information needed to make choices was not available. As a result, those within the system felt powerless to make necessary changes (Picot *et al.* 1988: xi). It recommended a major devolution of management responsibility to the school level, and that the previously powerful Department of Education should lose its management role and focus solely on the provision of policy advice. Many of the Picot recommendations have a strong similarity to the 1987 Treasury brief, leading Codd (1990) to argue that there was collusion. Grace (1990) also argued that the restructuring of education administration served to secure the role of the Treasury as the pre-eminent policy voice in education. Historically, the Treasury had very little role, other than fiscal overview, in the area of education. However, with the restructuring of the Department of Education, the Treasury had effectively secured their position and their ideological dominance in the area of educational policy:

> The replacement of a mediated relationship between the state and the school by a direct relation raised large questions about exactly who had become empowered as a result. A diffuse collection of boards of trustees and community forums throughout New Zealand was unlikely to constitute a significant power bloc, which Treasury would have to deal with in future struggles over education policy.
>
> (Grace 1990: 181)

Within three months of the issue of the Picot Report, the Minister of

Education released his policy statement, *Tomorrow's Schools*, which announced that most of the Picot proposals would be implemented by 1 October 1989. The key structural changes contained in Picot and *Tomorrow's Schools* became incorporated in a major revision of the Education Act (the Education Act 1989 and the Education Amendment Act 1990). Therefore, in 1990, a Ministry of Education, which was concerned only with providing policy advice, replaced the Department. The support functions of the education boards and the Department of Education were turned into private, and therefore contestable, service providers. Other functions of the Department of Education were separated into new 'stand alone' organisations (the Parent Advocacy Council, the Early Childhood Development Unit, the Special Education Service, Quest Rapuara (The Careers Service), the Education and Training Support Agency, the Education Review Office (ERO), and the New Zealand Qualifications Authority (NZQA).

The Department of Education and the local education boards were disbanded, and responsibility for school management was devolved to the school level. The basis of the devolved management structure was the creation of boards of trustees within each school. In 1990, parents were invited to stand as trustees of primary and secondary schools, after being informed, through a government-funded advertising campaign, that if they could manage a child they could manage a school (Gordon 1992b: 188). In 1991, the Education Reform Act changed the rules and allowed anyone, not just parents of children at the school, to be elected to a board of trustees. This was specifically aimed at encouraging businesses to become involved in school management (Gordon 1992a: 288). The trustees are legally responsible under Section 64 of the Education Act 1989 for the performance of all aspects of the school and, while they have the freedom to decide how to run the school, they are required to respond to community educational needs and to comply with national guidelines for education.

The key aspect of devolved management in New Zealand was that funding would go directly to the school, rather than indirectly through the Department of Education or through the various education boards. This was the case for the operational grant, which covered administration, ancillary support, maintenance and the non-salary aspects of teaching. However, the teachers and the teachers' unions strongly resisted the devolution of the teaching salary grant (Gordon 1992b: 285) and it remained the responsibility of the Ministry of Education (Education Act 1989, Section 89).

However, the devolution of management autonomy to the school level was accompanied by a number of new forms of control and visibility.

Under the Education Act 1989 and the Public Finance Act 1989, each school was required to prepare annual financial statements for the Crown in accordance with private-sector accounting standards. Under Section 84 of the Education Act 1989, the financial statements and the school financial management system are subject to audit by Audit New Zealand. The audit report is to comment on the school's compliance with the Education Act 1989 and the Public Finance Act 1989, and on whether the statements fairly reflect the financial state of the school. Elementary-school league-tables were also produced by the Ministry of Education on an annual basis, as the statistical annex to the Ministry's annual report; however, these reports were discontinued from 1996.

Many of the key responsibilities of the school were defined by the government. The national guidelines provided an important mechanism for the State to specify particular aspects of education and for translating central policy into local reality. Guidelines were issued, covering areas such as: codes of conduct for trustees and Principals, expressions of the principles underpinning educational administration, and details of national curriculum objectives.[2]

The establishment of a national curriculum was retained as a responsibility of the Ministry of Education. The curriculum objectives standardise the curriculum taught in New Zealand schools, and specify the achievement aims and the objectives for learning. All schools are required to comply with the curriculum objectives. Together with the standardisation of curriculum came the establishment of a unified, national system of qualifications. The government policy document *Learning for Life* (Lange and Goff 1989) and the Education Amendment Act (1990) saw the establishment of a single qualifications authority with responsibility for all nationally recognised qualifications: the NZQA. The NZQA established a modular qualifications and curriculum structure, known as the 'national qualifications framework'. Unit standards were established by the NZQA for a wide range of academic and vocational topics. Secondary schools have to gain accreditation from NZQA and must adjust their teaching curriculum to comply with the unit standards. To maintain their accreditation, schools have to participate in a moderation system, and are subject to review by the NZQA.

The key to enforcing the new administrative and educational obligations in the devolved management environment is the ERO. The ERO provides a monitoring mechanism to ensure that schools fulfil their contractual obligations and comply with the education guidelines and curriculum framework. To ensure their compliance, each school is subject to a regular assurance-audit review once every two or three years. The ERO also developed a second review process, which they called an effectiveness review. Based on the concept of 'value added', the ERO attempts to measure what a student has learned from the programmes provided by the school.

In many ways, the relationship between education and the State can be seen as a pendulum, swinging between State control over the operation of schools at the periphery and the desire to shift the problems of operation, management and funding away from the centre. Redvall's (1993) study of the decentralisation of Swedish schools illustrates this tension. He found two contrasting tendencies: first, the decentralisation provided an increasing freedom of choice, both for parents in the selection of schools, and for the schools in how they operated. The second tendency was a centralising drive for a common curriculum, and for national testing and examination of results. This tendency restricted the freedom to develop different curricula and teaching styles in the schools, therefore restricting parental choice among schools. Codd and Gordon's (1991: 22) study of the New Zealand reforms goes one step further and argues that the strategic aims of devolution were first to give the central agencies of the State more control over economic supply and political demand; and second to shift the focus of legitimation problems away from central government. While the rhetoric indicated that schools would have more autonomy, the creation of new organisations such as the NZQA and the ERO indicated that the devolution was limited and was accompanied by a new form of centralism and control that facilitated management from a distance.

To summarise, the New Zealand education reforms involved a massive restructuring of central and regional administrative functions. Many of the financial responsibilities previously handled by the Department of Education or the regional education boards were delegated to the school. In this sense, the changes were similar – in general – to the LMS reforms in England and Wales and the Devolved School Management reforms in Scotland. However, the delegation of responsibility was associated with a new form of centralism based on the creation of new review agencies. The question addressed in the next part of the chapter is how schools actually responded to the new responsibilities and the new forms of visibility.

Description of the research project

The project on which this chapter is based involved an empirical study of the effects of devolution and education reforms in New Zealand. Four schools were selected in the city of Christchurch, from a Department of Education list of local schools. As it seemed likely that the size, the nature of the school (primary or secondary) and the socio-economic area would be likely to affect the response of the organisations to the reforms (see Gordon *et al*. 1994), the schools were selected to provide a variety in type, size and socio-economic area, although no attempt was made to obtain a 'random' sample in a statistical sense.[3] The schools are:

- Matai is a state primary school in a poor socio-economic area. Much of the local housing is state owned (council flats), and a large number of the residents are on some form of state support. Matai is a small school, with a roll of only 160 students and 15 teachers on the staff, and they find it difficult to attract and hold students. Many of the students in the school have social and learning difficulties.

- Deans is a state primary school situated in a wealthy socio-economic area. Many of the residents are employed in professional and managerial jobs (73 per cent of the parents in the school) and have degree qualifications. The net family income is NZ$10,000 p.a. higher than the national and the city-wide average. Deans is a large primary school with a roll of just under 500 students in 1995.

- Straven High is a state secondary school. It is situated in a middle-class neighbourhood, although it draws students from a wide area. The roll in 1995 was over 2,000 students and there were more than 100 teaching staff, which makes Straven one of the largest schools in the region. The school has a reputation for high levels of academic achievement in state examinations.

- Aroha College is a state secondary school. It is located in a working-class area, where most of the residents are on an average or below-average income. Although the school was built for nearly 1,000 students, in 1995 Aroha had a roll of only 480 students.

The research method was based on the work of Moustakas (1990) and Broadbent and Laughlin (1997), and involved interviews, discussions and non-participant observation. The research process involved a number of different individuals – the Principal, teachers, administrative staff and school trustees – and was conducted over a twenty-seven-month period between August 1993 and December 1995. Most of the interviews were unstructured and involved a single participant, although several – particularly trustee meetings – involved more than one individual. The interviews and meetings were taped, transcribed by the interviewer, and returned to the participants for comment and amendment. The key themes addressed in the interviews were first how the schools were managing the devolved management responsibilities, and second how the agencies such as ERO and NZQA were influencing the school.

Impacts and outcomes

Surrounding the *Tomorrow's Schools* reforms was the rhetoric of devolution: that education was too controlled by the centre and captured by bureaucratic interests, that it was inefficient, and that autonomy should be devolved to the local, and indeed the school level (Grace 1990). This rhetoric provided the logic for the restructuring of the Department of Education, the closure of the education boards and the creation of Boards of Trustees within each school.

The major impact of the restructuring at the school level was the devolution of financial and administrative responsibilities. Under the *Tomorrow's Schools* reforms, operational funding was allocated directly to schools as a bulk grant, with the exception of teachers' salaries, which continued to be administered by the Ministry. The change in funding arrangements led to a massive increase in the amount of money that individual schools had to manage. The Principal of Straven explained:

> Prior to the reforms we were responsible for the government grant of about $140,000, now it is $1.2 million. But $600,000 is salaries that come into our bank account and go out straight away. We receive funding for non-teaching staff salaries. If we were funded for teaching staff salaries also the total would be up about $5 million.

Under the reforms, schools were given some discretion as to how the state funding was spent. This was a dramatic change from the strict spending restrictions that had been in place, and was generally welcomed. The Principals interviewed thought that the increased autonomy meant that the school could be more flexible in how it spent its grant. The decision-making process was also quicker because the school no longer required the approval of the Department of Education. Straven's Principal argued:

> We do have a lot more autonomy in that we do not have to ring the department whenever we need to employ an extra teacher. No, perhaps that is not a good example since there remain restrictions on the use of the bulk grant for employment of teachers; minor capital works would be better. We don't have to waste time negotiating with the department; we just go out and do the maintenance we need.

The Principal of Aroha further illustrated this point:

I like the independence for making decisions that have come from the reforms. The delegated autonomy of *Tomorrow's Schools* has allowed us to let our own contracts and employ our own carpenter and therefore bring minor maintenance in house.

Responsibility for governing the school, and for approving a budget prepared by the Principal and staff, rested with the trustees. Although they were not liable for a 'loss in good faith', they could be personally liable for fraud or wrongdoing (Education Act 1989, Sixth Schedule, Section 4). At Straven and Deans, a high level of financial and management expertise was readily available within the local community. The Principal of Straven remarked that:

We have been able to get a very well qualified board from the [local] parents. We have expertise in the accounting and finance area from both the previous treasurer and in [X]. [X] used to be on the PTA committee and has a child in form three. We are also strong in the property area. [Y] is an engineer and is responsible for property management at the airport. The ability of these people has been a big help in coping with our responsibilities under *Tomorrow's Schools*.

In contrast, neither Matai nor Aroha found it so easy to recruit professionals on to the board of trustees. At Matai, the Principal was forced to absorb the responsibility for the financial aspects of school management. However, while the trustees did not have financial and administrative skills comparable to those of the trustees in the wealthier areas, they were often actively involved in the operation of the school, as the Chair of Matai's Board of Trustees explained:

I do a little bit of administration but mostly I help in the classroom as a teacher aid. I play parent for some of these kids, I teach them social skills, watch them while they do homework, the things that their parents should do but don't.

The Principal of that school pointed out the difficulties:

People who stand for the board are of the people. The president, the secretary and many of the board members are unemployed. They find it hard to make ends meet themselves. It is difficult for many to get to board meetings. It is also difficult to commit themselves to being at meetings. We don't get the 'professional types' many other schools have on their boards. Someone has to make the decisions therefore I do ... I have had to deal with it all [building and maintenance]. I also did the books from 1989–91. I had done some commerce in my degree studies. However, the load got too big. Now we employ an accounting firm to do the accounts.

The process of devolution also led to changes in the internal arrangements within the schools. As shown in studies of the LMS process (Laughlin *et al.* 1994), a local management group emerged, centred on the Principal and key members of the administrative staff. In this case, the role of administrative staff within the school increased significantly. All of the schools studied developed a financial and administrative position, designating one staff member as the school financial officer. In the primary schools, this tended to be less formal and centred on the school secretary. At Aroha, they restructured the job of the School Executive Officer, making her responsible for overseeing the financial management and administrative responsibilities within the school. They also created a new administrative position – the school bursar – who was directly responsible for handling cash and keeping financial records. The personnel arrangements were explicitly designed to absorb the changes and to protect the teaching staff from financial administration. These arrangements were described by the Principal of Aroha:

> Teaching staff do not handle money. That is all handled by the Bursar now. Teaching staff are inclined to lose money or leave it around where it could get taken. So we have improved the system for cash control. Teaching staff do not naturally consider financial issues so we attempted to institute systems to help them be better managers.

Aroha's bursar explained the role:

> I have just spent the afternoon with the principal discussing the finances. I have responsibility for all of the finances. I handle all of the money and banking, I hold the invoices for the teachers to sign and code them for the computer and I keep an eye on all of the school grants.

At Straven, the reforms also led to the appointment of a new administrative position. In 1991 they employed a consulting firm, Ernst & Young, to review their staffing situation. Ernst & Young recommended that a new position, a Finance and Administration Manager, be created to oversee the accounts and administrative staff. This position was established from 1991, and a professional accountant was employed to take responsibility for the accounting system, internal and external reporting, and the administration computer network. The Manager described the responsibilities involved:

> I have responsibility for the accounting system and the internal and external reporting system. I answer to both the principal and the finance sub-committee, rather like a chief accountant, reporting directly to the board but also reporting to the chief executive officer.

However, the administrative staff could only absorb some of the new workload, and there were significant changes in the role of the Principal. All of those interviewed found their administrative responsibilities increasing, meaning that they had less time to devote to the curriculum, teaching and pastoral support. Here is how the Principal of Matai put it:

> The administration responsibilities now take up much of my time. Principals should be responsible for the development and implementation of curriculum and for looking after the welfare of students and teachers. Once I had the time to get to know each of the kids personally, but now the administrative responsibilities take up 95 per cent of my time. I only have 5 per cent to devote to curriculum and welfare issues.

A teacher at this school remarked:

> We also spend a lot of time doing social work. One girl's sister got raped a few days before. You can't send them down to the Principal like you used to – he is too busy with administration.

As the role of the school Principal changed, some of the Principals interviewed started perceiving themselves in more managerial terms. Thus the Principal of Deans described himself as the chief executive officer for the school and as an entrepreneur. He was keen to introduce new management practices into the school. Other Principals interviewed were not so managerialist in their orientation and, although they sought to retain much of the pastoral role of the Principal teacher, they found themselves increasingly drawn into administrative and political concerns, as was, for example, the Principal of Matai:

> As Principal most of what I do now has little directly to do with the school. I have to deal with all sorts: today there was an engineer, an architect, an electrician and a plumber.

The financial and administrative responsibilities devolved to the schools had little direct impact on the teaching staff, as they were intentionally protected by their Principals, administrative staff and trustees. This finding is consistent with the findings from studies of the LMS reforms (Bowe and Ball 1992; Broadbent *et al.* 1993), and of devolved management in Scottish schools (Bailey in this volume: Chapter 3). However, teaching staff were affected by the changes. New indirect forms of visibility, control and review associated with the national curriculum, the NZQA and the ERO, accompanied the devolution of management to schools. All of the teaching staff interviewed found themselves under pressure to cope with the changes in curriculum and the requirements to comply with the new forms of performance measurement. The tendency towards measurement was reflected in the Ministry of Education 'Assessment Initiative' and measurement requirements of the NZQA qualifications framework, which required teachers to explicitly measure and quantify student performance and the regular ERO reviews of school performance. A teacher at Deans complained:

> All we seem to do is measure everything. When the ERO and the Ministry visit, you feel that you should produce more data – you should have numbers for everything. They try to prove that teaching is more effective with statistics.

A colleague at the same school elaborated this point:

> It is hard to do assessment because of the way that we teach. We try to take a personal approach and adjust what we do for individual student needs. That makes it difficult to measure. Accountability involves statistics, paperwork and measurement. I have to conduct my physical education classes with a clipboard in one hand and a whistle in another. This is because I have to write everything down in order to be accountable and satisfy the Ministry. There is more paperwork for everything.

Concern was expressed that the process of measurement that characterised the new centralisation would have a negative impact on student learning, and there was some criticism of a number of the measurement proposals. For example, Straven's Principal aired misgivings:

> But my concern is that we are trying to drive a tack with a sledgehammer, that the assessment part is overtaking the learning. And every extra hour you spend on assessment you are going to spend one

less hour on learning. And that is a great concern to me. It is the assessment part that I think is getting too much time and I am not sure why. And some of the solutions they have for the difficulties worry me as well. I have one department setting re-tests after school. If you don't pass your unit you have a chance to do it again. But most teachers are not going to re-test their students after school. This department is involved in a trial, but most teachers can't do that. It is this jolly re-testing all of the time. The NZQA's latest solution is for teachers to walk around the class and look at their books. If it looks like they are doing their examples well, there is no need to re-test them and you can tick them for it. From the sublime to the ridiculous.

While the financial and administrative tasks associated with devolved management were absorbed, the process of quantification and measurement associated with control from a distance began to alter significantly the role of the teacher. However, this increasing shift to indirect forms of control is not limited to the New Zealand education sector. Power (1994) argued that the British public sector was shifting away from control over direct provision and towards oversight and rule-setting. He argued that because audit offered a technology to resolve the tension between central control and devolution and to facilitate steering at a distance, the emphasis on audit in the UK had exploded, and that in the 1990s, Britain had effectively become an 'audit society'. The increase in audit technologies signals a change in accountability relationships because the style of accountability associated with audit 'displaces trust from first order to second order verificatory activities' (Power 1994: 49). However, this is not a neutral process, as Power (1994) argues that in an audit culture there is a danger of devoting more resources to policing quality rather than creating it.

The emphases on the explicit audit role of the ERO and the indirect audit function of the NZQA and the Ministry of Education have done much to construct the schools studied as an audit society. With such an explicit shift from direct to indirect forms of control and accountability, one may well ask whether the management of schools was ever devolved in a true sense or whether there was only a shift from one form of control to another. Power's (1994) concern with the costs of policing quality is also relevant in this context. In seeking to eliminate the 'folk devils' of 'provider capture', the New Zealand changes have undermined the basis of trust in the teaching profession and placed faith in those responsible for external verification activities. The problem is that while these activities can police the teaching process, they may not improve it.

Conclusion

While small groups within the schools studied successfully absorbed the managerial responsibilities associated with the delegated financial and administrative tasks, the changes in the national curriculum and the growing emphasis on quantifiable performance measurement have significantly changed the education system. This shift from direct forms of control to indirect control mechanisms has clearly extended beyond a focus on budgets and finance to change the nature of the teaching profession.

It is interesting to contrast the devolution of financial and administrative responsibilities to the school level with the new forms of control and monitoring that were introduced at the same time as this devolution. The interviews indicate that key individuals were unwilling to relinquish the central powers of the State to monitor the education process, and with the removal of the direct forms of control came the introduction of indirect forms of audit and review. In New Zealand, these indirect controls took the form of the financial reporting mechanisms, the ERO, the national curriculum and the NZQA.

In conclusion, devolved school management in New Zealand has led to a transfer of administrative responsibility from the centre to the school level. This has led to three consequences: first, administrative structures are replicated at the school level; second, the role of the Principal teacher has changed from a concern with education to that of a full-time administrator; and third, teaching staff have found themselves spending more of their energies on measurement and quantification and less on teaching children. The creation of new forms of quantification and measurement was a clear policy associated with devolved school management. However, it remains to be shown that these new forms of verification, based on standard setting and audit technologies, will be better than more direct forms of control and administration, and whether the elimination of 'provider capture' will result in better educational performance in New Zealand.

Notes

1 The 1983 OECD review indicated that the New Zealand system was performing well.
2 A sub-set of the national guidelines which defines a common curriculum for all New Zealand schools.
3 In order to maintain confidentiality, the identity of the schools participating in this study have been disguised. This has involved using pseudonyms, such as 'Matai', in place of the school names and removing any references to special features of schools that would identify them.

References

Bowe, R. and Ball, S. (1992) 'Doing What Should Come Naturally: an Exploration of LMS in One Secondary School', in Wallace, G. (ed.) *BERA Dialogues 6, Local Management of Schools: Research and Experience*, Clevedon, England: Multilingual Matters.

Broadbent, J. and Laughlin, R. (1997) 'Developing Empirical Research: an Example Informed by a Habermasian Approach', *Accounting, Auditing and Accountability Journal*, 10, 622–48.

Broadbent, J., Laughlin, R., Shearn, D. and Dandy, N. (1993) 'Implementing Local Management of Schools: a Theoretical and Empirical Analysis', *Research Papers in Education*, 18(2): 149–76.

Codd, J. (1990) 'Educational Policy and the Crises of the New Zealand State', in Middleton, S., Codd, J. and Jones, A. (eds) *New Zealand Education Policy Today*, pp. 191–205, Wellington: Allen & Unwin.

Codd, J. (1993) 'Managerialism, Market Liberalisation and the Move to Self-Managing Schools in New Zealand', in Smyth, J. (ed.) *A Socially Critical View of the Self-Managing School*, London: Falmer.

Codd, J. and Gordon, L. (1991) 'School Charters: the Contractualist State and Education Policy', *New Zealand Journal of Educational Studies*, 26(1): 21–34.

Cummings, I. and Cummings, A. (1978) *History of State Education in New Zealand 1840–1975*, Wellington, New Zealand: Pitman Publishing.

du Chateau, C. (1987) *The Lost Generation: Victims of the Great Educational Experiment*, Auckland, NZ: Metro.

Gordon, L. (1992a) 'The New Zealand State and Education Reforms: Competing Interests', *Comparative Education*, 28(3): 281–91.

Gordon, L. (1992b) 'The State, Devolution and Education Reform in New Zealand', *Journal of Education Policy*, 7(2): 187–203.

Gordon, L., Boyask, D. and Pearce, D. (1994) *Governing Schools: a Comparative Analysis*, Education Policy Research Unit, Christchurch, NZ: University of Canterbury.

Grace, G. (1990) 'Labour and Education: the Crisis and Settlements of Education Policy', in Holland, M. and Boston, J. (eds) *The Fourth Labour Government*, Auckland, NZ: Oxford University Press.

Jesson, B. (1989) *Fragments of Labour: the Story Behind the Labour Government*, Auckland: Penguin Books.

Lange, D. (1987), Leader's Speech, in *New Zealand Labour Party Conference Proceedings*, Wellington, NZ: New Zealand Labour Party.

Lange, D. and Goff, P. (1989) *Learning for Life: Education and Training Beyond the Age of Fifteen*, Wellington: Government Printer.

Lauder, H. (1987) 'The New Right and Educational Policy in New Zealand', *New Zealand Journal of Educational Studies*, 22: 3–23.

Laughlin, R. (1995) 'Empirical Research in Accounting: Alternative Approach and a Case for "Middle Range" Thinking', *Accounting, Auditing and Accountability Journal*, 8(1): 63–87.

Laughlin, R., Broadbent, J., Shearn, D. and Willig-Atherton, H. (1994) 'Absorbing LMS: the Coping Mechanism of a Small Group', *Accounting, Auditing and Accountability Journal*, **7(1)**: 59–85.

McGovern, R. (1992) 'A View from the Front', in Wallace, G. (ed.) *BERA Dialogues 6, Local Management of Schools: Research and Experience*, Clevedon, England: Multilingual Matters.

Macpherson, R. (1989) 'Radical Administrative Reforms in New Zealand: the Implications of the Picot Report for Institutional Managers', *Journal of Educational Administration*, **29(1)**: 29–44.

Moustakas, C. (1990) *Heuristic Research: Design, Methodology and Applications*, Newbury Park, CA: Sage.

New Zealand Council for Educational Research (1987) *How Fair is NZ Education? Part II: Fairness in Maori Education*, Wellington: NZCER.

OECD (1983) *Review of National Policies for Education: New Zealand*, Paris: OECD.

Osborne, D. and Gaebler, T. (1992) *Reinventing Government*, New York: Plume.

Picot, B., Ramsay, P., Rosemergy, M., Whetumaramu, W. and Wise, C. (1988) *Administering for Excellence: Effective Administration in Education*, Report of the Taskforce to Review Educational Administration, Wellington: Government Printer.

Power, M. (1994) *The Audit Explosion*, Paper No. 7, London: Demos.

Redvall, G. (1993) 'Decentralising Swedish Schools Since 1980', in Wallace, G. (ed.) *Local Management, Central Control: Schools in the Market Place*, Bournemouth, England: BERA, Hyde Publications.

Smyth, J. (1993) *A Socially Critical View of the Self-Managing School*, London: Falmer.

The Treasury (1987) *Government Management: Brief to the Incoming Government 1987*, Volume II, Educational Issues, Wellington: The Treasury.

9 Governance and devolution in the Danish school system

Jørgen Grønnegaard Christensen

Introduction

During the 1980s, education reform was constantly on the Danish political agenda. An entrepreneurial minister of education took any opportunity to push for radical change. His basic idea, launched again and again, was to increase school autonomy by giving parents a democratic say in the management of schools and by giving more managerial authority to school Principals. It was also to give schools an economic incentive to adapt to changing signals and to improve their performance. Therefore, his reform programme intended to give parents a choice among schools, while at the same time making schools bear the direct economic consequences of changes in student enrolment. This liberal prescription was to be applied to all Danish schools, be they public primary schools, secondary (grammar) schools, or vocational training schools. In all these cases, the minister found problems ensuing from low economic efficiency, deficient pedagogical effectiveness, and an overall lack of responsiveness to societal needs and demands.

This chapter deals with this series of reforms, initiated in the second half of the 1980s and implemented in the early 1990s. The analysis is comparative, because the general question is: Why did the same general goals lead to very different outcomes for different types of schools? The hypothesis is that this was due to two factors. First, each type of school represents a distinct historical legacy that constitutes an institutional endowment to which a specific cluster of interests is attached. Second, the fragmentation of the Danish political system increases the probability that this endowment will, to a large extent, prevail. Neither of these factors excludes reform, nor does either deprive an entrepreneurial minister of the hope of success. Rather, they pave the way for reforms that, in spite of their common rationale, point in partially different directions and vary in scope. Still, as changes in the governance of schools were put into force around 1990, affected actors had an incentive to reconsider their strategies both during the implementation stage and in issues concerning the future governance of schools. The issue is whether institutional reform has created opportunities for strategic adaptation that may change future policy, or whether established interests are so strong and so adept in adapting their strategies that path dependency will be the best bet for the future.

Devolved management in the Danish school system

Administrative devolution is a complex and multidimensional phenomenon (Whitty *et al.* 1998), involving other matters besides school autonomy and school choice. To grasp fully the scope of devolution, it is necessary to consider the extent to which schools are subject to national regulation and how tight this regulation is. Finally, the procedures through which resources are allocated to schools decisively influence the conditions under which schools operate. Table 9.1 presents a comparative framework for evaluating the amount of devolution for different types of schools. It includes all types of schools offering teaching to children from the age of six (the non-compulsory preparatory year) to the age of 19–20 (grammar-school graduates and/or basic vocational training[1]). As parents have a constitutionally guaranteed option to choose a private school for their children at both the primary and the secondary level, private schools are included. Table 9.1 describes the formal scope of devolution after the reforms were put into force around 1990.

The general pattern shows strong variation among different types of schools. First, when it comes to school autonomy, the legal status of schools varies. Public schools, primary as well as secondary, are integrated in the public-sector hierarchy. However, as basic education is a local responsibility, primary schools and grammar schools are owned and run by municipalities and counties, respectively. These political bodies are responsible for financing their activities, for setting up buildings, for staffing, and for planning the local and regional school structure. Local hierarchical governance does not exclude variation in managerial autonomy. This is mainly a matter of delegation from the council and its central administration to Principals. In contrast to public schools, private schools and vocational training schools enjoy legal independence. According to the law, both types of schools must be self-governing, non-profit trust funds. Their Principals are appointed by the school board, which is responsible for all other decisions concerning the organisation and management of the school. For neither type of school is there any element of hierarchical governance in these respects.

Table 9.1 The governance of Danish schools

Schools	National curriculum	National tests	Legal status of schools	Managerial autonomy	User democracy	Exit option to other public schools	Exit option to private schools	Allocation of resources
Primary schools								
Public	Broad legal standards Advisory guidelines	Yes	Local government	Pending on council delegation	Directly elected school board – council delegation	Pending on council policy	Constitutional right	Local-government budgets
Private	Very basic legal standards	Yes	Self-governing trust funds	Pending on delegation from board	Board elected according to school statute	—	—	Government subsidy and parents' fee
Grammar schools								
Public	Compulsory and tight	Yes	Regional government institution	Pending on council delegation	Board representing parents, students and local interests	Pending on council policy	Constitutional right	Regional government budgets
Private	Compulsory and tight	Yes	Self-governing trust funds	Pending on delegation from board	Board elected according to school status	—	—	Government subsidy and parents' fee
Vocational training schools	Broad regulation	Yes	Self-governing trust funds	Pending on delegation from board	Board representing employer and union interests	—	Quasi-market	Central government funds allocated according to number and types of students

Organisationally, public and private/vocational schools diverge in another important respect. All schools have boards with decision-making powers. In the case of public schools, the boards are partly democratic bodies, elected by parents and students. The boards also include staff representatives, but the council decides whether they shall be allowed to vote on the board. In grammar schools, the board also includes representatives from the local political and economic community. For private schools, the statutes of each school specify how the board is selected. It may consist of representatives for parents or representatives for the founding community behind the school. In the case of vocational training schools, the board is a corporatist body that mainly consists of representatives for local employer associations and unions.

The legal status of the boards diverges between public schools and self-governing, private or vocational schools. For the latter type of schools, national legislation makes the board responsible for the management of the school and its human and financial resources. The boards of public schools are placed in an ambiguous situation. On the one hand, the law specifies the minimum responsibilities of the board. In principle, school boards are responsible for setting up a general policy for the school and for approving the school budget. On the other hand, as public institutions, schools are integrated into a local hierarchy of governance, subjecting them to political guidance and supervision from councils. Among other things, local councils can delegate responsibilities to these boards that exceed the basic authority defined by law. Therefore, in public schools, national legislation only provides a framework to be filled in by political decisions taken by individual councils.

All children are entitled to free education in public primary schools, but parents have the option to send their children to a private school. In principle, school choice also applies to the public school system, but the law makes its implementation a matter of local policy.[2] Finally, vocational schools operate in a quasi-market where students can enrol in any school that offers the relevant specialisation.

To a large extent, the principle of free education has been expanded to cover teaching at private schools as well, as fees are heavily subsidised by central government. On average, government subsidies cover 75 per cent of private schools' operational costs (Department of Finance 1994: 166). Although the subsidy is allocated among schools according to a complex formula, its aggregate sum as well as the subsidy received by each school vary with the number of students (Department of Education 1991). A similar mechanism is used to allocate resources to and among vocational schools, thus creating a fully government-financed quasi-market for vocational training. Nothing excludes the use of similar quasi-market principles in allocating resources to public primary and grammar schools. The integration of these schools into a hierarchy led by local politicians and fully financed through the council budget leaves it to these local democratic bodies to set up their own procedures and mechanisms for resource allocation and resource management.

All types of schools are subject to substantial national regulation when it comes to the content and standards of teaching. Thus, whatever the status of a school and whatever the level of teaching, national tests are compulsory for students who are graduating. When it comes to curricula, class-size, and the number of lessons taught per year and per subject, national regulation allows for marked variation in the degree of school autonomy. Grammar schools, both public and private, have virtually no autonomy in any of these respects, as these matters are tightly regulated by national legislation or by government decree. Public primary schools are similarly subject to a vast set of national regulations, dealing with virtually all aspects of teaching and school life, but their regulation is different. This sets advisory guidelines – broad standards often defined as a basic minimum – and then leaves the rest to local councils. For private primary schools, regulation is even less strict. Vocational training schools enjoy similar autonomy, as the principal instrument of regulation is national approval of their schemes for specific types of courses or trades.

How the past shaped the present

Danish schools of the 1990s constitute an extremely complex set of institutions. Several types of schools offer teaching to students belonging to the same age and target groups. Simultaneously, these schools differ in a number of their dimensions, thus creating a complex pattern of devolution, local political governance and national regulation. This variation is remarkable. During the 1980s, Minister of Education Bertel Haarder launched his *perestrojka*-programme for institutional reform, which presented an integrated attempt to reform the entire school system along the same lines (Haarder 1988). Implementation of his neo-liberal reform would have approximated the governance of public and government-financed schools to the governance of private schools. During the same period, the mechanisms through which private schools received government subsidies were tightened without compromising their managerial and pedagogical autonomy.

In spite of the coherence and synchronisation of these reforms, the outcome was strikingly different, although in all cases the minister succeeded in mobilising political support to change the governance of schools. However, the minister had to renounce his original ambitions because they ran counter to a set of distinct historical legacies. Around each of them a cluster of interests was grouped, all of them with a stake in both policy within and power over the particular sector. As the history of the school system has demonstrated, this has not precluded successive reforms. The problem with the institutional reforms launched in the late 1980s was that they threatened to upset the institutional equilibrium that ensured some interests a privileged position when it came to influencing both the governance and management of individual schools and policy-making at the national level. Table 9.2 presents the logic behind this path dependency.

First, each school type has preserved its own institutions of governance and management over a long period. This is the case with both intra-organisational management and decision-making in schools and the extra-organisational regulation of schools. Second, for each school type, national policy-making has followed a distinctive pattern. This mirrors a strong institutional variation and differences in the distribution of power within each policy-making segment. Third, these institutional patterns have created strong path dependencies. For each school type, they have created a set of institutional safeguards that are not easily circumvented. The prospective policy entrepreneur aiming at a radical reform of past policies will have to accommodate the interests that are protected by these institutional clauses. Fourth, the implication is that devolution of authority to a large extent depends on its compatibility with the distinc-tive institutional paths that represent the historical legacies for each school type.

This strong and extremely varied legacy confronted the Minister of Education with a double challenge. First, he could not follow the same strategy when he moved from one part of the school system to another. Second, the odds of achieving his programme were not identical for all parts of the system: for public primary schools, the minister had to operate within a highly politicised system, where several actors took a strong interest in policy and governance. They were the political parties repre-sented in Parliament, the municipalities organised within the Association of Local Governments (ALG), the Teachers' Union (TU), and finally the more anonymous Skole og Samfund, an organisation representing parents elected to the advisory school boards. For two reasons, the voices of these actors were going to be heard on the proposed reform. First, the minister knew that changes in primary-school policy traditionally depended on support from a broad coalition in Parliament, and second, that such support again depended on prior accommodation of the interests organ-ised by at least the ALG and the TU.

These political constraints did not deprive the minister of all

Table 9.2 Path dependency and devolution in Danish school policies

Historical legacy	School type				
	Public primary	Private primary	Public grammar	Private grammar	Vocational
Governance and management					
Extra-organisational	Local government	Ex-post-supervision	Central-government bureaucracy	Central-government bureaucracy	Labour-market corporatism
Intra-organisational	Collegiate	Hierarchical	Professional bureaucracy	Hierarchical	Hierarchical
User democracy	Advisory boards	Boards	Professional bureaucracy	Boards	Boards
National policy-making					
Educational	Parliamentary democracy, public-sector corporatism	Parliamentary and private school associations	Parliamentary democracy, public-sector corporatism and central bureaucracy	No independent policy segment	Labour-market corporatism
Labour relations	Tight collective agreements	No independent segment	Tight, collective agreements	No independent policy segment	Weak collective agreements
Path safeguarded by?	Local democracy and public-sector corporatism	Constitutional principle and corporatism	Central-government bureaucracy and public-sector corporatism	Central-government bureaucracy	Labour-market corporatism and corporatist bureaucracy
Is devolution compatible with this path?	Yes, to a very limited extent	Yes, it is the very foundation of these schools	No	No	Yes, within the confines of labour-market corporatism

opportunities for reform. He could exploit local governments and, less importantly, the parents' interest in more local autonomy. Therefore his strategy was to form an alliance with local governments, in order to increase their formal authority over primary schools. For their part, local governments had to swallow the transformation of advisory boards into directly elected bodies with some decision-making powers (Lindbom 1995). However, local governments and teachers formed another alliance, based on their common dislike of a policy of devolution that gave schools managerial autonomy while subjecting them to compulsory school choice and to quasi-market regulation of resource allocations to individual schools. Together, these political and institutional constraints defined the strategic field within which the minister could operate. Limited devolution could win parliamentary support as long as the minister did not challenge local democracy and public-sector corporatism.

For public grammar schools the situation was different. First, there was no tradition of user democracy and therefore no institutionalised support for the creation of strong school boards. Second, there was a strong tradition of centralised regulation and unchallenged control. Third, as owners of the grammar schools, the counties strongly disliked the idea of devolved management and, even more, the idea of quasi-market reforms. Strategically, this gave the minister very few options, and, except for the nearly symbolic creation of school boards, the proposed reform came to nothing.

In political terms, vocational training is defined as a labour-market issue. This stems from the history of the field. Up to the 1960s, vocational training was the responsibility of the then Department of Trade and Industry (Christensen 1980). Although the department had to accept a transfer of vocational training to the Department of Education, the corporatist institutions characteristic of the field have stayed intact ever since. So, both when it comes to making policy and to management of the sector, corporatist institutions prevail. As the prime concern of employers and unions was to protect their strong hold on the sector, they did not oppose the proposals for devolution and quasi-market governance as long as the introduction of these mechanisms did not challenge their political control of the sector. Thus, the result was a compromise, barely discussed in Parliament, that led to radical reform without challenging the existing distribution of political power.

Private schools hardly constitute separate segments, and neither were changes in their status and governance a political issue during the 1980s. Still, their situation is fundamentally different. The autonomy of private primary schools is safeguarded by both a constitutional principle and corporatist practice for hearing any affected interests, in this case the associations of private schools. The full incorporation of private grammar schools in a general grammar-school sector follows similarly from the existence of a strong and centralised bureaucracy. While private grammar schools do not possess many political resources, private primary schools have consistently been able to resist local governments' arguments that parents' option to move their children from a public to a private school undermines their long-term planning and their possibility of exploiting economies of scale. Even the revision of the rules that regulate the allocation of government subsidies to private schools, so that local governments have to refund central government the countervalue of the subsidy for children living within their borders, has not made it possible for them to upset the traditional political protection of private-school autonomy.

Patterns of devolved management

Only in the case of vocational training did the reforms definitively change the governance of schools. As schools were subjected to quasi-market competition, they were no longer guaranteed a fixed budget. They had to compete for students and funds with other vocational schools and, equally important, with grammar schools. If they could not attract students and bring them through to graduation under the new regime, vocational schools would see their resources shrink.

With the deals struck between the minister, affected interests and parties in Parliament, nothing precluded the introduction of similar principles of governance in the public-school sector. However, nothing like this has happened. Without exception, the counties have kept within the strict minimum rules defined by law; that is, local grammar schools are integrated in a politically led hierarchy where funds are allocated through the annual budget. The extent to which resource allocations correlate with the number of students and other demand indicators is not regulated by the semi-invisible hand of an artificial market, but through political and administrative discretion (Pallesen 1998).

Local governments have had the same preference for hierarchical governance, although some municipalities during the 1990s have gradually introduced more fine-grained budgetary systems to allow for stronger economic responsiveness to changes in student enrolment (Christensen 1998a). Under these modern systems, the number of students (together with a norm specifying the number of teaching hours), is used as the criterion for allocating resources to schools (*5-by Analyse* 1997: appendix B5). This is a unilateral decision by the council. However, the council is heavily constrained by the collective agreements negotiated by the ALG, which represents their interests as employers. The agreements specify how teachers have to split their time between classroom teaching and preparation. For each lesson of class teaching, teachers are entitled to one hour of preparation and related tasks. In addition, the council has to negotiate a contract with the local branch of the union that specifies the number of hours to be spent on other tasks, such as student counselling, supervision, post-entry education, and union-related work as shop stewards and board members. The size of this resource is decided locally, but, according to the national agreement, it has to make up at least 50 per cent of the resources allocated to class teaching. However, the percentage is often higher. An analysis of the five biggest cities outside Copenhagen found that in the 1996–97 school year, teachers' resources corresponding to 58.5 to 64.2 per cent of the resources allocated to teaching were tasks outside the classroom.[3] Consequently, about a third of teachers' pay for work-time was spent on classroom teaching. In spite of two successive and radical changes in the collective agreements, this pattern is very similar to the pattern of the early 1990s (*5-by-Analyse* 1997: 49 and 56–67; Department of Finance *Folkeskolens Økonomi* 1995: 33–7; Christensen 1998a). A different but equally constraining collective agreement covers grammar schools, where less than 30 per cent of teaching resources are allocated to classroom teaching.

Still, with budgetary models to some extent linking schools' teaching resources to student enrolment, the introduction of free school choice might seem an obvious solution. However, local governments have been reluctant to take this step. Typically, local governments allocate children living within a precisely defined geographical area to each school. Then parents can apply for enrolment of their child in another local school. But local policy excludes any direct competition among schools for students. One quite restrictive policy is to allow schools to enrol children from other districts on two conditions: first that there will still be excess capacity in the class, and second that the enrolment of these children will not lead to the creation of extra classes (Aarhus Skoleforvaltning 1995). Even seemingly more liberal regimes stress that 'in legal terms there exists no "free school choice," as … the city council has never made such a policy decision … However, over time administrative practice has led parents to think that they can decide where their child has to go to school.' With this reminder of official policy, schools are instructed that 'no school can commit itself to enrolling children from outside its district, until a negotiation has been arranged between the schools involved' (Odense Kommune 1996). In either case, local authorities have regulated parents' school choice in order to protect themselves against the structural consequences of parents' choices. In the former case, the solution is a bureaucratic procedure, setting up strict rules, while in the latter case it is a procedure that allows schools to negotiate a solution among themselves within the existing school structure.

Grammar schools operate within the same combination of constraints set by legal regulations and collective agreements, and, as is the case with public primary schools, school choice is heavily circumscribed by bureaucratic procedures that protect county councils against any structural consequences from choice. Compared to public schools, vocational training schools and private schools are in a very different situation. As already described, both types of schools receive resources that reflect changes in student enrolment: in the case of private schools in a very direct way and in the case of vocational schools more indirectly, as the quasi-market mechanisms used for the allocation of resources to some extent distinguish between fixed and variable costs. Moreover, the principle of free choice subjects both types of schools to competition from other schools. In the case of private schools, this competition is very direct, as there is always a public and free alternative in the local area, while for vocational training schools, geographical distance may create *de facto* monopolies (Department of Education *et al.* 1998).

Although private and vocational training schools have a status as self-governing trusts, they are integrated in the public-sector labour market. Because in both cases they receive more than 50 per cent of their funds as central-government subsidies, central government decides and negotiates the rules that regulate teachers' work; that is, the relationship between classroom teaching, preparation, etc. as well as other tasks (Department of Finance 1995: 40–1). For private schools, the implication is that teachers here work under the same collective agreements as their colleagues in public primary schools and grammar schools. In vocational training schools, separate agreements have been negotiated between the Department of Finance and the organisations representing their teachers. This centralised bargaining system has been upheld after the quasi-market reform. Like other agreements for the education sector, they specify the relationship between lessons taught in class and other activities (preparation, examinations, etc.).

However, in important respects, the mechanisms work out differently. First, the rules are comparatively simple, specifying compensation at the individual level in terms of time to be paid for lessons taught, examinations, and grading. Second, this individualisation allows for an extreme differentiation among teachers, where teachers are paid in cash for taking more classes, and where it is possible to compensate them in the form of overtime payment. Thus, the maximum number of lessons taught per week by teachers increases to 26–28, even allowing for more against extra compensation. The result is a marked wage differentiation among teachers at each school (Department of Finance 1995; 1997; National Auditors 1994), but it remains questionable whether teachers in vocational training schools deliver more classroom teaching than their colleagues in public schools.[4] In 1997, a new agreement opened for a decentralisation of the bargaining procedure, so that teachers' work time could be regulated in local agreements at individual schools. The goal was to allow for more flexible planning rather than to save money (Department of Finance 1997).

In public schools, user democracy was launched as an important aspect of devolution. School boards that have existed since the early twentieth century have been transformed from advisory to decision-making bodies. In two respects, this experience has been disappointing. First, interest among parents in this new instrument for democratic influence has been limited. At the first elections to the new primary-school boards in 1990, the election was uncontested in 57 per cent of all schools; in the remaining schools the turnout was 43 per cent. During the same period, many parent representatives resigned. Four years later, the corresponding figures were 77 and 40 per cent (Cranil 1994: 102–104; Department of Education 1996: 26). In the 1998 election, the election was uncontested at 83 per cent of the schools, with a turnout of 36 per cent at the remaining schools (www.uvm.dk/nb/nb9810).[5] Second, both municipal and county councils have been reluctant to delegate authority to school boards. Therefore, in most cases, school boards do not seem to have received more than the minimum authority defined by national legislation (Cranil 1994; Sørensen 1995; Department of Education 1996).

However, this reluctance toward user democracy has not excluded delegation from councils – and their bureaucracies – to schools. But, as discussed below, councils have preferred administrative delegation to Principals rather than a transfer of authority to school boards. Especially when it comes to the financial management of schools, Principals have seen an expansion of their authority. In the 1990s, they often receive a budget in the form of an envelope that allows them to transfer money from one item to another, and also to transfer savings to the following budgetary year. The rationale behind this policy is well expressed in a policy document prepared by the central school administration for the Council of the City of Aarhus that emphasises its preference for 'delegation of authority – compared to decentralisation – as the City Council retains the last word and thus keeps the option to repeal delegated authority.' (Aarhus Skoleforvaltning 1995). Thus, in a local government perspective, school boards may have gained decision-making authority, but as in the old days before the reform, their principal task is to give their opinion on proposals prepared elsewhere.

Conclusions: devolution, management, and politics

The reforms in the governance of Danish schools that took place in the early 1990s represent a mixed record. In important respects, they have changed the conditions under which schools operate, and local governments have clearly seen an increase in their formal authority (Christensen 1996). In the highly centralised grammar-school system, the counties have not experienced a similar gain in authority, although it is within the powers of the county council to shape the school structure according to its own preferences. Thus the extreme centralisation of the standards applied to grammar schools have not excluded a marked variation in operating costs between the counties (Pallesen 1998). The creation of school boards in public schools has introduced a new actor with decision-making powers and democratic legitimacy. However, the importance of this institutional innovation is limited, because municipal and county councils have been reluctant to delegate authority to them, and because users (parents) have shown extremely little interest in this new democratic channel. While user democracy in general has not made schools more responsive to parents, some incidents during the 1998 elections for primary-school boards indicated that the directly elected boards have created a channel for the articulation of critical demands that were not formalised under the previous system.

School choice provides another mechanism for increasing user responsiveness. Here, little has happened because local governments have upheld their restrictive policies. However, parents increasingly use the private-school option, so that, since the mid-1980s, the percentage of children attending private schools has increased from 8.9 to 10.3 on average (Statistiske Efterretninger 1997). In this way, public primary schools are subject to competition from an alternative provider, even if they do not compete among themselves. There is no evidence that allows conclusions concerning the effect of such competition on either the responsiveness towards parents or the quality of teaching.

With the lack of a mechanism that directly links changes in student enrolment with resources allocated to schools, the question arises as to what extent and in which way schools should adapt their costs. This was a tremendous problem in public primary schools during the 1980s and early 1990s when student enrolment decreased. The result was not just increased costs per student, because teaching resources were not adjusted for the drop in student enrolment. It was also a result of improvement in teachers' collective agreements that did not allow for an improvement of quality – for example, through an increase in the number of lessons – as slack resources were, at least theoretically, made available through decreasing enrolment. There were important exceptions to this general pattern. Local governments that have linked the allocation of resources to the number of students enrolled have demonstrated a relatively high degree of efficiency in controlling the level of costs. The City of Aarhus, which operates more than fifty schools, provides an excellent illustration of the success of this strategy (Christensen 1998a).

Two types of reorganisations at the local level may have changed this. First, local governments have delegated more authority to Principals and other managers at the operational level (see Table 9.3). Second, they have simultaneously changed the mechanisms used for allocating resources to schools that more directly establish a correlation between resources and student enrolment. However, this happens within a context of hierarchical governance that bears no similarity to the quasi-market mechanisms applied for vocational training. Probably these changes mirror several concerns among local politicians and bureaucrats. Through delegation of authority to Principals, they introduce an element of managerial and administrative flexibility that does not exist in a centralised hierarchy, while at the same time making Principals more directly responsible for the management of their schools. However, they keep the option to intervene in the management of schools, if, for some reason, this seems opportune from a political point of view (Christensen 1998b). Financial concerns seem equally important for municipal and county councils. They know from experience that structural adaptations involving closure of schools mean tough confrontations with both users and staff. They also realise that in a situation where the survival of a local school is at issue, directly elected boards, despite their few powers, may turn into opponents with considerable democratic legitimacy. By sticking to the principles of hierarchical governance that allow little choice to parents and a minimum of self-regulation in the allocation and realloca-tion of resources, they try to protect their own room for manoeuvre in critical situations.

Private and vocational training schools are in a very different situation. In both cases, changes in student enrolment have direct consequences for the school's financial situation. Even if they can build up financial assets as a buffer, they are still in a position where their own board is responsible for taking the adaptive measures provoked by a decrease in enrolment-linked subsidies. The linkage of the school's income to enrolment may partly explain why private schools operate at 90 per cent of the costs per student as compared to public primary schools (Department of Finance 1994: 165–66).

Although devolution has not gone as far as indicated by the first policy announcements of the minister, both public primary and vocational

Table 9.3 Principals' authority in Danish schools

School type	Type of budget	Inter-period transfer of funds	Budget holder	Authority to hire and fire	Principal accountable to:	Main constraints on Principal
Public primary	Envelope with binding specifications; strong variations	Transfer of savings up to a certain period to next level in some municipalities	Principal	Local council	Local council	Local council hierarchy, collective agreements and teachers' co-determination
Private primary	Envelope determined by enrolment	School capital serves as buffer	Principal	Principal and board	Board	Board, collective agreements and current income
Public grammar	Envelope with binding specifications; strong variations	Transfer of savings up to a certain level to next period in some counties	Principal	Principal or county council	Local council	County-council and central-government hierarchy, collective agreements and teachers' co-determination
Private grammar	Envelope determined by enrolment	School capital serves as buffer	Principal	Principal and board	Board	Board, central-government regulation and current income
Vocational training	Envelope determined by enrolment	School capital serves as buffer	Principal	Principal	Board	Board and current income

Note: Due to the decentralisation of Danish public education, a precise account of the position of Principals cannot be given. It will vary according to local-government and county policies (Christensen 1998a; Pallesen 1998). For vocational and private schools, two recent reports shed considerable light both on the position of Principals and the constraints within which they operate (Department of Education et al. 1998; National Auditors 1998).

training schools enjoy more autonomy than before the reforms (Department of Education *et al.* 1998; National Auditors 1998). For grammar schools this is hardly the case. The question then is to what extent this has changed managerial behaviour at school level. To see whether this has been the case, it is necessary to look at both the constraints and the incentives that operate at the managerial level. For both public and vocational training schools, the role of Principal is now defined as a leadership role with some distinctive responsibilities when it comes to resource and staff management. This is most clearly seen at vocational training schools, where the quasi-market mechanisms for resource management create the risk that a school may end up in financial trouble. The school's survival is hardly at risk, as the closure of a school in a particular geographical area would raise serious political concerns. However, a school in financial trouble risks its autonomy. The Department of Education can withdraw its authorisation of certain courses offered by the school, withdraw certain delegations of administrative authority, dictate tough financial measures, and can eventually remove the board of directors. The latter has not happened yet, but more than half the managing directors have been replaced during the first few years of the reform (Department of Education *et al.* 1998: appendix E).

For public primary schools the situation is different. Although their Principals have also seen their managerial role clarified, they operate within other constraints. One is schools' unbroken integration in a public-sector hierarchy where local politicians occupy a pivotal position. Another is their integration in strong corporatist institutions characteristic of the Danish public sector. The weak formal position of school boards, together with the absence of regulative mechanisms that subject schools to unmediated signals from a quasi-market, give Principals a comparatively strong incentive to accommodate teachers. One indicator of this is that even in cases where schools receive more teaching resources than required to cover the minimum number of lessons required by law and by local school plans, schools show no inclination to offer more lessons to students. Rather than expanding output, these extra resources are typically allocated to a *de facto*, but well-disguised reduction in the student/teacher ratio; for example, by putting two teachers in certain classes or lessons or by splitting a class in certain lessons (*5-by-Analyse* 1997: 47). Apparently, this works differently at private primary schools. Although labour relations are regulated by the same collective agreements, private schools exploit the wide formal margins for school-level agreements in a way that allows for more classroom teaching and for teachers attending after-school care as part of what is defined as 'time for other tasks' in the general agreement.

The controversial nature of the reforms introduced in the early 1990s also raises the question as to whether the system of governance is now in equilibrium. One reason that this is not the case is that opponents of the reforms might have an incentive either to reverse the reforms or at least to adapt to them in a way that balances or even neutralises their presumed negative effects. Municipal and county councils clearly have been placed in a favourable position to exploit such strategies. While they have seen their authority expanded, the same legislation lets them decide both to what extent and in which ways further steps toward devolved management are going to take place. For teachers and their union this represents a new challenge to which they seem to have adapted efficiently. Instead of focusing their efforts at national-level policy-makers in government and Parliament, they have directed their attention toward the ALG, while at the same time strengthening their organisational apparatus at the local level. As part of this strategy, they work to set up tougher national standards to protect them against the whims of local politics, and to create collegiate bodies at the municipal level – also to protect their interests against school boards and Principals. The latter have seen their role strengthened because of legislative specification of their tasks and delegation from local councils. However, this strengthening has also put them in a situation where their interests do not always coincide with those of their teachers (Fremtidens Skoleledere 1996). As a result, Principals broke from the TU in 1997. The limited scope of the reforms undertaken in the grammar-school sector characteristically has led to similar adaptive strategies.

For vocational schools the situation is different. They have won more autonomy, while, at the same time, the creation of a quasi-market has made them more vulnerable to fluctuations in demand and has exposed them to competition from other vocational schools and from other private and public providers of courses. One adaptive strategy is the introduction of a very visible and very commercialised marketing strategy, which is also known in private schools. But as these schools are well integrated in the corporatist institutions of the Danish labour market, another and partly successful strategy has been the negotiation of better subsidies from central government. After the first few years of quasi-market regulation, schools, through their sponsors in trade unions and employer associations, secured themselves a better deal as the central-government budget was negotiated in Parliament.

Notes

1 Vocational training schools also offer a broad range of courses to adults. Such courses comprise full-time studies and shorter courses to both individuals and employer-financed groups.

2   According to the primary schools' act (lov 438, 20.6. 1989, 36,2) 'parents are entitled to have their child enrolled in the school district where the child lives ... Parents can further demand that their child is enrolled in a school outside the district, if the school is willing to enrol the child, and this is possible within the general financial guidelines decided by the council.' The grammar schools' act (lov 431, 13.6. 1990, 5,3) simply states that 'applicants are enrolled at the school they prefer, allowing for capacity'.

3   These estimates cover the teaching of normal classes. For 'special classes' a higher compensation for preparation is applied, while for bilingual children (immigrants and refugees), local governments decide and negotiate their own teaching standards, which again have implications for the compensation of teachers as concerns the number of hours paid for a given teaching load.

4   The figures are not exactly comparable, because the collective agreement regulating teachers' work time at vocational training schools also specifies a number of tasks involving student counselling and supervision for which these teachers are compensated specifically (Department of Finance 1995/97). An estimate at one large commercial college concludes that approximately one-third of the school's teaching resources is devoted to classroom teaching, a figure very close to what seems to be the pattern for public primary schools (Deloitte & Touche 1997).

5   At grammar schools, the interest in school-board elections has been extremely low from the beginning. However, no statistics are collected.

References

Aarhus Skoleforvaltning (1995) *Et Fælles Skolevæsen med Lokale Muligheder. Vilkår for Yderligere Decentralisering ved Aarhus Skolevæsen*, October 1995.

Christensen, J. G. (1980) *Centraladministrationen: Organisation og Politisk Placering*, Copenhagen: Samfundsvidenskabeligt Forlag.

Christensen, J. G. (1996) 'Reshaping the Welfare State: the Dynamics of Decentralization and Recentralization', Paper presented at the annual meeting of APSA, San Francisco, 29 August to 1 September.

Christensen, J. G. (1998a) 'Institutioner, Politikere og Brugere', in Blom-Hansen, J., Grønnegaard Christensen, J., Damgaard, J. B., Nannestad, P., Pallesen, T. and Pedersen, L. D. *Offentligt og Effektivt? Institutionelle Valg i den Offentlige Sektor*, Copenhagen: Gyldendal.

Christensen, J. G. (1998b): 'Institutionelle valg i den Offentlige Sektor', in Blom-Hansen, J., Grønnegaard Christensen, J., Damgaard, J. B., Nannestad, P., Pallesen, T. and Pedersen, L. D. *Offentligt og Effektivt? Instituitonelle Valg i den Offentlige Sektor*, Copenhagen: Gyldendal.

Cranil, M. (1994) *Decentralisering og Selvforvaltning i Folkeskolen*, Copenhagen: Undervisningsministeriets Forlag.

Deloitte & Touche (1997) *Auditor's Report on the 1996-Account*, Aarhus Købmandsskole.

Department of Education (1991) *Betænkning om et Nyt Tilskudssystem for de frie Grundskoler*, Copenhagen: Department of Education.

Department of Education (1996) *Rapport om Skolebestyrelser i Folkeskolen*. Folkeskoleafdelingen, Copenhagen: Undervisningsministeriets Forlag.

Department of Education et al. (1998) Rapport om Taxameterstyring, Copenhagen: Undervisningsministeriets Forlag.

Department of Finance (1994) Budgetredegørelse 1994, Copenhagen: Schultz Information.

Department of Finance (1995) Budgetvejledning, Copenhagen: Schultz Information.

Department of Finance et al. (1995) Folkeskolens Økonomi, Copenhagen: Schultz Information.

Department of Finance (1995/97) Cirkulære af 4.7 1995/19.8 1997 om Arbejdstid m.v. for Lærere og Ledere ved Erhvervsskolerne.

Department of Finance (1997) Cirkulære af 19.8. 1997 om Rammeaftale om Forsøg med Arbejdstid for Lærere ved Erhvervsskolerne.

5-by Analyse af Folkeskoleområdet. Rapport Udarbejdet af 5-Byerne: Aarhus, Odense, Aalborg, Esbjerg og Randers, September 1997.

Fremtidens Skoleledere (1996) En Analyse af Kravene til Skoleledelse i Folkeskolen. Copenhagen: Mandag Morgen.

Haarder, B. (1988) Perestrojka i Uddannelsessystemet. Uddannelse Undervisningsministeriets Tidsskrift, Copenhagen: Department of Education.

Lindbom, A. (1995) Medborgerskapet i Välfärdsstaten. Föräldrainflytande i Skandinavisk Grundskole, Stockholm: Almqvist & Wiksell International.

National Auditors (1994) Beretning om Lønforhold ved Erhvervsskolerne. De af Folketinget Valgte Statsrevisorer 11/92. Copenhagen.

National Auditors (1998) Beretning om Erhvervsskolernes Ændrede Økonomiske Adfærd. De af Folketinget Valgte Statsrevisorer 15/97. Copenhagen.

Odense Kommune (1996) Circular Letter to All Principals Concerning the Enrolment Procedure for 1997. Skoleforvaltningen, Magistratens 5. Afd., 18.12. 1996.

Pallesen, T. (1998) 'De Danske Amter – Politikere Eller Administratorer. Gymnasieskolen som Eksempel', in Blom-Hansen, J., Grønnegaard Christensen, J., Damgaard, J. B., Nannestad, P., Pallesen, T. and Pedersen, L. D. (ed.) Offentligt og Effektivt? Institutionelle Valg i den Offentlige Sektor, Copenhagen: Gyldendal.

Sørensen, E. (1995) 'Democracy and Regulation in Institutions of Public Governance', Ph.D. Thesis. Copenhagen: Institute of Political Science, University of Copenhagen.

Statistiske Efterretninger (1997) Uddannelse og Kultur, No. 8.

Whitty, G., Power, S. and Halpin, D. (1998) Devolution and Choice in Education. The School, the State and the Market, Buckingham, UK: Open University Press.

Index